How to Attain Enlightenment

# How to Attain Enlightenment

## The Vision of Non-Duality

## JAMES SWARTZ

SENTIENT PUBLICATIONS

First Sentient Publications edition 2009
Copyright © 2009 by James Swartz

A paperback original

Cover design by Kim Johansen, Black Dog Design
Book design by Timm Bryson

Library of Congress Cataloging-in-Publication Data

Swartz, James Bender.
  How to attain enlightenment : the vision of non-duality / James Swartz. -- 1st Sentient Publications ed.
      p. cm.
   ISBN 978-1-59181-094-0
   1. Vedanta. I. Title.
   B132.V3S95 2009
   181'.48--dc22

                              2009033858

Printed in the United States of America
10 9 8 7 6 5 4

## SENTIENT PUBLICATIONS

A Limited Liability Company
1113 Spruce Street
Boulder, CO 80302
www.sentientpublications.com

# CONTENTS

# INTRODUCTION

The knowledge contained in this book is a great secret that hides itself. Even when it is clearly presented, it is rarely assimilated, because you need to be prepared to understand it. Ordinarily we gain knowledge by experience, but the object of this knowledge lies beyond the scope of perception and inference, the senses and the mind. To know it, another means is required. There is such a means, but it is unlikely that you have come in contact with it…until now.

It is also a secret because it is extremely valuable. Things that are very valuable are not kept on the coffee table; they are locked away and are only displayed on special occasions. If you find yourself reading these words, it is an occasion to solve a problem that has been trailing you since the day you were born.

This knowledge is valuable because it eliminates suffering. This book will not tell you that you are free of suffering; it will prove that you are free. It will relieve you of your sense of smallness, inadequacy and incompleteness. When you appreciate what you are shown here, you will no longer try to be something you are not. You will no longer wonder who you are and why you are here.

The knowledge that you are about to be given is the king of all forms of knowledge because it is self shining. Other forms of knowledge do not shine on their own. But this knowledge—self knowledge—stands alone and rules all others because what you know depends on you, but you do not depend on what you know.

This rare knowledge resolves all divisions. All other forms of knowledge reinforce the duality of subject and object, the division of the knower/experiencer and the objects of knowledge/experience. It is the separation of the person you believe yourself to be and the objects of your experience—from which you gain knowledge—that causes you to experience yourself as a limited, incomplete and often inadequate being. When the knower is thought to be different from the known, each limits the other. If I do not understand that the knower is non-separate from the world, I will feel small…even though I am not small at all.

When I assume that things are divided, I become one of the divided things. I find myself as a distinct unique entity, qualified by any number of factors. From this standpoint, I am forced to transact business in a vast complex world that does not always seem to have my best interests at heart. As the small person I think I am, I can understand a few things, but I can never understand everything I need to know to survive, much less to thrive. The assumption that I am separate from what I know creates many unnecessary problems. For example, although I am not actually subject to time, I believe I am mortal and see my life inexorably slipping away. I erroneously believe that I am limited by health, wealth, love, and many other things.

Knowledge is true to the object of knowledge. When you experience a tree, you know a tree, not a dog or a cat. When you know anything in this world, you are always different from it. However, you are not a known object. The knower of the self and the object of knowledge are the same. The knower/experiencer and the objects of knowledge/experience all depend on you. The knower is awareness with reference to what is known and knowledge is just thoughts manufactured out of you, awareness. They are not different from you, although they seem to be. When you understand this, the division between you and what you know is resolved, destroying all other differences.

Everyone here is a seeker of one of the four categories of knowledge: pleasure, security, virtue or freedom. When you pursue knowledge that depends on the subject/object division, there is always something that you do not know. In every type of relative knowledge, what you do not know is always greater than what you do know. What you think you know often turns out to be false when new information comes in, or when you look at the object of your knowledge from a different standpoint. But self knowledge cannot be falsified, because you are eternal and always present. It is not subject to negation.

Furthermore, no ordinary knowledge is ever complete. Because the universe is a whole, every piece of knowledge is connected to every other piece of knowledge. In the whole, how can you have a piece of knowledge and still call it knowledge? Knowing an aspect of something, you cannot say you know it completely. But self knowledge is complete, because you are a partless whole.

This book is more than a mere book. It is the ancient science of self knowledge. It is not the philosophy, beliefs or opinions of some musty ancient sages or the author, although you will find some of the author's opinions relating to the topic of enlightenment in it. It is the result of the realization of the non-duality of all things and forty years of study of the science of self inquiry. Do not read this book. Immerse yourself in it. Had you been able to solve the riddle of your existence on your own, you would have done so by now. Allow it to guide your investigation. It will certainly demystify the mystery of existence and awaken the realization of your non-separation from everything.

# CHAPTER ONE

# Inquiry into Object Happiness

## Security, Pleasure and Virtue

Every living being responds to life according to its programming. Although barely conscious, plants unfold their complex and wonderful forms from within tiny seemingly intelligent seeds. Somehow they learned how to ingest water, turn towards the light and reproduce.

A hound hunting a rabbit does not question its own behavior. A force hidden deep within it interprets a scent and sends adrenaline flooding through its system, compelling it to bay loudly and salivate excessively as it moves relentlessly toward its prey. It sinks its sharp teeth into the soft flesh and happily wolfs down its meal without a trace of guilt. Whether its victim munched tender organic grass in the wild or fed on hay contaminated by agribusiness' pernicious chemicals is of no concern to it; it is not programmed to think.

In the never-ending search for the edge in the survival game, consciousness evolved the intellect. Somehow apes figured out that ants living in the trunks of trees could be extracted with the help of a blade of grass or a thin twig, providing them with an easy source of protein. Although incapable of understanding mathematics or composing symphonies, monkeys, dogs, cats and many other species have somehow developed a rudimentary capacity to think. Fido brings the evening paper to the master sitting in his easy chair after a hard day's work and is rewarded with a bone. A pair of dolphins guide a confused whale caught in a maze of delta waterways to the freedom of the open ocean.

Humans sit on the roof and crown of the pyramid of life, much to their undying satisfaction. In them intellect is more subtle and sophisticated and appears as free will, the power to consider various alternatives and choose among them.

What we call reality is governed by the uncertainty principle. Because our source of food, animal or vegetable, is unconcerned about our need to survive, we are forced to either pursue it or cultivate it. Shelter does not simply happen on its own but requires effort to obtain. Caves may have been useful during mankind's infancy but make unsuitable dwellings today. Money is of little use in itself. It is neither edible nor a suitable building material. It does, however, provide various forms of material security. Security through power is another primary human pursuit. Most of us spend the lion's share of our lives trying to secure ourselves in an uncertain world.

Once my material needs are met and I am ensconced in a cozy home with money in the bank, I may discover that I am still not completely fulfilled. Time hangs heavy on my hands and I feel that I have earned the right to a little pleasure. I may pamper myself with luxuries: a vacation home, romantic holidays in foreign countries and expensive playthings, hoping to remove an uncomfortable sense of lack that bubbles up from within. I might begin dating, thinking that love will do the trick. Perhaps I discover the high in drink and drugs or extreme sports. No matter what brand of pleasure I pursue, I pursue it for a reason: I want to feel good. I want to feel whole and complete. But although the good feelings are intense as they happen, they are short lived. Consequently, I either become dispassionate because I see the futility of this pursuit or I pursue pleasure more ardently.

If I find that wealth and pleasure are unable to satisfy me in a meaningful way, I may seek consolation in religion. Every religion entertains the notion of heaven and hell. Because hell is not desirable, I opt for heaven and commit to doing good deeds, which requires virtue. To attain virtue, my sins need to be removed. I believe that once I am pure I will be happy, both here and hereafter.

Even if I already count myself among the virtuous and eschew religion, I may be deeply troubled by the lack of virtue in the world and set out to make a difference. I reason that if the world is a better place, I will be a happier person. But whether the object of my efforts is the salvation of my own soul or the salvation of other souls, my primary motivation is the removal of the sense of limitation. Most of us are engaged in the pursuit of any or all of these three goals, or some variation of them, throughout our lives.

## Subject and Object

Although life is one seamless whole, for the purpose of our analysis it can be divided into two categories: subject and object. The gross and subtle things that I pursue are objects. Objects are known to me through perception, inference and other means of knowledge. Even the faculties of perception—the senses, mind, and intellect—are objects from my point of view. Objects include physical forms, activities, situations, environments, sensations, feelings, thoughts, ideas, beliefs, opinions, memories, dreams and states of mind. All experiences, solicited and unsolicited, are objects. Anything that I desire or desire to avoid is an object. Objects are not conscious, but the subject, that which I am, is conscious.

Life is the pursuit of objects, by conscious beings, for the happiness that seems to reside in them. When I take a job, fall in love, read a book, eat a meal, go to the dentist, pray or meditate, I expect the activity itself or its results to make me feel better than I do at the moment. No matter how good I feel, I can always imagine a state of greater happiness. If I am miserable, my actions will be calculated to remove or lessen the misery and bring about an increase in happiness. When a better state is inconceivable, I refrain from activities that might compromise the one I'm in. The world's tropical beaches are packed with happy people lying flat on their backs, not moving a muscle.

Several facts need to be considered when we pursue objects for the happiness we think they can provide. First, I want to be happy all the time. Bits and pieces of happiness spliced between periods of unhappiness is not good enough. What I need is an object that contains limitless happiness that I could possess and enjoy every minute of my life.

Leaving aside the question of whether or not such an object exists, let us consider the way experience works. Experience is the continuous interaction of a subject with objects. Nothing can be done about it. I am here and the world of objects is there and we are somehow inextricably bound to each other. The proof lies in the fact that I am always experiencing something. Even deep sleep is an object in which I experience limitlessness and bliss.

Also, everything in the world of experience is in a state of change. As part of that world I am never the same from one moment to the next. One minute I feel good, the next minute I do not. One moment I want this, the next moment I want that. The objects around me and within me that I depend on for my happiness are also in a state of flux. When I connect to or obtain the object of my desire, the happiness or satisfaction lasts as long as the connection lasts.

At first glance it would seem that happiness resides in objects. I purchase a house and a new car and I feel happy. I go on vacation and I feel happy. I jog, garden, meditate or ski and I feel happy. Literally millions of apparently happiness-producing objects and activities fall within the categories of security, pleasure and virtue. But if happiness is inherent in an object or activity or a particular state of mind, the object or activity or state of mind would produce happiness for everyone equally. A pair of Nike running shoes makes a jogger happy but provides little joy for an amputee. A granny who knits for fun will not take pleasure in bungee jumping. Giving away millions makes philanthropists happy, yet letting go of a dime is anathema to a miser. A man divorces his wife because he sees her as the source of his misery. Before the ink is dry on the divorce decree, he finds her in the arms of another who sees her as his darling bundle of joy.

Some try to attain happiness in subtle and abstract ways. Poets, writers, artists and actors find it by interacting with thoughts and ideas, feelings and emotions. Academics, convinced that it can be gained through knowledge, subject themselves to years of disciplined study. Religious types seek happiness in prayer and ritual. Spiritual questers seek fulfillment in meditation, chanting and mystic techniques that are meant to give them access to higher states of consciousness. The psychological world maintains that happiness can be attained by removing subjective obstacles: disturbing memories, self limiting concepts and unforgiving thoughts lodged in the subconscious mind.

## Limitation of Object Happiness

Both approaches, the physical and the psychological, share the belief that effort can alter the objective and subjective factors inhibiting happiness. Conventional wisdom supports this view, and the kernel of truth it contains probably accounts for the universal pursuit of happiness through objects.

Why do we feel happy when we get what we want? The pursuit of happiness in objects is driven by a two-faced monster: fear and desire. A desire hides behind every fear and behind every fear lurks a hidden desire. If I do not get what I want I will be unhappy. Avoiding what I do not want makes me happy. So the fear of unhappiness is just the desire for happiness. These two primal psychic forces, which cause our attractions and repulsions, attachments and aversions, color every aspect of our lives. They are caused by ignorance of the nature of the subject.

Because fear and desire are uncomfortable feelings, I have a strong need to be free of them. I need to be fulfilled and happy. When I say that I want a new car, a new relationship, a better job or a vacation abroad, I do not want the object for its own sake. I want the happiness apparently wrapped up in it. If there was a permanent happiness pill, I would quickly forego my desires for objects.

## Removing the Wall

Why does happiness seem to come from objects? When desired objects are attained or feared objects avoided, the wall of fear and desire separating me from the subject—the source of happiness—dissolves, and happiness fills me.

How does this work? When a fear or desire is removed, the mind associates the happiness with the object, rather than with the removal of the subjective limitation. If this fact were clearly understood, people would discontinue the search for happiness in objects and directly remove their fears and desires. Unfortunately, what I want and do not want does not seem to be under my control. Desires appear in my mind from an unknown source and more or less command me to scurry off into the world in search of the relevant object.

While there are myriad objects that human beings pursue in the quest for happiness, the familiar belief that happiness lies in relationships with people is a good example of how the mechanism works. I find someone to love and if that person returns the love, it makes me happy. But what happens when the love object no longer satisfies my desire for love? The feeling of love disappears and now I believe that the removal of the love object will make me happy. Why does the love dry up? Because the idea that it was coming from the object acted like a switch and closed the door between the desirer and the desirer's true nature. Although the desirer's true nature is love, he or she does not know it.

That switch, the belief that the joy is in the object, can also open the door. For instance, loneliness causes fantasies of an ideal someone who will bring happiness. When life presents an approximation of the fantasy, the dam encompassing the inner ocean of love is breached because the desire has found its object and love cascades freely into the heart, producing the experience of intense happiness. Because the process is unconscious and love appears miraculously in the presence of the object, I assume that the love is coming from the object or my interaction with the object, but they are only catalysts that trigger the inner switch.

You may wish to argue that if love is everyone's nature, I can get love from someone else. It is possible, but getting love from conscious beings is difficult because their likes and dislikes, which are not under their conscious control, operate their inner switches and whimsically turn the love on and off. Giving love is equally difficult for the same reason. Even if I am fortunate enough to be loved unconditionally, my conditioning may prevent me from appreciating the object's love. To avoid this trap I should understand that although love is in everyone, I can rely on it only when I have realized that it is my own nature.

To accomplish this, I need to sacrifice the fears and desires separating me from my own nature.

## Object Happiness Not Permanent

The fly in the ointment of the belief in object-dependent happiness is the fact that life is impermanent. All objects, including the minds and emotions of every subject, are in a state of continual flux. Additionally, if permanent happiness is attainable by possessing and enjoying objects, the desire to have another object would never arise once the desired object was attained. Conversely, if permanent happiness was attainable by removing an object, it would never have to be removed again. But experience shows that getting rid of an unwanted object does not prevent it from reappearing. Additionally, the desire for objects continues, often increases, when they are possessed and enjoyed. I may want more of a particular object, less of it, or something else altogether. The satisfaction of my desires and the removal of my fears do not leave me permanently satisfied.

For instance, people who associate happiness with a certain object, say a drug- or alcohol-induced state of mind, try to achieve that state over and over, up to and often beyond the point where it no longer yields pleasure. Nobody is ever permanently satisfied by a successful sexual encounter or any other supposedly happiness-producing object or activity. In fact, happiness-producing objects and activities often suddenly produce unhappiness. It is common knowledge that what I want changes when I get what I want, causing me to no longer value the object. Or even if my value for the object does not change, the object will eventually change and rob my happiness.

## A Zero-Sum Game

The lid on the coffin of the object happiness business is the sad fact that life is a zero-sum game. It is a zero-sum game because it is a duality. You cannot win. Every upside has a downside. For example: the way to remove my sense of being bound by time is to fulfill my desires because then my sense of time limitation disappears, but desires are endless and fulfilling them takes time; I need money for security but my desire to spend—what good is it if you can't spend it?—makes me insecure. The more pleasure I get, the more pleasure I want. Wanting is not pleasant; I want power to be free of my sense of inadequacy and smallness but power depends on circumstances not under my control, causing me to feel powerless. I want to be perfect, but the more perfect I become, the more hidden imperfections come to light.

## The Fourth Pursuit – Freedom from Limitation

If you think about it, the common denominator in all pursuits is freedom. Each pursuit is meant to remove a sense of incompleteness and inadequacy, but they all fail to deliver. Does this mean that I should abandon my quest for freedom? Or does it mean that I am barking up the wrong tree? Perhaps my problem has nothing to do with the world at all. Perhaps there is something I do not know about myself.

A careful study of the voluminous and ancient body of literature that deals with the topic of freedom reveals two distinct but not unrelated paths to freedom: the path of experience and the path of knowledge.

# CHAPTER TWO

# What Is Enlightenment?

## The Path of Experience

Existence is consciousness. From the human point of view it is experienced as three states: waking, dream and deep sleep. Sleep is the absence of differentiated experience. Dream is similar to waking in that the subject-object distinction obtains. Waking state consciousness can be divided into two sub-states: *samsara* and *nirvana*, to use two Sanskrit terms.[1] Samsara describes the

---

1. I am sorry to introduce Sanskrit terms, but it is virtually impossible to dispassionately discuss the self and the inner world exclusively in English. And even though Western poets, mystics, and religious figures investigated the inner world in a personal and happenstance way, no science of self knowledge developed. Consequently, there is no established terminology. Sanskrit, the native language of self inquiry, arose out of the need to communicate about the nature of consciousness as a result of the investigations of untold numbers of subjective scientists over several thousand years. It is a particularly elegant and precise language that divorces the investigation into consciousness-awareness from mysticism and religion and makes it straightforward and easy to understand. The science of self inquiry is discussed in detail in chapter 3.

experience of life as we know it. It is conceived of as a whirlpool or a wheel, a state of mind that goes around and around more or less forever. A whirlpool is difficult, if not impossible, to escape. Desires and fears emerge from an unknown source, disturb the mind for a while and disappear, only to reappear and disturb it again. We do actions intended to remove them but the actions only serve to reinforce them. As the wheel of life goes around and around we go up and down, elated one minute and depressed the next. Samsara is an entropic perpetual motion machine that never takes us anywhere, slowly wears us out and eventually sends us on.

Sometimes, however, we are granted a reprieve and lifted out of the samsaric state of mind. One is never sure how or why it happens. *Grace* is the only word that seems applicable. During these episodes we feel open, expansive and free. Typically, we observe our minds and bodies as objects. Perhaps we feel connected to everything. Maybe we melt into the world or experience a radiant inner light or the peace that passes understanding. It may feel as if we are not there because the ego has temporarily dissolved. Fear and desire, our more or less constant companions, are conspicuous by their absence. Hence, this transcendent otherworldly state is called *nirvana*. Nirvana literally means *without flame* or *extinct* and symbolizes a desireless, fearless state of mind or the extinction of the sense of separateness. This state is invariably accompanied by wonder and bliss. These epiphanies vary from a few seconds to minutes, days and occasionally weeks or even months. Eventually we come back to samsara, the everyday state of mind.

When we get back we long to return because a vacation from the monotonous uncertainties of life is a great relief. A few serious epiphanies and we are tempted to drop out and head for India. Epiphanies are the basis of all religions and give their doctrines of divinity an experiential foundation. They are sometimes called visions of God or revelations and are highly valued. Many ardent prayers are offered to invoke them.

These experiences, large and small, happen infrequently but are so compelling they cannot be discounted. At a certain point in an individual's evolution they become intense and frequent. Over the course of human history they have been catalogued, discussed and analyzed and these studies constitute a large body of literature. In due course a science of meditation evolved from them.[2] Meditation makes it possible to experience nirvana, the transcendental state or God consciousness, with enough certainty to give it a scientific basis.

Meditation is often conceived of as a flight, a journey to the beyond. It takes considerable practice to master, but eventually the meditator is able to transcend the mind more or less at will. As the practice becomes routine, the meditator spends increasingly longer periods in nirvana, where there is no suffering, and less time in the samsaric state where there is. Eventually the state is meant to become effortless and continuous so that the individual can even go about daily life in nirvanic consciousness, i.e., fulfilled and happy.

The last word in terms of freedom from samsara is called *nirvikalpa samadhi,* a state of absorption that erases duality.[3] The subject and the objects merge into one experience that lasts for some time. It is the opposite of deep sleep because the mind is awake. In deep sleep duality is erased because the knower-known-knowledge division is gone. When the duality of subject and object does not obtain, freedom obtains. This state does not destroy the ignorance that causes the samsaric state of mind, because the one who has the ignorance has been absorbed into awareness where no duality obtains. If you achieve this samadhi it indicates a high degree of mastery of the mind, which may be useful once you are back in samsara.

It comes up short in terms of lasting freedom, however, because when you leave the samadhi and enter samsaric consciousness the inbuilt dualistic orientation, the subject-object distinction, returns. Unconscious tendencies begin interpreting experience and the same old problems resurface. And one important fact needs to be taken into account when we are considering the pursuit of this kind of enlightenment: all experiences are in time so nirvana or samadhi can never become a permanent or continuous experience.

The theory of experiential enlightenment does not explain why we are caught up in samsara. It takes for granted that the solution to samsara is exclusively experiential and offers to convert samsara into nirvana. The bible

---

2. Chapter 13 discusses meditation in detail.

3. This and other states are discussed in detail in chapter 15.

for the proponents of this view of enlightenment is the Patanjali *Yoga Sutras*, written a few hundred years before the Christian era. It informs us that our conditioning stands in the way of the experience of nirvana and instructs us how to remove it so that we can experience freedom. It is a dualistic doctrine based on the apparent reality of subject and object. I, the subject, am limited by my state of mind. Because limitation is not acceptable to me I would like to free myself of it. I practice some form of meditation and gain mastery of my mind by removing the thoughts that obstruct the experience of limitlessness. My experience of limitlessness is the object. Buddha's Eightfold Path and Ashtanga Yoga are the traditional methods for gaining experiential freedom. Buddha did not bring God into it but Patanjali did, saying that surrender to God is an indirect aid for attaining freedom.

Success in meditation does not destroy duality. I am still me, the subject, but I now experience freedom. Patanjali does not put it exactly this way. He says that once the mind is brought under control, "the seer dwells in its own nature" and "the indweller shines forth as pure consciousness," words that amount to freedom but do not take into account the fact that the seer, awareness, dwells in his own nature and shines forth irrespective of the condition of the mind. Nor does it take into account the fact that the meditator is consciousness, i.e., free already. In any case, enlightened or not, a mind free of desire is certainly not undesirable for anyone seeking happiness. The Eightfold Path is also an experiential journey that is said to end with enlightenment. This view is fairly reasonable and would not have endured for two thousand years if there was not some truth to it, but it is a very arduous path requiring an austere lifestyle and many years of rigorous practice.

When passion is king and instant gratification is queen, the mind becomes agitated if more than a few minutes are required to satisfy its desires. Fortunately, the samsaric state of mind is its own worst enemy, and sensitive individuals seek a way out. Invariably, the first enlightenment view that presents itself to them is the experiential view. From womb to tomb, life is one long series of experiences, so it is natural to become attached to experience and define ourselves by our experiences. Who would I be without them? The idea that we do not need experience to be happy never occurs to us. Although it is a natural and inevitable experience, death terrifies us as it seemingly spells the end of experience.

Experience obviously takes place in time. It is clear that experienced objects change, but what about the experiencer—me? I change too. Can I honestly say that I have not changed since the day I was born? Absolutely everything about me changes: my body, my feelings, my thoughts and ideas. I am never the same from one day to the next. Time is having its way with me and there is nothing I can do about it. If experience did not modify me, what would be the point of experience? And because experience is dualistic it is sometimes positive and sometimes negative. Positive is fine, but negative is not fine, so I am open to suggestions that might free me of the negative and generate the positive. In fact, a significant fraction of my energy goes into calculating which course of action will make me feel good and which will make me feel bad. As I cannot know for sure what the results of my actions will be, I often find myself hopelessly confused and unable to do anything at all.

If somebody says that there is a special kind of experience that feels good and never ends, I am ready to sign up. If I have an experience of uncaused bliss, one that is not dependent on an outside event, I may be even more inclined to accept the idea of experiential enlightenment. Perhaps I reason that I can make the experience permanent, even though every time it happens, it ends. When the great sage Patanjali says that all I have to do to make it permanent is to remove my thoughts, I am ready to become a yogi. How hard can it be?

This is wishful thinking because samsara, the world of experience, is change. There is no special experience in samsara that does not change. The experiencer, me, is in time, and the objects of experience are in time, including all states of mind. How is it possible for two things that are constantly changing to produce a state of mind that does not change?

The experiencer changes because he or she is limited. Even deep sleep changes the experiencer because he or she wakes up rested. The experience of oneness also changes the experiencer because he or she wants to experience it again when the effects wear off. If it had no effect, the desire to regain it would not occur. To experience changelessness, there would have to be an unchanging experiencer outside of samsara that could experience it, assuming there is something beyond samsara. But where there is no change there is no experience, so what is the point of trying to become another experiencer even if it is possible?

If you believe that through a yogic technique or willpower or some other way, the experience of limitless freedom could be made permanent, who would make it permanent? The experiencer could not do it, because he or she does not even know what his or her next state of mind will be. No state of mind is under the conscious control of the experiencer. Even if the experiencer could control its state of mind or the thoughts in it, what happens when he or she loses control? To maintain control, concentration is necessary. What happens to the experience of limitlessness when I get sick and lose my concentration? It seems that my enlightenment is going to disappear along with my health.

Furthermore, the experiencer would have to be limitless to keep the mind permanently under control. But I am definitely limited. If I were limitless I would not be concerned about enlightenment as I would not be limited by suffering. It is precisely because I feel limited that I am interested in freedom. How can an action—concentration, meditation or any other action—by a limited entity produce a limitless result? Freedom is limitless and cannot be the result of any action.

Finally, the idea that I can obtain the experience of enlightenment means that I am not experiencing the self—the light of awareness—now. It so happens that the non-experience of the self is impossible because consciousness is eternal and omnipresent and non-dual. It is everything that is. How can I get what I already have by doing anything? If I am going to get what I already have, I am going to have to lose my ignorance of who I am. This is not to say that meditation, epiphanies, or other spiritual practices are not valuable. We will later argue that epiphanies are very helpful as they give us an idea of what we are seeking. And we will also argue that spiritual practice is essential, not because it produces enlightenment, but because it prepares the mind for enlightenment. Without a prepared, qualified mind, enlightenment will not happen.

# The Path of Knowledge

To attain enlightenment I need to know what it is. The experiential view of enlightenment is based on the idea that reality is a duality. I am here, the world is there. I am here, enlightenment is there. But what if reality is not a duality? What if it is actually non-dual consciousness?[4] Would I try to experience the self through meditation or some other method?

If I have a mystic experience like a non-dual epiphany, it is unlikely that I will think about its meaning as it unfolds. The experience itself will be so strange, welcome and exhilarating that I will just get into it and enjoy. As it happened unexpectedly—perhaps I was just walking to the post office with many mundane things in my mind—the cause is unknown to me. If I take LSD and my mind is blown, the cause is obvious. But non-dual experiences, melting into everything in love for example, come unsolicited. They can only be chalked up to the grace of God. And in the absence of the knowledge of the nature of reality, I have no way to evaluate their overall meaning. Even if they tend to come with regularity, each one is unique, making it difficult to divine the meaning. Experience usually needs to repeat over and over, in the presence of an inquiring mind, before its secrets are revealed. Epiphanies may temporarily motivate me to change, which oddly enough is not desirable, or they may make me think I am quite exceptional, perhaps enlightened, but usually they simply produce a strong craving for more. The attempt to re-experience the self is futile because the experiencer thinks the self is not presently experienced. But ironically it is present when I want it because it exists prior to the experiencer. It is not prior to the experiencer in time, in which case it would not be present. It is prior in terms of understanding. It is present and apparently hidden.

Experience, worldly or spiritual, is only raw information that has no meaning apart from the way it is interpreted. What if the purpose of experience is not experience but knowledge? What if experience is just an envelope containing

---

4. The science of self inquiry uses the word *non-dual* and not the word *one* because one implies duality and multiplicity.

messages from consciousness about our identity? What if experiences are not telling us what to want or to avoid in samsara? What if they are telling us who we are?

Just as there are scriptures that tout experiential enlightenment, there are scriptures that tout enlightenment as self knowledge. If you find yourself suddenly disinterested when you hear the word *knowledge*, keep reading. Please do not succumb to the strong anti-intellectual bias that pervades the spiritual world. If you think enlightenment is all about heart or a special experience and that knowledge is merely intellectual, keep reading. Knowledge is not opposed to sensations or emotions or any experience. In fact, what you feel is enhanced by understanding. What is about to unfold could very well move you along on your path. If you react unfavorably to the word *knowledge*, substitute the word *understanding*.

Knowledge cannot be dismissed or negated. For example, when scientists want to send a spaceship to Neptune, they do not aim it at Neptune but send it toward another planet in the opposite direction. You say, "Hey, Neptune is over there!" But they do not listen. When it arrives it circles around planet X, picks up momentum and is shot off into the depths of space where there is nothing for a zillion light years. You cannot believe what they are doing because Neptune is presently a bit to the left of planet X. You politely mention it but they do not care. A few months later it enters the orbit of planet Y, picks up more momentum and is again shot off in a direction that has nothing to do with the present position of Neptune. After a year or two it meets up with Neptune right on schedule. You cannot count on personal experience as it is conditional and can be dismissed. If you relied on personal experience you would never get to Neptune. The odds of stumbling upon enlightenment are a million to one if you rely solely on your personal experience and the knowledge you extract from it.

Knowledge is object-dependent, not subject-dependent. Two plus two is four, no matter how you personally see it. Objects accelerate at thirty-two feet per second whether you are a Christian, Muslim or an Australian Aborigine. It has nothing to do with you. It is like sleep; a king sleeping on his silk sheets in the palace has the same experience as a drunk sleeping in his vomit in the gutter. When you realize the truth, you realize what everyone else realized. The idea that there is my truth and your truth does not work, because knowledge is object-dependent and there is only one self. Knowledge is valuable because nothing in this world is what it seems to be. The world of time, experience, is a world of appearances. If you take it to be real you will suffer. It does not exist apart from awareness. It seems to be real because you do not know who you are.

Awareness, you, is always here. You are always the same. You are what is real. You are the truth. Without you the world of appearances does not exist. Self knowledge—I am awareness—is always good because the self is always free, and it is most desirable because freedom is our most cherished value. You can count on it because it never changes. You cannot dismiss it, because you, the object of knowledge, are always present and cannot dismiss yourself. If this knowledge "stands under" you, you are free. Hence, the path of understanding.

The scriptures that tout enlightenment as self realization or self knowledge are based on the contention that reality is non-dual, unlike the scriptures that tout experiential enlightenment. Non-dual reality means that there is only one principle operating in reality, not two or more, appearances to the contrary notwithstanding. It means that the subject and the objects are actually non-different, although they seem to be different. Unlike experiential enlightenment, self realization is a hard sell because experience seems to completely refute it. We cannot be faulted for unthinkingly interpreting the information we get from our senses to mean that the subject is different from the objects. We are born into a world where everyone has unwittingly made this assumption. We are conditioned by it every minute of our lives because we accept our senses as our only means of knowledge.

Just as the scriptures on Yoga offer methods for experiencing the self, the scriptures on knowledge use a sophisticated methodology to reveal the self. This method, which will be unfolded throughout this text, is called self inquiry. We inquire because we want to know something. There is no contradiction between these two methods. Experience is not good and knowledge is not bad. Nor is experience bad and knowledge good. If the relationship between them is clearly understood, a great obstacle to enlightenment has been dismissed.

From the point of view of consciousness there is no difference between knowledge and experience. Knowledge is experience and experience is knowledge. What you see you know and what you know you see, because consciousness is all there is. But from the point of view of an individual seeking freedom, experience and knowledge are quite different. This is so because the individual experiences objects through the mind, which makes them seem to be something other than the mind, and the mind, based on past experiences, interprets what it sees as knowledge whether or not the knowledge is actually true to the object.

If we look at the claim of the proponents of the experiential view of enlightenment from the non-dual point of view, the attempt to gain the experience of consciousness, however I formulate it, is unnecessary. Why? Because, if there is only one self and it is everything that is, then everything I experience at any time or place can only be the self including me, the experiencer. In short, I am experiencing awareness because I am awareness. And because awareness is limitless it is always free. And because there is only awareness, I am already free. I do not need an experience to set me free. Therefore, the attempt to get a discrete experience of the self is gratuitous, like going out for a hamburger when you have a filet mignon in the refrigerator.

This may sound like the negative teachings of the instant enlightenment schools—there is nothing to do, no path, no teacher, no scripture, no this, no that, you are already enlightened—that have muddied the spiritual waters since time immemorial. The view from the self does negate everything, but negation is only the preliminary portion of the self inquiry story, as we will see. Neo-Advaita,[5] the latest iteration of the instant enlightenment idea, makes it the whole story because the teachers, all Westerners, never actually exposed their minds to the teaching tradition of the science of self inquiry[6] in a disciplined way. They kept a Western orientation and picked the easiest self serving teaching—not this, not this—from a guru who neglected to teach

---

5. Chapter 16 discusses Neo-Advaita in depth.

6. The teaching tradition of the science of self inquiry is explained in detail in chapter 3.

the complete science of consciousness, if he knew it at all, passing it off as the whole loaf. In fact the guru explicitly stated that he did not give the whole teaching as his disciples were not qualified.

In any case, one of the most important functions of the statement that reality is non-dual awareness and that if you exist, which you do, you can only be awareness, is to convince you that you do not have an experience problem as far as enlightenment is concerned. In fact, you cannot actually experience awareness as an object, because you are awareness. The best you can do is to experience its reflection in a pure mind. This can be a help or a hindrance, depending on what you make of it.[7] What use is it to try to experience awareness, if in fact everything that you experience within yourself and beyond the body is it?

If I am experiencing awareness all the time because it is me, then I have a knowledge problem, not an experience problem. If you do not realize that you have a knowledge problem, then unfortunately you will have to keep groping around in the experiential wilderness until you do realize it. "By knowledge alone is the self realized," says Ramana Maharshi and innumerable texts of the science of self inquiry. When this fact has been properly assimilated, you are qualified for self inquiry.

So what is the knowledge that constitutes enlightenment? It is the hard and fast conviction based on direct observation that I am ever free awareness and not the body-mind. It is the understanding that I am everything that is. It is the rock solid conviction that no matter what happens, good or bad, I am completely OK. This knowledge frees the self from the belief that it is an individual, limited being and destroys its attachment to objects as defined in chapter 1.

The words *hard* and *fast* mean that binding fears and desires have been neutralized by the knowledge and that the pursuit of security, pleasure and virtue is no longer active. If you say you are enlightened but continue to chase and cling to objects in samsara, you are not enlightened. You may know who you are intellectually but you do not actually know who you are.

---

7. Chapter 8, Inquiry into Practice, will discuss the value of spiritual practice.

Enlightenment is the unassailable understanding that because you are eternal, you are completely secure. Wealth cannot make you more secure. It is the bedrock knowledge that the pleasures available in the world of appearances are but dim reflections of the pleasure that you are. It means that you need not strive to be virtuous, because you are goodness itself.

## The Value of a Means of Knowledge

If you are in the middle of a non-dual epiphany, the self[8] does not suddenly appear and say, "Yo! Seeker! Pay attention. What you are experiencing is you, although it seems to be an object. I am telling you this so you will not try to repeat this experience once it ends. If you are wondering what to make of this experience I will tell you now. It means that you are whole and complete actionless awareness, just like me. It means that henceforth you will not desire or fear anything, because nothing can be added to you or taken away from you. If, when this experience wears off, you set out to get it back or do something with it, you have not properly assimilated the meaning of my words. Good luck."

The self will not say this, because it sees you as whole and complete consciousness. The beliefs and opinions you picked up in life will not help interpret your epiphanies either, because you picked them up when you were ignorant of whom you are. You will see them as you want to see them, not as they are. Knowledge is seeing things as they are, not as how they appear to you. So to gain enlightenment you need to shed self ignorance and to do that, you need a proven means of self knowledge. It will help you make sense of what happens to you spiritually and otherwise.

---

8. In Western spiritual literature about the topic of self realization it has been a habit for many years to capitalize the word *self* to distinguish it from the ego, the "lower" self. It is a useful convention on one hand, but on the other, it encourages us to think in a two self paradigm, which feeds our sense of duality. Because reality is non-dual there is actually only one self. The ego, the individual, is not actually a separate self. It is a "self" created out of ignorance of the nature of consciousness. I have elected to refer to this self as the apparent self, therefore, I have not capitalized the word *self*.

Epiphanies are useful if they are accompanied by self inquiry. Self inquiry does not mean asking "Who am I?," because the answer is known. If you have a doubt, a glance at scripture will set your mind at rest. You are awareness, not the person you have been led to believe you are. Self inquiry is a systematic body of proven knowledge that looks at experience and knowledge, from the point of view of consciousnesses and from all the basic samsaric reference points. It does not summarily dismiss experience and knowledge as illusion. It shows you that you are the big picture and if you cannot see yourself that way, it shows you how you fit into the big picture. You need an impartial guide, not your own interpretation of experience, because ignorance can make what is false seem to be real. You are the last person who should be an expert on who you are.

## Enlightenment Myths

If you can see that the question of freedom is due to a lack understanding, you will be open to a means of self knowledge. A means of self knowledge does not actually give you self knowledge, because everyone actually does know who they are, as will become apparent as we proceed. Unfortunately, there is usually a lack of clarity about the nature of the self, which impedes the full appreciation of it. This lack of clarity manifests as ill considered beliefs and opinions, particularly the belief that the self is limited. If you expose your mind to a time-tested, experienced based means of self knowledge, it will patiently strip away these beliefs and clarity will return. When the last vestige of ignorance is removed, you will realize that you knew who you were all along. You will find it amusing that you went through so much seeking to find out what you already knew.

We are going to accept the contention that reality is non-dual and examine a number of popular enlightenment teachings from the non-dual perspective. If they come up short as means of enlightenment, it does not mean that they have no value. Indeed, there is some truth to all of them and they may be useful in some form as practices that prepare the mind for self knowledge. If you find yourself attached to one or more of these beliefs, it will benefit you to consider them from the non-dual perspective. Ultimately, you will have to determine the nature of reality through your own investigation, but if your inquiry is disinterested, you can only come to one conclusion: "I am ever free awareness."

## No Mind, Blank Mind, Empty Mind, Stopped Mind

The experience of deep sleep and waking state epiphanies, characterized by an arrested mind, are probably responsible for the no-mind theory of enlightenment. In both cases no objects are present, or have been neutralized, so the mind—which is only capable of experiencing objects—is not there to own the experience. When the mind is reconstituted, it has no memory of the experience.

Because reality is non-dual the mind is actually the self, awareness, under the spell of ignorance. On the absolute level awareness knows that it experiences itself when the mind is both present and absent, but when it tries to express this at the mental level, all it can do is represent the experience as an empty or blank mind. This causes a problem because a blank mind is an object, albeit a subtle one. Therefore, to get back the experience of itself, the experience that it never lost, it thinks it needs to get a blank mind to experience what it is!

A simpler explanation for the idea that liberation is the elimination of all thoughts is the fact that the scriptures that comprise the science of self inquiry describe the self as thought free. But between two thoughts there is a tiny gap, an absence of thought. If the absence of thought for a split second is not enlightenment, the absence of thought for an hour or two will not amount to the liberating knowledge "I am whole and complete actionless awareness."

The most obvious defect of this theory is the fact that all enlightened beings think. As long as the mind is awake, it thinks. If you cannot accept this, the way around it would be to simply go to sleep as the mind is non-existent in sleep. But this kind of enlightenment is not terribly useful, because you always wake up.

As the self is always enlightened, the idea that "no mind" is enlightenment implies a duality between the awareness and thought. To say that the self is not experienceable when the mind is functioning means that the mind and the self enjoy the same order of reality, like a table and a chair. But experience shows that this is untrue. Do you cease to exist when you are thinking? Is there thought without awareness? In fact, thoughts come from you but you are much more than a thought. They depend on you but you do not depend on them.

Or, let us put it in a slightly different way. Let us say that you are awake and the mind is stopped. For you to know that it is stopped, you would have to be aware. Now, let us say that the mind is thinking. You would also have to be aware to know that it is thinking. In both cases, with and without thought I, awareness, am present. If I am aware when it is stopped and when it is thinking, I am not hidden by thought nor am I revealed by no thought. Whether they are present or absent, you, the ever-free, ever-present self, can always be directly known.

However, if I define enlightenment as an experience that is different from my waking, dream or deep sleep state experience, it can easily be hidden because it is not always present. Experience is always present because experience is the self even though the self is not experience, but the subsequent or next experience, mystic or otherwise, will always be hidden when the present experience is taking place.

Awareness, the self, is always present. It is self evident. It reveals itself. It is self experiencing. There is nothing you can do about it except know what it is and look for it. If your mind does not want to cooperate with your investigation, you may have to do some work to get control of it and direct it to the self. Nothing hides you from you, except ignorance. Action, removing thoughts, will not remove ignorance because action is not opposed to ignorance. It is ignorance of who I am that causes me to believe that I am hidden from myself and attempt the actions that I believe will stop my mind.

Ignorance exists as beliefs and opinions in the mind. It can only be destroyed by knowledge. Knowledge only takes place in the mind because the mind is the instrument of knowledge. So the mind needs to make an investigation to get rid of its ignorance. Just because awareness is subtler than the mind does not mean that the mind cannot, with the help of scripture, investigate it.

In fact, scripture is the result of the disinterested and successful investigations of untold numbers of minds over thousands of years. If you deny the existence of the mind, then how can you even say that enlightenment is no mind? However, using the logic of its own experience, the mind can discover its inherent limitations and no longer support them. When ignorance is no longer supported by beliefs and opinions, it collapses under its own weight.

Thought is not the devil; it can reveal the truth. Self inquiry does not ask you to kill your mind and destroy your thoughts. It gives you the right self thought, and shows you how to use it, assuming you are seeking freedom. The right thought is *I am awareness*. The *I am awareness* thought is as good as awareness because when you think a thought, the mind goes to the object of the thought. The object of the *I am awareness* thought, the "I," is awareness and it has to be present or thought cannot happen. So when you think *I am awareness* it turns the mind away from other thoughts, the mind goes to awareness and awareness is revealed. Try it.

It certainly makes sense to eliminate thoughts that are not in harmony with the nature of reality as such thoughts cause suffering. But it remains to be considered whether all thoughts are a problem. Must I get rid of kind, positive, compassionate, happy thoughts too? The thoughts that cause happiness do not stand in the way of enlightenment because a happy mind is perfectly suited for self inquiry.

The upside of this teaching: a modified version of the no-thought idea is very useful and will be discussed in detail later, but it is not enlightenment.

### No Ego, Ego Death

This popular so-called teaching vies with the no-thought teaching for top spot on the list of enlightenment myths. Before considering its value, we will be well served by exploring four definitions of the word *ego*.

The first definition is *that which identifies with any activity*. It is called the doer and its relationship to the self and enlightenment is explained in detail in chapter 7, "Inquiry into Karma and Dharma."

The second definition is *embodied consciousness*, a conscious being with a body. Animals, insects, microbes and humans are embodied beings. You can even make a case that plants are embodied beings. Embodied beings are sometimes conceived as rays or emanations of formless consciousness, man cast in the image of God, and they seem to be separate from their source, consciousness. They seem to be separate if they are viewed from the point of view of their bodies, but viewed from the self's point of view, they are non-separate. They do not stand in the way of consciousness because they are consciousness in form, just as waves do not stand in the way of the ocean. Humans are the only egos that think, although certain members of the animal kingdom seem to be evolving the capacity to think.

All embodied beings are the self, but an embodied human being can be enlightened or unenlightened. An enlightened being is one that knows, appearances to the contrary notwithstanding, that it is not separate from consciousness, assuming as always that this knowledge has neutralized its binding likes and dislikes. An unenlightened being is someone who takes the appearance of separation to be real and is at the mercy of his or her binding likes and dislikes.

The third definition of ego, the "I" notion, relates exclusively to human beings because they are the only embodied beings that think. Dogs do not know they are dogs. They do not think they are better or worse than other dogs or any other embodied beings. Human beings, on the other hand, entertain all sorts of ideas about who they are. "I am rich, poor, gay, straight, intelligent, stupid, good, bad, Republican, Democrat," etc. The list of identities that humans are capable of concocting is virtually limitless. All these identities are limited and fall under two categories: I am a knower or I am a doer/enjoyer. The doer is someone who identifies with an activity and thinks it is solely responsible for its actions, gross and subtle. The doer is a doer for the sake of the results of its actions—which it wishes to enjoy. When a doer enjoys the result of its actions, it becomes an enjoyer. The knower is the one who identifies with what it experiences and knows.

Aside from the fact that there is no evidence that such an "I" exists, the destruction of the notion that the "I" is limited is a restricted formulation of enlightenment because the absence of a limited identity does not equal enlightenment. If it did, plants and animals, even microbes, would be enlightened.

And you would be enlightened in deep sleep because you are not an ego there. For enlightenment you need the hard and fast knowledge of who you are in the waking state. If you conflate ego death with enlightenment, you may very well find yourself a void. The life of a void is not particularly pleasant.

Assuming there is an ego that is standing in the way of enlightenment, the ego death teaching is still unworkable because it asks the ego to kill itself. If the ego is the embodied being, it would only kill itself if it thought that it would derive a benefit—such is the nature of egos—but most egos are smart enough to realize that if they do not exist, no benefits will accrue.

Also if ego is the "I" notion, it cannot kill itself, because it is not conscious. So on both counts, the idea comes up short. This leaves the Hollywood ending: the ego remains, gets the permanent enlightenment experience and enjoys endless experiential bliss.

In actuality, enlightenment is freedom from the "I" notion, not the embodied being. The embodied being is actually limitless consciousness with an incorrect understanding of its nature. For it to free itself from erroneous self notions, it should expose itself to the means of self knowledge and contemplate the teachings dispassionately. The death of the "I" notion happens as a result of self knowledge, not something you do.

What is self knowledge with reference to the ego? It is the knowledge that the embodied being is me but I am not the embodied being. This is tantamount to ego death because it shifts the ego from the center of consciousness to the periphery where it belongs, not that consciousness has a periphery. Self knowledge is the best of both worlds, not that there are two worlds, as it allows you to live freely as embodied consciousness, without suffering the results of actions.

Pride, the final definition of ego, does not relate directly to the question of enlightenment but bears mention nonetheless. Pride is willful ignorance of the fact that everything you take to be yours is actually borrowed from the world. If you are proud of your good looks, you need to realize that you had nothing to do with it. If you have a particularly brilliant mind, it was not created by you. If you are proud because you accomplished something, it was only because the world provided the opportunity. Pride is a problem for seekers because it supports the ego's notion of specialness, uniqueness and duality. Its absence, however, is not enlightenment. Many humble people have no idea who they are.

### Nirvana

This idea, explained above, is another negative formulation of enlightenment. *Nir* means *not* or *without* and *vana* means *a flame*. Fire is a common symbol of passion or desire so nirvana, which is meant to be enlightenment, is said to be a desireless state. Desire makes samsara go around and around. Desire includes fear, its kissing cousin. Fear that I won't get X equals desire for X. Desire to keep X equals fear of losing X.

This view is based on the idea that desire is suffering. It may take a while for the ego to completely assimilate this truth but it is obvious: if you want something, it means that you are not happy with what you have. If you are happy not being happy, fine, but normally people are not happy with unhappiness.

The same criticism raised against the no thought mind applies to the desireless mind. Desireless mind is an oxymoron. When, except during sleep, do you not want something? Even at the end of life you want to continue living, if life is still good, or to die if it is not.

On the surface the logic makes sense, but what is the cause of desire? Is it self-caused or is it the result of something else? If it is self-caused, then eliminating desire should eliminate suffering. But what if desire is an effect of self ignorance? Will removing the effect remove the cause? Will ignorance collapse when it is no longer supported by desire? Or will it just keep manufacturing more desires? In mythological literature there are many examples of the difficulty of removing desire, the Hydra for example. Cut off one head and another grows back, sometimes more than one. However, unreasonable it is as a definition of enlightenment, the upside of this idea is discussed in chapter 8.

It remains to be seen whether desire is only suffering. It is possible to entertain a desire and not be agitated by it. In fact, if desire disappeared altogether, the world as we know it would disappear, not that that is necessarily a worst-case scenario. It seems desire is the cause of much good and much evil. If I desire to develop a cure for cancer and enjoy my work, is this desire a problem?

If I am building a bridge across a river and fear that it may collapse and take extra care to see that it is properly reinforced, is it a bad fear? Desire is just awareness functioning as the creator, sustainer and destroyer of the world. As long as my desires do not cause me to violate the physical and moral laws operating in the creation, why should I remove them? And finally, if I accept the contention that desire is suffering, how will I remove my desires without the desire to remove them? Why should the desire to remove them be less painful than the desires themselves?

You need not get rid of your desires to realize the self. You will have to get rid of the gratuitous desires that prevent you from making a dispassionate inquiry, but without a burning desire to know who you are, you will not have the perseverance necessary to overcome the many obstacles to self realization. When you realize who you are, you know that objects cannot complete you.

## The Now

Not to put too fine a point on it, the basic idea of the "now" teachings is: I am enlightened when I am present. Living in the past and the future means I am unenlightened. Aside from the fact that there is no time in our non-dual reality, let us inquire into this idea.

Does the word *now* refer to a period of time, which it certainly seems to, or is now a symbol for something else? If it refers to time, is there such a thing as objective time? If now is a period of time sandwiched between the past and the future, when does the past end and the now begin? When does the now end and the future begin? It is impossible to determine because time is relative to the desires and fears of individuals and to the relative intervals between experiences. If my desires are being met and I am enjoying, time passes quickly. If I am suffering terribly, time passes slowly. If different experiences occur in a rapid sequence, time passes quickly with reference to the observer. If the distance between two experiences is great, time passes slowly.

Are the past, present and future actual divisions in consciousness or only conceptual divisions? If time is objective, then everyone would be able to determine just when the past ends and the now begins. Furthermore, when I am in the now, how long does the now remain the now? Is it one second? Two? One minute? More? Assuming I am in the now and want to remain enlightened, I should have this information because when it ends, I need to avoid travelling into the future. Perhaps I need to hop up out of the time continuum just before the end of the now and jump back into it just before the past appears, keeping in mind how much time passes until I have to hop out again. Even if I am sitting still in the now I need to worry about the past and the future creeping into it. It doesn't take an advanced degree to understand that in reality the past, present and future are just concepts that help individuals who are caught up in their desires and fears navigate through an apparently changing world.

Let's assume that there is only now. Am I ever out of it? Experience only takes place in the present. How can you experience the past if it is not here? You can experience a memory but the experience of memory does not take you to the past. The memory appears in awareness and is experienced now. The experience takes as long as it takes and means whatever it is interpreted to mean. The same logic applies to the future. Nothing is ever experienced in the future. You may think about something that you imagine will take place at another time but it if happens, it only happens in the present, when it appears in awareness.

Time is not linear. Objects appear in consciousness, last as long as they last with reference to your desires and then disappear back into consciousness. When they appear in that part of awareness called the mind, they seem to change, but in reality it is only the mind that changes.

If this is true, maybe *now* is a code word for the self, awareness. It is the humble opinion of the author that *now* is a misleading and inaccurate term for the self and should be banned from the spiritual debate because it is not helpful to refer to something that is eternal and out of time with a word that conveys a sense of time.

However, if now is a synonym for awareness, you still cannot be in the now because you are the now. Aside from the obvious duality of "in" and "out," to say that you are not in the now means that you are paying attention to a present thought that represents either of these two fictitious time periods and not to the one to whom these thoughts appear. And to say that you are not in the now, means that you take yourself to be something other than the awareness that you are. When I am "out" and want to be "in" effort is required, but aware-ness cannot be gained by action, so being in the now is not enlightenment or a valid means of enlightenment.

To complete this inquiry we need to ask what the word *in* means. To say that I am in or out of my self means that there are two selves, me and myself or, if you insist, the now. Experience shows that reality is non-dual, so there cannot be two selves. So who exactly is going into and out of the self? By tak-ing reality to be a duality and using inaccurate words, we are simply confusing ourselves.

We need not dismiss this teaching completely because it has value as a prac-tice for someone who thinks he or she is caught up in time, takes his or herself to be a doer, and is trying to gain a certain degree of mastery of the mind.

### Experience of Oneness

This idea suffers the problems of other experienced based teachings. The sci-ence of self inquiry uses the location of objects inquiry to show that there is no need to experience oneness with yourself or anything else—if you see otherness—because you are already experiencing oneness with yourself and everything.

How so? You are already experiencing oneness with everything because re-ality is non-dual. You are awareness and the objects are awareness. It is all you. If it seems that there is something other than you, consider this: how far is a wave from the ocean? How far is a gold ring from gold or a clay pot from clay? Every object is just awareness-consciousness in a particular name and form. A name and form cannot be separated from its substrate. How can you separate the pot from the clay?

There is no need, however, to take scripture and the author's contention about the non-dual nature of reality. Investigate on your own. Ask yourself where you experience objects. Do you experience them out there in the world or do you experience them in your mind? I experience them in my mind. How far is the object from your mind? Is it floating off the surface of the mind? No, it is not. Where is it then? It has merged into the mind and the mind has taken the shape of the object. The mind is formless, like water or air, and can take any form, just as gold can become any kind of object, a ring a bracelet or a necklace.

How far are you from your mind? Is your mind floating above the surface of your awareness? Is there a gap between you and your mind? Do you need a bridge to travel over the gap? Catch a flight, perhaps?

I do not. Why? Because my mind is me. It is awareness. If this is true, then what you experience is not only in awareness but it actually *is* awareness. The objects in awareness and the subject awareness are one. If this is true, then why do I need to experience oneness? I am already experiencing oneness with everything.

I want to experience oneness with everything when I am already experiencing oneness because I have identified with the thought of separation, which causes suffering. Instead of trying to remove the want by experiencing a particular situation, I should inquire into the thought of separation. Is it true? Am I really separate from my self? Or do I already have the bliss that the object is meant to deliver?

### Transcendental State

The mind is sandwiched between pure awareness and the material world. It is an interface or buffer through which awareness interacts with itself in the form of the gross elements.[9] It is awareness but awareness in a form called *chitta*. The chitta makes it possible for awareness to think, will, feel and remember. The mind is capable of a wide range of states, from the gross feelings associated with the physical body up to the most mystical and sublime samadhis of Yoga. All states are in the mind and all change because they are in the dream of duality.

The self is non-dual and therefore it is out of time. It does not, nor can it, change. It is that because of which the mind's many states are known. It is conscious but states of mind are not conscious. They are subtle material energies capable of reflecting consciousness but they are incapable of thought or action.

---

9. How the body and the mind evolve from non-dual awareness is explained in chapter 6.

The higher you go in the mind, the more ethereal and luminous the states become because they are further removed from the gross level. When you get to the interface between the self and the mind, the mind stuff is so refined and the self so close, that radiant light and intense bliss is experienced. It is very easy to mistake these higher states of mind for the self and think enlightenment is an amazing heavenly state or a state of endless experiential bliss. Experience belongs neither to the self nor to the mind. It occurs when awareness shines on the mind. Awareness and mind is the most fundamental duality.

It may seem like splitting hairs to distinguish these pure states of mind from the self but if you are chasing freedom, you can easily get sidetracked in the blissful mystic states because you become attached to them. Attachment to bliss is a problem because the mind, the instrument of experience, changes. Just when you are settling in for a nice long blissful experience, it morphs into another state. Nothing can be done about it because the states are governed by factors beyond human control.

So, enlightenment is not a transcendental state, a higher state, an altered state, the fourth state beyond waking, dream and deep sleep or any other kind of state. It is simple, unchanging awareness and cannot be directly experienced as an object as it is subtler than the mind, the instrument of experience. A subtle object can illumine a gross object but a gross object cannot illumine a subtle object, a fact that seems lost on the proponents of the experiential view. However, the self can be experienced indirectly as a reflection in a pure mind. It is possible to gain knowledge of the self through indirect experience with inquiry. This topic is discussed in detail in chapter 12.

### Enlightenment as Eternal Bliss

When someone accustomed to identifying with the ever changing content of the mind wakes up to non-duality, the awakening is interpreted as a very positive event. When the mind reasserts itself, agitation and dullness reappear; when agitation and dullness are no longer acceptable, the mind becomes a seeker. The feeling of peace and bliss, which is an interpretation of non-duality by the mind, is brought on by the absence of suffering and not because awareness feels good. If you have been suffering a toothache for days and the tooth is extracted, it is the absence of pain that feels good, not the bliss of the extraction. You have actually just gone back to normal, not attained an exceptional state.

Enlightenment does not feel like anything. It is simply the hard and fast knowledge that I am limitless, partless awareness. When this knowledge is firm, it has a very positive effect on the mind but it does not convert the mind into an endless bliss machine. However, it infuses the mind with a sense of authenticity, wholeness and rock solid confidence. Henceforth the individual knows that it can weather any existential storm. When you know beyond a shadow of a doubt that you are awareness, you no longer desire to feel good because you know you are the source of goodness. This is not to say that a more or less constant feel good happiness is not possible. It can be attained by the consistent application of self knowledge to the mind or by the practice of the yogas discussed in subsequent chapters.

When enlightenment or self realization is touted as the experience of limitless bliss, it is usually believed that the bliss of the self is superior to the transitory bliss encountered in daily life. But all experiences of bliss, whether they are born of sensory experience, the discovery of some unknown object or spiritual practice like meditation, are the fullness and limitlessness of the self reflecting in the body-mind. The bliss belongs neither to the self nor to the body-mind. It belongs to the relationship between them.

## Levels of Enlightenment

If the problem of happiness is ignorance of my nature, and enlightenment is the hard and fast understanding that I am limitless, whole and complete, actionless, ever-free awareness, to say that there are stages of enlightenment is like saying that a woman can be a little bit pregnant. Everything is the light and the light falls equally on everything, so there is no standard for comparison.

Duality provides a basis for judgment, evaluation and comparison. When you are in duality you do not know who you are, so you are forced to evaluate yourself with reference to objects. You can compare yourself to an idea of what you want to be, to what you were yesterday, to other people or to absolutely anything. Seekers, worldly people dressed in spiritual clothing, evaluate themselves with reference to their idea of enlightenment as they perceive it to be embodied in themselves or in others.

An enlightened being is just the self functioning through a mind whose self ignorance has been removed. But the removal of self ignorance does not automatically remove the tendencies in the mind, although it eventually renders them non-binding, since they bind only because of self ignorance. Because all the mind's tendencies are equal from the self's point of view, it has no preference concerning the type of tendency it illumines. Therefore, it expresses through the existing tendencies. If you view clear water though a colored glass, it appears to be colored. If you view the self through the mind, it appears to be a person with various tendencies. If the individual has been blessed with a very pure mind from birth, has had many epiphanies, is particularly single pointed in his or her pursuits or lives an austere and disciplined life, he or she will have radiance or charisma.

Radiance is awareness reflected on a pure mind. It so happens that many enlightened people do not have radiance, although many do. It is also a fact that many unenlightened people have radiance and many do not. Additionally, the quality of radiance is in time and is conditioned by two other qualities that render the mind less than radiant.[10] Therefore, because an individual is radiant, brilliant, powerful or compassionate, does not mean that he or she is enlightened. So while it is natural to associate radiance with enlightenment and try to correlate relative degrees of enlightenment with relative degrees of radiance, it is not a sign of enlightenment. Enlightenment is just the hard and fast experience-based knowledge "I am awareness." Knowledge does not show and is therefore impossible to evaluate directly.

ENDARKENMENT

To say that there are no levels of enlightenment is not to say that in samsara there are no stages of enlightenment. The first stage might well be called endarkenment. We come into this life experiencing limitlessness and oneness with everything but, because the intellect has yet to develop, we do not

---

10. The topic of radiance and how to attain it is discussed in chapter 10.

understand the nature of what we experience. When the intellect does develop it is trained to think of the self as a limited, incomplete, inadequate creature and encouraged to solve the problem of inadequacy by picking up experience in life. At a certain point, the individual comes to realize that no matter how much experience he or she can garner, the experienced objects and activities do not solve the happiness issue. This is usually an unpleasant realization and often results in profound disillusionment. It is frequently referred to as the dark night of the soul in religious literature or hitting bottom in popular culture.

Most react to this existential crisis by sinking into distracting habits, ingesting mind numbing substances or pursuing frivolous entertainments. But for unknown reasons, a few are blessed with a variety of peculiar and invariably confusing religious or spiritual experiences that lead them to the idea of God or the pursuit of the inner light or a higher state. At some point during this period the person becomes convinced that he or she can find happiness within or in a relationship with God.

## SELF REALIZATION/SELF INQUIRY

The second stage could be termed the seeking or questing phase, which heads off in two apparently different directions. The religious path leads to the development of a personal relationship with God, who is usually conceived as a pure and perfect someone other than one's self. The idea of the self as inadequate, incomplete and separate is retained and the self is thought to be corrupted by sin. Salvation is meant to lie in invoking the grace of God through prayer and the study of scripture as well as working hard here on earth for a place in an afterlife far from this vale of tears. The religious life offers a positive, if somewhat intellectually challenged, alternative to the belief in the world as a source of meaning.

The other branch of the road leads in a less doctrinaire and belief-laden direction to the experience of the inner world and an investigation of the self. In its worldly form, it may incline one to the study of psychology but it can as well lead to various epiphanies that give rise to the conviction that the truth dwells within, as the higher or inner self or as a transcendental state of consciousness. The changes that take place in an individual's world view during this phase are often referred to as awakening.

Although the experience of the inner self is invariably uplifting and intensifies the quest, it is always confusing because the knowledge gained from these experiences challenges the view of oneself as a needy, incomplete, inadequate isolated creature. Many of these experiences can accurately be described as the experience of oneness with all things, limitlessness, and transcendent bliss.

During this stage, which might also be called the meditation stage, the mind, formerly riveted on happenings in the outer world, turns inward and fixes itself on the self, the light within, and at some point, usually after intense investigation, realizes the self. This realization is invariably formulated in experiential terms and is thought by many to be the end of the search, the ultimate state. But the science of self inquiry says that while this is a welcome and enjoyable state, it is not the end, because there is still a sense of separation between the experiencer and the object of experience, the self. When there is separation there is doubt, and the doubt is always that this state, like all states, will end, plunging the experiencer back into darkness. This fear is invariably fulfilled as the experience is not the direct experience of the self, which is impossible for reasons already discussed, but a reflection of the self in a still mind. No blame. However, the mind is subject to change, so the experience inevitably ends.

This doubt is due to the failure of the experiencer to understand that what is experienced is just his or her own self, in which case it could never be lost, because when do you not exist? The failure to convert the experience to knowledge is usually caused by the twin beliefs that knowledge is merely intellectual and that there is such a thing as a permanent experience. Experience is permanent in samsara but discrete experiences are not. So when the experience happens, the intellect is submerged in the bliss, peace and radiance, switches off, as it does in most intense sensuous experiences, and stops inquiring.

To enter the final stage, which is not a stage, inquiry must continue during the experience of the self. In ordinary perception, a thought wave arises in the mind corresponding to the nature of the perceived object. You see a tree and you know it is a tree because the self, awareness, illumines the tree thought as it arises in the intellect. Similarly, when the ego experiences the reflection of the self in a pure mind, a thought corresponding to the nature of the self, an unbroken "I" thought, arises, and this thought needs to be owned. When it is taken as one's own, the "I" thought, backed by experience, destroys the notion in the mind that it is limited, incomplete and separate.

## ENLIGHTENMENT

At this point, due to inquiry, everything stops and there is a subtle shift. The ego and the self switch places. The self, which heretofore had mistakenly been seen as the object of inquiry, "becomes" the subject, and the ego, which had mistakenly been taken to be the subject, "becomes" the object. This knowledge/experience never changes, because it was obtained through the realization that although what I experience is me, I am always free of what I experience. In other words, I "become" the self. Unlike a discrete experience of the self, self knowledge can never be lost, because it is not separate from me, awareness, the basis of everything. In fact, there is no actual transformation of the ego into the self because the ego cannot be transformed in so far as it is only a belief that the self is limited. The becoming is in terms of understanding and the understanding transforms your understanding of the relationship between the subject and the objects. It confirms the actual truth of experience by destroying the false belief that the self is an object. You see that there are no objects, that there is only the self.

But we said that reality is non-dual. If it is non-dual and enlightenment is non-dual wisdom, how do we account for the subject-object distinction when one is enlightened? We said that the object becomes the subject and the subject becomes the object and this never changes. There should be no subject and no objects.

When you view water on the surface of the desert you know that it is not water. It is experienced as water but you will not try to drink it because you know it is apparent water. When you realize who you are, subject and object remain but they are known to be apparently real. It is only when you take the subject-object distinction to be real that you pursue happiness in samsara and suffer accordingly.

SEVEN STAGES OF ENLIGHTENMENT

Within this general outline seven stages can be delineated: ignorance, obscuration, superimposition, indirect knowledge, direct knowledge, the cessation of grief and the rise of perfect satisfaction.

Ignorance of the self causes obscuration and superimposition. Obscuration is the self identified with the belief that there is no self and revealed by the fact that the individual pursues happiness solely in the world of objects, even though the self itself is the actual source of happiness. It is followed by identification with the body-mind, which results in the belief that the self is a doer and enjoyer that experiences pleasure and pain. This is called superimposition. At some point, it momentarily experiences itself or hears of the self from scripture or an enlightened teacher. This is the stage of indirect knowledge. It says "the self exists," not knowing that it is talking about itself. Then by means of discrimination born of inquiry, it realizes "I am the self." This is direct knowledge. Direct knowledge cancels the doer/enjoyer idea, and reveals the self and suffering stops. It appears as the realization in the intellect that the self is self evident. Finally, the self realizes that it has accomplished everything that needs to be accomplished and experiences lasting objectless satisfaction.

## Enlightenment Is a Special Status

Humans are fascinated by status and spiritual types are no exception. The belief that enlightenment is a special status accounts for the fawning, sycophantic, self abnegating behavior toward the enlightened that is common in the spiritual world. Enlightenment is not a special status. It is the default, the nature of the self. You are not getting something you do not have; you simply realize that what you sought so frantically you had all along. Enlightenment should be cause for embarrassment, not jubilation. When an obscenely obese person goes back to normal, he or she is lauded as a courageous super being, someone who has overcome long odds in the brutal game of survival. Would not it be equally realistic to condemn the person for allowing his or her self to get into such a miserable condition in the first place?

### Enlightenment as Energy[11]

A major misconception brought on by the fascination with and craving for experience is the belief that enlightened beings have a special kind of energy and that energy is a sign of enlightenment. But experience confirms and scripture states that the self is free of energy, so if I am the self I have no energy. Then how does it appear as if enlightenment is energy?

Energy does not happen until the self illumines a given mind. The mind is just the subconscious tendencies of a given individual entity. The subconscious tendencies are subtle matter. Matter is inert. But when it is illumined by the self it becomes dynamic, just as a seed will remain dormant until it gets water and sunlight. The subconscious tendencies are conditioned by three types of energy: sattva, rajas, and tamas.

Tamasic energy is heavy, dull and sleepy. Rajasic energy is passionate, dynamic, outgoing and unsettling. And sattva is the state when the mind is luminous, clear, still and aware. When the self illumines tamasic tendencies, the person appears to be ignorant and sleepy and lacks motivation. When the self illumines rajasic tendencies, the person is exceptionally dynamic, powerful and highly motivated. When the self illumines sattva, the person is clear, bright, knowledgeable and loving. The state of one's energy, therefore, is a consequence of the nature of the tendencies of the mind, not self knowledge. Because it is impossible to rid oneself of these three energies completely, even the greatest sage will occasionally manifest dull or passionate energy.

Sometimes an individual can transmit powerful energy into receptive minds and awaken them to the self. Conventional wisdom has it that such people are enlightened. They may be if the knowledge "I am limitless awareness" is firm

---

11. A technical explanation of the three energies can be found in chapters 10 and 11.

and the mind is particularly pure, but there is another way to account for this phenomenon that has nothing to do with enlightenment.

There is an ancient yogic practice that accumulates energy. It is based on the fact that energy flows from the subtlest layer of reality, the unconscious mind, into the conscious mind and out through the senses into the world at large. If the energy is not allowed to flow into activities that dissipate it, it will accumulate in the mind. The practice involves considerable will power because the subconscious tendencies are dynamic and need to express themselves, so when they are restrained, they transform into heat. The purpose of this practice is to eradicate subconscious tendencies to prepare the mind for enlightenment. When enough heat accumulates it produces a kind of radiant light. This kind of energy is like water behind a dam. It appears still and luminous but it has a tremendous potential. So when it is transmitted, it produces an epiphany. If the yogi is unclear about his or her goal, he or she may be tempted to capitalize on this power and tout it as enlightenment, but extraordinary energy is not a sign of enlightenment. If the person has purified the mind before enlightenment, he or she will have strong energy. If not, not.

### Fulfillment of All Desires

Many who are unsuccessful in life take to the spiritual path believing that enlightenment will make it possible for them to fulfill their unfulfilled desires. If this is your motivation, you need to know that enlightenment is not the fulfillment of all your desires. If this is not acceptable, remain in samsara and keep trying to get what you want.

The understanding that enlightenment is not an experience and that experience does not necessarily lead to enlightenment is not meant to take the wind out of the sails of your seeking. If it did, it would be unfortunate. There is no actual contradiction between experience and the path of understanding. Unexamined experience only leads to perpetual rounds in samsara, but experience backed by inquiry can lead out of samsara, assuming the inquiry is guided by proven knowledge. Self inquiry is a proven means of self knowledge, the distilled essence of the experience of countless enlightened beings.

Finally, although enlightenment is not experiential, it has tremendous implications in terms of experience. It is true that what you experience after you have realized that you are awareness is not different from what you experienced before, because karma does not care if you are enlightened. It continues as always. But since the essence of experience is interpretation, self realization represents an experiential sea change because non-duality, not likes and dislikes, is now the basis for interpreting what happens. Interpreting experience from the self makes it possible to assimilate and appreciate any and all experiences. It does not hinder the appreciation of pleasant experiences and makes it possible to appreciate unpleasant experiences.

# CHAPTER THREE

# The Means of Knowledge

If I am going to subject myself to a means of self inquiry, I should know its credentials. Nowadays, the pure quest for knowledge plays second fiddle to the desire for power, security, pleasure and virtue. Scientists regularly tout data that bolsters the claims of their corporate sponsors and disregard information that does not. Individuals routinely lie and exaggerate to achieve their goals. Religious types famously ignore common sense evidence because it challenges long standing beliefs. This pervasive disregard for truth has unfortunately prejudiced many spiritually inclined individuals against knowledge. Many do not find discriminating thinking to their liking and prefer to trust feelings, "surrender to the energy," mindlessly chant mantras without understanding, or sit in silence hoping to transcend their minds. The teachers too seem to have little regard for truth. They regularly pass off as knowledge not only their own beliefs and opinions, but also what they have cobbled together from disparate traditions or culled from books and questionable sources, too numerous to mention as knowledge.

If you allow beliefs and opinions to guide your life, you will continue to spin around in the samsaric whirlpool until you appreciate the value of knowledge. The discussion that follows will show that self inquiry has a long and successful history, that it is much more than an outdated philosophy, and that you can accept it without the fear of being exploited or confused.

I know that through effort I can attain something I do not have, but how would I attain something I do have? When a secretary answered the phone, she put her pencil behind her ear. After a lengthy conversation, during which many important subjects were discussed, she began searching for the lost pencil. A co-worker asked why she was agitated, and upon discovering the reason, revealed the pencil's location. In this case, her search was ineffective as she had the object all along. It was revealed by knowledge.

It would indeed be wonderful if one fine day knowledge dropped out of the sky like rain, but for knowledge to take place, a means is necessary. It so happens that our God-given means—the senses, mind and intellect—are not capable of knowing the self, because they require objects to function. To know sounds, ears are necessary. A heart or mind is required to feel emotions. Ideas can only be grasped by the intellect. But the self, awareness, is not available for objectification because it lies outside the scope of these means. A light bulb can illumine the objects in a room but it cannot illumine the electricity of which it is a transformation; the effect cannot comprehend its cause. When the heart tries to feel the self or the intellect know it, they come up short. It seems, then, that as we are created we are at a distinct disadvantage concerning self knowledge.

## What Is Self Inquiry?

Yet it so happens that a systematic means of self inquiry has been with us for a very long time. Self knowledge, which is the result of investigation, is not a philosophy. Philosophies come from the minds of human beings. They are an individual's—or group of individuals'—idea of the nature of reality. Their authority rests solely on the mind of individuals. If another individual has a contradictory philosophy, it is equally true. In our world there is my truth and your truth, my god and your god, but *the* truth does not exist.

In empirical reality, knowledge transcends the minds of individuals and groups of individuals. Knowledge is true to its object. We all agree that a tree is not an elephant. Anyone who claims that a tree is an elephant needs help. Two plus two is four for both idiots and savants. It is something that is always true. Our thoughts or beliefs may be in harmony with the truth, but they in no way validate nor invalidate it. Truth needs no validation. It is self validating.

The vision of self inquiry is an equation of the identity between awareness, the subject, and the objects appearing in awareness. Awareness is everything that is. This vision of non-duality, which Yoga claims to achieve through certain disciplines, is not contradicted by direct perception or by inference as it is beyond the scope of these means.

Self inquiry is not a salvation theology that requires an individual to change. According to it, the soul—the individual—is perfect and already free. So the release of the individual from his or her feeling of limitation is the result of the understanding that the subject and the objects share the same nature, limitless awareness. All the remaining teachings of self inquiry are only meant to prove the equation between the subject and the objects.

Another ill-considered belief that enjoys considerable currency in the modern spiritual world is the idea that self knowledge is intellectual and that enlightenment is experiential. Because of this confusion, it is believed that scripture is merely for knowledge while other practices, like the samadhis of Yoga are for practical, experiential enlightenment.

The confusion between intellectual knowledge and experiential realization is caused by a failure to recognize the invariable presence of consciousness in all situations. If the self is always present and available, the scriptures that make up self inquiry, wielded by the self in the form of a skillful teacher, are a direct way of experiencing the self because they reveal the nature of the self. In fact, if reality is non-dual, knowledge and experience are one. My experience of a tree and my knowledge of the tree are the same because experience and knowledge take place in awareness and are not separate from awareness. Furthermore, if only knowledge is freedom and ignorance of my wholeness is the problem, a technique that gives experience of the self would in fact be indirect realization (since the experience would have to be converted into knowledge for it to last). When you focus on experience exclusively you take what is eternal to be non-eternal. Information is time sensitive, but self knowledge is eternal because the self is eternal. Finally, whatever experience is taking place is the self, but the self is not a particular experience. Finally, experience is the self but the self is not experience.

In fact, since all knowledge takes place in the intellect, including the absence of knowledge, both knowledge and ignorance are only intellectual. The self is never interested in knowledge or experience, because it is the illuminator of both and is therefore free of both. Furthermore, if the self is experienceable as an object and the problem of self recognition is due to ignorance of the nature of the self, as self inquiry contends, how can experience erase the ignorance? And experience, no matter how apparently non-dual it is and how long it lasts, does not erase thought patterns, although it may temporarily suspend them. Invariably, those who experience non-duality retain a dualistic orientation when the experience ends. As reality is nothing but a projection of an individual's thinking, a dualistic mentality is a ticket to suffering.

However, analysis of experience, in line with a proven means of self knowledge, leading to the discovery that experience is nothing but awareness, will remove the intellectual notion that experience is superior to knowledge. After all, someone who strives or longs for the experience of oneness does so because he or she holds an intellectual conviction that enlightenment is only experiential. The dismissal of the very reasonable idea that we can only get what we already have through understanding, requires us to also dismiss as merely intellectual the more unreasonable notion that the self is only available experientially.

Self inquiry is called *Vedanta* in Sanskrit. In deference to the Western reader, who may have a certain resistance to the wisdom of non-Western cultures and exotic languages, I have elected to call Vedanta "the science of self inquiry" or simply "self inquiry." It is important that I discuss this science openly at the beginning of this book, however, because the reader should not think that the knowledge presented here belongs to the author. Although my own experience confirms the truth of these teachings—it would be equally accurate to say that these teachings confirm the truth of my experience—self inquiry does not come from the mind of an individual, just as no scientific discipline is attributable to the mind of a single individual. Science is knowledge gained through observation, investigation and experimentation, dealing with a body of facts or truths that are presented systematically to show the operation of general principles. The considerable resistance to the idea that Vedanta is a science stems from the idea that the self is not a valid object of inquiry, first because it is subjective—which it is not, although it seems to be—and second, because of the inadequacy of perception as a means of knowledge for consciousness. Perception and inference (which is based on perception) is the foundation of the epistemology of Western material and psychological sciences.

The claim that self inquiry is scientific generally irritates the spiritual, scientific and religious communities. Scientists think that consciousness is subjective and can never fall under the scope of its methodology. The spiritual world thinks spirit or consciousness is a matter of mystic experience or grace and can never be rationally investigated, and the religious community sees it as a matter of faith. If we are interested in lasting happiness—the science of self inquiry shows that happiness is the nature of everyone—it is important that we investigate all the factors operating because reality, life, is one. Nothing stands apart from anything else. So to examine only one aspect of reality at the expense of another will not work. We need a comprehensive science of life. Our science should have a cosmology because the physical world is part and parcel of our experience. It should have a psychology, because matter has no meaning apart from the mind's experience and interpretation of it. Also, it should have a "theology": knowledge and a means of knowledge that makes the investigation of the apparently unknown factor, spirit or consciousness, possible. It should tie together these three factors in such a way that our understanding of ourselves and the field in which we are pursuing happiness is conflict free. As this teaching unfolds, it will become apparent that self inquiry meets these criteria. Additionally, it will also become clear that self inquiry is not a religion, although it does link us back to our source. So, by unfolding this science, I am not trying to convert anyone to an exotic Eastern religion.

In these chronocentric times, it may be hard to believe that a solution to the fundamental problems of existence has been with us for thousands of years. It is hoped that the reader will overcome any resistance to this wisdom because of its seemingly foreign origin. In fact, self inquiry evolved long before the nation state existed and before the ideas of East and West had meaning. Self inquiry is the science of consciousness. Consciousness is everything that is. It transcends time and space. If you believe that the ancients were intellectually and spiritually primitive and concerned only with parochial interests, exposure to self inquiry will quickly disabuse you of that notion. You may rather conclude that *we* are intellectually and spiritually challenged.

In a footnote at the beginning of the last chapter, I pointed out that Sanskrit arose out of the need of untold numbers of subjective scientists to communicate the nature of consciousness to others and that it has an established terminology for expressing their findings. Having said that, I have employed Sanskrit terms only when an English equivalent is obviously insufficient. I also explain these terms in English as I go, to give the reader a clear idea of the topic under consideration.

In any case, self inquiry looks like a philosophy or a school of thought because it is comprised of a body of ideas that originated in the Vedas, about which more will be said presently. Intellectuals to whom the self had never revealed itself assumed that self knowledge was just another philosophy and attributed differing interpretations about the nature of reality to different teachers, and so it became several schools of thought for them. Had they understood that self inquiry is simply a means of self realization, this misconception would not have arisen. In any case, at some point self inquiry was divided into several schools: dualism, qualified non-dualism and non-dualism.

Contrary to the prevailing belief, the word *non-dual* is not an adjective meant to modify a particular type of self inquiry; it is a word that describes the nature of the self. Keeping in mind that words are always symbols, although non-dual implies dual, it is more appropriate to refer to the self as non-dual than as one because one is a number that implies two, many, and even zero, nothing. Furthermore, it would be inappropriate to label self inquiry, which is merely a means of self knowledge, as non-dual, as it is a dualistic device operating in a dualistic situation, one that ironically delivers non-dual knowledge. If you take self inquiry to be a philosophy, then you might count yourself as a follower of one of its schools or some other path altogether. But a means of knowledge is not a belief or dogma that an individual follows; it is a tool that makes understanding possible.

Because of the cryptic nature of the statements that contain the ideas of self inquiry, the subtle nature of the subject matter—awareness/consciousness—and the fact that a single Sanskrit word often has many possible meanings, it is possible for people to interpret the statements of self inquiry's source texts[12] differently. Over the course of time, a number of teachers have interpreted them in different ways. But this does not amount to different schools of thought, because all of them accepted self inquiry as a means of self knowledge.

So if self inquiry did not come from the minds of humans, how did it get here? In the beginnings of history did somebody stumble on a capsule from outer space, sitting in the Himalayan snows, that contained the teachings with a note, "This is the truth. Pass it on to human beings. It will set them free."?

If it did not come from the human mind, then perhaps it came through the human mind. This idea is equally problematic. Clean water passing through a dirty pipe will be contaminated by its passage through the pipe. Invariably, when someone claims to be a channel for the truth, some of the channel's ignorance wears off and pollutes it. It is not clear who wrote the Old Testament, but it is a good example of truth and ignorance sitting side by side. God, "The Eternal," kindly leads the Israelites out of the darkness. However, when Moses asks him what to do about another tribe that is getting in the way of their march to the "land of milk and honey," which is a symbol for freedom, he says to kill them. Evidently, The Eternal is an "us and them" kind of god. Channeled information also presents the same problem that philosophies present. Channel A sees it one way and channel B another.

If it did not come from humans and it did not come through humans, how did it get here? It was "seen." It was "heard." It was revealed. It came from an objective source. It came to me, not from me or through me. I saw it. I heard it. The people to whom it was revealed are called seers. It is important to understand that these seers were not mystics. They were ordinary people who were

--------

12. The Upanishads

called mystics by other ordinary people who didn't understand what the seers saw or heard. It was a mystery to them. Seer is not an identity. Mysticism is not an occupation. Seeing happens. It can happen to anybody, anywhere.

If the truth does not come from us but to us, then it is possible for everyone to whom it has been revealed, assuming there is nothing wrong with their minds, to agree on what it is. This is how the science of self inquiry developed. Tens of thousands, perhaps hundreds of thousands, of minds experienced consciousness, the self, with and without objects, and verified the knowledge of the previous generations. Because it is objective, personal views that inevitably try to gain a foothold stick out like a sore thumb. Consequently, they are easy to identify and reject. If Einstein saw the truth of relativity and said it was $E=MC^2$, and others did the calculations according to the rules of mathematics and arrived at the same result, $E=MC^2$ is the truth. If a scientist, using his or her own rules, claims that $E=MC^3$ is the truth, we can take it only as a belief or an opinion. If self inquiry says consciousness alone is real and the world is an apparent reality and it has been confirmed independently by countless individuals over millennia, it is true. As is true with any science, individuals who have realized the truth and understand the importance of keeping the science pure become its guardians. They continually refute erroneous notions with reference to the original non-dual vision: thus the science retains its purity.

Different minds may see the truth from different angles and express it in different ways, but this only enriches and enhances the means of knowledge, as long as the fundamental vision conforms to tradition and the nature of reality. It is important to know this about self inquiry because it gives an objective standard by which an individual can evaluate his or her experience. Nowadays you have many individuals claiming to be enlightened who rain down what they call the truth, without so much as a nod to the grand tradition of self knowledge, perhaps because they are unaware of it; although it seems more likely that personal motivations are at work.

Everyone is awareness, but not everyone understands this fact and its importance. Even a person who actually does know who he or she is will be an ineffective communicator if his or her words do not conform to tradition. Undeniably any Tom, Dick or Harry who has had a major non-dual epiphany, which is just consciousness recognizing itself, is attractive and inspired, at least for a while. Without reflection and without considering how the words stack up against an impartial source, the individual may believe that he or she speaks the truth. People are lifted up by the inspiration and fail to detect the ignorance that inevitably contaminates the words. They will suspiciously check their bank statements to make sure they have not been cheated, but will swallow the inspired words of so-called enlightened beings without question.

Revelations of non-duality cause a problem. Once the revelation is over and you return to your normal state of mind, doubts arise. "Is it really true that I am non-separate from everything? Is it true that I am not this body-mind assemblage? Perhaps that experience was just a hallucination." If you expose your mind to the means of self knowledge, it will either validate or invalidate the conclusions you have come to as a result of your experience. If it validates your understanding, you gain confidence. If it does not, you have been saved from a mistake. Unfortunately, individuals who have seen the light tend to entertain grandiose ideas about their self worth and are usually loathe to subject their visions to scrutiny.

When self inquiry actually began is anybody's guess. It may have begun when the inner eye of the first human opened and saw the whole luminous creation sitting in the Heart Cave shining "like a city in a mirror." Somehow the wonder of it—that this whole universe lives in me, that it is me!—inspired the words necessary to communicate it to others. It must have happened like that, because the science of self inquiry says that the world is there because I see it. To our everyday way of thinking this view is patently absurd, although on investigation it turns out to be true. We are quite convinced that we see the world because it is there.

But we need not involve ourselves with this sticky issue presently. How or why the creation began should take a back seat to the question of how our self ignorance creates a thicket of beliefs that makes the world seem to be an implacable foe, rather than the benign mother that it actually is. Just as a debate rages today between the scientific and religious communities about the nature of the creation—Big Bang or Intelligent Design—the ancient texts chronicle an endless argument between the non-dualists and the dualists and many others about the nature of reality.

Everyone, even the most hard-nosed individual, is a mystic and a seeker because everyone is actually consciousness seeking itself, whether they know it or not. Even cynical materialistic atheists believe in the experience of love, which is just consciousness experiencing itself and formulating its knowledge in terms of the experience of an object. While it is true that the public tends to discount the knowledge and experience of individuals of a spiritual or religious disposition who do not share its values, the self reveals itself to individuals blessed with practical and scientific natures in equal measure. So over the centuries, dispassionate individuals with no particular religious inclinations who experienced mystic or altered states of consciousness patiently investigated them and connected them to certain causes. Slowly a body of knowledge about the nature of consciousness and its relationship to the cosmos and the human psyche developed. Science is inquiry and inquiry is a means of knowledge. So not only is everyone a mystic, the craving for knowledge is perhaps the most salient characteristic of the human mind. If humans have established the investigation of material and psychological reality on a scientific basis, why should it be difficult to accept the contention that a science of consciousness evolved, in so far as there is nothing dearer than the self?

So what is the difference between material science and self inquiry? Material and psychological sciences continue to evolve because their fields are complex and always changing, but self inquiry has remained the same for a long time because consciousness is simple, self evident and never changes. Also the method that proves the theorem that self ignorance is the cause of suffering works, so there is no need to improve the methodology. Furthermore, the stated aim of material science is knowledge of the cosmos for the sake of pure knowledge, but the purpose of self knowledge is to end suffering. When the self is known as non-dual consciousness, suffering ceases.

Skepticism with reference to the claim that self inquiry has a scientific basis is understandable because consciousness is subtler than the senses. Inference does not work either, as consciousness is subtler than the intellect.

However, this does not mean that it cannot be known. In any case, whether or not the means of self knowledge has mystic or scientific origins or whether it came to us by some other means, it does destroy suffering. It is hoped that the reader will consider the teachings about to be presented with reference to common sense and the logic of his or her own experience. In any case, at some point more than a thousand years ago, a systematic verifiable experienced-based body of knowledge that is the last word on the topic of existence crystallized.

Self inquiry deals with two kinds of knowledge: relative and absolute. Relative knowledge has to do with everything we experience with our senses, mind and intellect. Each means of knowledge has its own field. The senses, for example, give us knowledge about the material world. The mind or heart, the feeling function, provides knowledge of a subtler field, the world of emotions. The world of ideas is the intellect's playground. The knowledge gathered by these instruments through direct experience or inference is relative because every object in each field is connected to every other object and each of the three fields is connected to each other. And to top it off, the three fields and the three means of knowledge are in a state of constant flux! Hard and fast knowledge is more or less impossible because so many changing variables influence it. The knowledge that a certain stock stood at twenty dollars a share at 1 pm may be invalid at 2 pm. The knowledge of the relatively eternal forces in nature, gravity for example, is not absolute, because creation is decaying.

Absolute knowledge is self knowledge. It is absolute because consciousness never changes. The problem with any means of knowledge, with reference to consciousness, is that consciousness cannot be objectified. Because it cannot be objectified it cannot be the object of any means of knowledge, including self inquiry. As we have pointed out, the individual who wants to know awareness is only capable of operating perception and inference. This shows that even before one perceives or infers, awareness exists. Unless you are aware, you will be unable to operate anything. Although awareness is not available as an object, it is not completely unknown. In fact, it is obvious that I exist and that I am aware. So there is room for self inquiry to operate as a means of self knowledge.

Self inquiry simply removes whatever ignorance I have about myself. It works for everyone because there is only one self. The removal of self ignorance is tantamount to self knowledge because knowledge always exists. Self knowledge exists because the self exists. Self knowledge is eternal because the self is eternal. An individual needs relative knowledge to negotiate his or her life through samsara, and self knowledge to get out of samsara.

Absolute knowledge is not subject to negation. Relative knowledge is negatable because it changes depending on the point of view from which it is gathered. If you say a particular item of clothing is a shirt, for example, it ceases to be a shirt when you look at it from the point of view of the threads that make it up. The knowledge of the threads is also subject to negation when you view them from the point of view of cotton. Self knowledge is not negatable because there is nothing other than the self to negate it. You cannot work your way out of samsara by doing things. Negate the doer, which is only a relative samsaric point of view, with self knowledge, and you are out in a flash.

Because nearly everyone seeks happiness in samsara, not freedom from samsara, the lion's share of each of the four Vedas deals with relative knowledge. The Vedas are self inquiry's source texts. People want security, pleasure and virtue and they often need to know how to get them, so the main part of the Vedas deals with karma. Karma means action and the results of action. Anything that happens is karma. The knowledge of karma is essential for anyone who wants to obtain something because you can get what you want—unless you want yourself—only by karma. Even if you believe that you can just will the objects you want to you, whatever actions you do with your mind, whatever thoughts you think, whatever emotions you feel, are all karma. Experience is karma. Absolutely everything in the time space matrix is karma. Karma, like rust, never sleeps.

Because the conscious being, the doer of karma, wants certain results from the world, it needs to have knowledge of the world and cannot always trust its own experience. Fortunately, the world is not a chaos, appearances to the contrary notwithstanding. It is intelligently designed, a deus ex machina—machine from God—meaning consciousness. Consciousness is both the substance of the creation and the intelligence that operates the laws that govern the behavior of all the objects in the creation.

The laws that govern the universe are called *dharmas*.[13] These laws protect us as long as we know what they are and do not transgress them. They protect us in the sense that they keep the vast field of existence orderly, so that we can go about the business of getting what we want. The karmic section of the Vedas is called the scriptures on dharma for that reason.

The dharma, or nature, of fire is heat. Stick your finger in flame and it will be injured. This is obvious to an adult, but a baby has no knowledge of dharma, so it often needs to transgress dharma to figure out the nature of things. The psyche has its own dharma too. Tell a lie and a feeling of guilt tells you that you have violated dharma. Eventually you are held accountable for transgressions of dharma, in one way or another.

Everything in the creation follows its dharma, its nature. Birds fly and fishes swim, plants photosynthesize light, and sugar is always sweet. If everything was blessed with free will as humans are, and they chose to exercise it on a whim, the whole world would come to a stop overnight because purposeful action would be impossible. What if trees get tired of eating our pollution and decide they like oxygen instead? Gravity gets fed up being what it is, has a sex change, and everything drops up! Humans make all sorts of minor rules, dharmas, to keep things orderly as well because the plethora of fears and desires that bedevil human beings, as a consequence of their lack of self understanding, constantly disrupts the world.

If you have any doubt about what is right and wrong, you can consult the karmic section of the Vedas. It prescribes rituals for getting what you want and doing it in such a way that the creation is not disturbed. Because we are not self-created and because we find ourselves in a conscious, well-ordered universe we have certain duties to ourselves, to our immediate environment and to the world at large. These are not just dry legal injunctions dreamed up by moralistic religious fanatics to control our behavior. Nor are they boring,

---

13. See chapter 7 for a more extensive discussion of dharma

scientific documents that take into account only what we know through our senses. The Vedas take consciousness into account because everything in the universe is consciousness or is ultimately beholden to it. Take away the conscious factor and you have nothing. Even if there were a world without consciousness, you would not know it existed, so what would it be? The texts in the karmic section personify consciousness as a number of deities or gods, so in that sense they are religious documents.

The knowledge in this portion of the Vedas is called lower knowledge. It deals with actions related to the pursuit of security, pleasure and merit. Because some humans seek virtue, believing they are morally flawed, it also deals with the topic of heaven and hell. It tells an individual how to live in such a way that hell is avoided and heaven is obtained. In the vision of the Vedas, heaven and hell are not eternal destinations outside samsara. They are subject to the same karmic laws that bedevil everything in it. Exhaust the merit that sent you to heaven and you come back to this vale of tears. Exhaust the demerit that sent you to hell and you get to come back and try again. In duality there is an upside and a downside to everything.

The knowledge that is relevant to the pursuit of freedom is called higher knowledge and is contained in a small number of texts that are appended to the end of each Veda, seemingly as an afterthought, since most humans believe that only the goods of the world can make them happy. Only those who realize that the temporary joys and sorrows of samsara are not for them are free to pursue the higher knowledge.

The section of the Vedas that reveals the higher knowledge is called Vedanta. *Veda* means knowledge and *anta* means end. Exoterically it refers to the texts at the end of each Veda that deal with the topic of self knowledge. [14] Esoterically, it refers to self knowledge. Self knowledge is "the knowledge that ends the search for knowledge." Or, it is "that, knowing which everything else is as good as known." This means that if you think you are small and limited and incomplete and are chasing objects because you think they will make you

---

14. The texts are called Upanishads.

happy, you need to know you are whole and complete. If you know this fact, you will no longer look for happiness in objects. You will live happily with whatever objects you have or do not have.

Many of the texts on self knowledge have been lost over time, but one hundred and eight remain, more than enough to give us a reasonable picture of this most unique and extraordinary means of knowledge. Self inquiry's statements pack considerable meaning into a single word and sometimes need to be interpreted. Occasionally the texts make seemingly contradictory statements because they came from different sources at different times. For example, although they state that "by knowledge alone is the self realized," they also tout Yoga, certain subtle and gross practices, and do not always clearly elucidate the relationship of knowledge and experience, as unfolded in chapter 2. In any case, self inquiry states that reality is non-dual consciousness. And as mentioned, it further states that the realization of this fact is tantamount to freedom.

The meaning of the statements of self inquiry is not a problem, because a long time ago a great sage came along and wrote the Brahma Sutras, clarifying their true meaning. *Brahman* means the self, awareness. A sutra is a thread, a symbol for a train of thoughts on a specific topic. Even today the topic of a particular forum on the web is called a thread. It is the basic idea that holds together all the secondary ideas on a given topic. All the teachings that make up self inquiry are like pearls strung together by the thread of consciousness.

The Brahma Sutras begin with the statement, "Now, the inquiry into Brahman." Unfortunately over time the word *Brahman*, like the word *God*, has taken on such an undeserved aura of majesty, grandeur and mystery that it can easily serve to confuse and hinder investigation. It just means consciousness or awareness. In the words of another text,[15] the self "is neither inward-turned nor outward-turned consciousness, nor both. It is not an undifferentiated mass of consciousness. It neither knows nor does not know. It is invisible, ineffable, intangible, devoid of characteristics, inconceivable, indefinable, its sole essence being the consciousness of its own self. It is the coming to rest of all

---

15. The Mandukya Upanishad

relative existence, utterly quiet, peaceful, blissful. It is without a second. This is the self to be realized."

The operative word in the beginning verse, in relation to a means of knowledge, is *inquiry*. It means that consciousness is something to be rationally investigated, not an object of faith. Inquiry is not an attempt to arrive at the truth because the truth is self evident; rather, it clearly explains the meaning of the statements of self inquiry by refuting erroneous notions about it.

The third primary source for self inquiry is the Bhagavad Gita. It is a more recent text, perhaps two thousand years old. It is a scripture on freedom that has the same status as self inquiry's source texts and shows how the teachings of self inquiry developed over the years. It makes clear the relationship between knowledge and experience and is a complete means of knowledge. It is both a scripture on karma and a scripture on liberation. It can enlighten you, and failing that, it can show you how to prepare for enlightenment. Or, if enlightenment is not your goal, it can tell you how to live a righteous life. There are also five layers of subsidiary literature involving thousands of texts, based on these three sources, which are part of this amazing means of self knowledge.

How does the means of self inquiry work? It does not promise to give you an experience of the self, because whatever you are experiencing at any time is the self. The self is just your being, your existence. Self inquiry is not intended to prove that you exist either. Awareness projects all objects, gross and subtle. There is nothing other than awareness to turn it into an object. Everything shines in its light, but nothing shines light on it. No proof is required to establish its existence. If you need someone or something to establish your existence, you need a psychiatrist, not a means of self knowledge.

If you investigate your being along the lines established by self inquiry, you will see very clearly that you are limitless, not separate from anything and eternal. But, because most of us are so busy trying to make life work, we forget to ask who the "us" is. In the process, we pick up all sorts of strange notions that cover up our core identity. A list of these notions would fill volumes.

Knowledge is only the removal of ignorance. Although the basic methodology of self inquiry is the same as it has always been, it has developed over the centuries into a very sophisticated body of teachings. Every time one of its truths is grasped, it brings to light something that is familiar but had been overlooked for some reason.

Self inquiry expands your mind, lifts it up, and gives it the big picture, the vision of non-duality. When you discover just how consciously the creation is structured, how the karma machine works, how ignorance works, how the body and mind function, how it all relates to the self and how you can transform your life with knowledge, you can no longer hold on to your small ideas about who you are and the nature of reality.

For it to work, you need to accept the following logic. I want lasting happiness. Lasting happiness is freedom from dependence on objects. I cannot get it through the pursuit of objects. I cannot get it through spiritual practice, because practice produces limited results. Knowledge is the only other option. For knowledge, I need a means. Self inquiry is a proven means. Therefore, I am ready to expose my mind to the teachings. Other factors that are required to make the teaching work are discussed in the following chapter.

Self inquiry is a refined means of enlightenment that appeals to intelligent individuals. Buddhism, another enlightenment vehicle, evolved from Sanatana Dharma, Vedic culture. Intelligent people are often saddled with a certain intellectual arrogance and believe that they can figure out enlightenment simply by reading the texts, but even a genius must sit down and listen, because the only means of knowledge under the control of individuals are perception and inference.[16] Perception and inference only operate with reference to objects, so they are not going to work with reference to consciousness. Just because you have control of perception and inference does not mean you have control of the means of self knowledge. Even Einstein needed to study physics up to a very advanced level before he could work out his famous equation. Yes, the existence of the self can be inferred but inference is indirect knowledge. Almost everyone accepts the idea of some sort of a god, either as a result of

---

16. Other means of knowledge available to humans are comparison or analogy, non-apprehension, postulation and supposition and verbal authority or the testimony of a competent witness but these are not germane to our discussion at this point.

the knowledge they have gained by observing the creation or as a result of epiphanies. Inference shows that there is a self but it does not show you that you are the self. Only direct knowledge will set you free.

A man went to a party hoping to meet someone he had been told could further his career. He had been given the person's name, Mr. Jones, but had never met him. It so happened he ended up speaking with Mr. Jones but did not realize it. During the course of the conversation, Mr. Jones asked why he had come to the party, and the man said because he wanted to meet Mr. Jones. Mr. Jones said, "I am Mr. Jones." The man perceived Mr. Jones all along but it did not remove his ignorance. The self is always present and always experienced, but you do not know it. You need an introduction.

The knowledge "Mr. Jones is here at the party" is indirect knowledge. Our person would have known via testimony of a competent witness, which is another means of knowledge, that Mr. Jones existed, but who Mr. Jones actually was would not be known. Everyone knows the self exists because they exist, but almost no one knows who or what it is. If you say, "I am experiencing the self" it is indirect knowledge because duality is still operating. You are not actually experiencing the self; you are experiencing the reflection of the self in a still mind and inferring the existence of the self. "I am the self" is direct knowledge.

Self inquiry gives direct knowledge and it needs to be operated on you, not by you. The only intelligence you need is the intelligence to realize that you cannot do it on your own. The ego cannot be involved if self inquiry is going to be successful. You need to set it aside and allow the teachings to reveal the true picture of the self and the world. When the vision of non-duality is complete, it is recognized as the truth and false notions drop off.

If you misperceive something and have the misperception corrected, you may still make the same mistake at another time because of a defect in your means of perception. But the existence of awareness does not depend on perception. You do not first see awareness and then interpret it. The you that sees is awareness itself, so no interpretation or memory is involved. Therefore, the ignorance will not return. You can forget something that is not present but you cannot forget the self once you know it, because it is always present. It is you.

Occasionally, people suffer amnesia and cannot remember who they are in a relative sense, but nearly everyone remembers his or her name until the day they die. This is so because the name actually refers to the self, which is always present. But we think, if indeed thought is involved, that the name refers to a limited entity, a perceived body-mind that suffered and enjoyed a long series of experiences. Because we think of ourselves as what happened to us, we think that we will cease to exist at death, which is true if we identify ourselves as perceived objects, in so far as all perceived objects begin and end.

Self inquiry has no quarrel with the information that comes from perception and inference. But perception has no meaning apart from your interpretation of it. To interpret experience, you are dependent on your means of knowledge: the senses, mind, and intellect. Apart from the obvious fact that beliefs and opinions, fears and desires, etc. skew any interpretation, perception and inference maintain the essence of duality, the subject-object orientation. For example, it is common to interpret the experience of consciousness as a void because it is free of objects. This often leads to a kind of existential malaise because it seems to indicate that enlightenment robs one of the pleasures of the world, since the perceived world does not actually exist the way it seems to exist. If the individual continued to inquire into the nature of consciousness in line with the means of knowledge, he or she would discover that what appears as a void is actually a fullness, a positive completeness that, when taken as one's identity, supplies much more pleasure than the small pleasures that come through subject-object transactions.

In any case, self inquiry teaches that you are not the perceiver, and in so doing, destroys your sense of duality. It says you are the very essence of the perceiver, the perceived and the act of perception. The dualistic process depends on you, awareness. But, you, awareness, do not depend on it. In other words, you are free of duality. Assimilate this knowledge and duality disappears.

This knowledge does not add anything to the perceiver, the person you think you are. You will not get knowledge. It cancels the perceiver, the feeler and the thinker altogether. When we say that self knowledge cancels the perceiver, what kind of cancellation is it? Does that mean that henceforth no perception takes place; that you will be left with just awareness shining on a big blank mind? No, it means that the perceiver knows it is not the perceiver. It realizes that it is the awareness that makes perception possible. An individual who gains self knowledge has the same knowledge as anyone else that gains it, because knowledge is true to its object. It is not personal. Two and two is four for both me and you.

There is no perceiver, feeler or thinker involved in the pursuit of self knowledge because the means of knowledge is not controlled by you. You put yourself in the teaching situation by your own will, relax and let the teachings take over. You are wrong if you think you can roam the spiritual world, pick up a bit of knowledge here and there and expect that one fine day it will miraculously jell into the knowledge that sets you free. Ignorance is not simply the absence of knowledge. It is very intelligent. It protects itself beautifully by aggressively projecting the entire universe like an image on a screen, filling the mind with desire and turning the senses and mind outward. The projection is so lifelike, so fascinating and hi-definition, that it fools everyone. For example, you actually believe that you are the person on your passport: a living breathing human being. If you were told that you exist without breathing, you would think it madness.

The welter of erroneous notions we pick up on our life journeys will not disappear with an epiphany, no matter how powerful it is. It may disappear temporarily when you are out of your normal mind but it will return in spades once the experience wears off. This thicket of unexamined ideas causes suffering. Self inquiry will destroy it. It is a proven, comprehensive, systematic, highly sophisticated attack strategy. It cannot fail, assuming you are ready for it.

Is self inquiry the only way to enlightenment? Yes and no. It is quite possible to pursue another path or no path at all and realize who you are; although if you are alive you are on the path because you are consciousness and consciousness will not rest until it has re-discovered itself. The realization "I am the self" is the knowledge that ends the quest for self knowledge, whether or not it arises in the context of the traditional teachings of self inquiry. Having said that, assuming you are qualified,[17] subjecting your mind to the teaching

---

17. Chapter 4 explains the qualifications in detail.

tradition of self inquiry is perhaps the most effective means of self knowledge available. It is impersonal, free of dogma and has worked for several thousand years. It regularly sets seekers free today.

As we pointed out above, the purpose of self inquiry is the removal of suffering by bringing about the experience based knowledge that there is only one self and that it is free of everything. Does this happen suddenly or is it a gradual process? Or is it some combination of the two? It is sudden and irreversible if the mind is pure when it is exposed to the teaching. It is gradual if the mind is impure to begin with and the impurities are removed by constant reflection, just as a tarnished object like a ring is restored to its original brilliance by rubbing it with a polishing agent. It can happen both suddenly and gradually. When a bit of ignorance is removed the self is revealed but when another belief takes its place, another teaching is required to produce the insight that dismisses it. In this way, a series of revelations or insights occur, until the last vestige of ignorance is removed. If you believe that enlightenment is sudden, it is wise to look into the basis of this belief because it may indicate an unrealistic evaluation of the purity of your mind.

Because its subject matter is awareness and because awareness is the content or essence of every experience, self inquiry need only reveal the self to grant permanent self experience. There is nothing more permanent than the self and the self is all that anyone experiences anyway. Discrete experiences come and go but the "I," the self, precedes, pervades and succeeds every experience. As stated above, the access to the self that self knowledge provides is in terms of the removal of ignorance and not in terms of a mechanical technique like arresting the mind, transmission of energy from one mind to another, or other methods.

The statement that self knowledge is the knowledge of everything, because everything is awareness, sounds grandiose and may be more discouraging than inspiring if it is not properly understood. Fortunately, everything can be reduced to two things: the subject and the objects. All experience and the interpretation of experience flows from this fundamental duality. Understand the nature of the subject and the objects and their relationship to each other and you are free. Self inquiry is not theory and practice. You will not get this knowledge and then set out to apply it. It does not work that way. The knowledge itself does the work. It is the practice. "And the truth shall set you free." However, if the knowledge is not firm, the practice of knowledge, which may seem contradictory and about which more will be said later, is recommended.

There is nothing you can do about the self. It is what it is. It will always be the same. You cannot make use of it in any way or transform it in any way. And there is nothing to be done about objects either. They are what they are and they behave the way they behave, at the behest of a power that is much greater than anyone. It is only when we confuse the subject and the objects—assume a connection that is not actually there—that problems arise. Self realization, enlightenment, is not just self knowledge. It is freedom from dependence on objects.

Knowledge is power. Before you can free yourself from objects you need to know what an object is and you need to know who you, the subject, are. The signature teaching of self inquiry is called the self/not-self discrimination and is unfolded throughout this book.[18]

## Importance of a Teacher

If self inquiry was a philosophy, one would only need to memorize the concepts to gain enlightenment. If it was a religion, only faith would be required. But this will not work, because the self ignorance that was in place before the study began would remain and a new layer of ideas and beliefs would be deposited on top of it, like silt. Just as any subtle discipline requires teachers, self inquiry requires a teacher, someone established in awareness as awareness, who can skillfully wield the teachings. To skillfully wield the teachings, the individual needs to have the disposition of a teacher who also must have been a successful disciple of a skillful teacher. If the teacher does not know who he or she is—or his or her enlightenment is formulated in terms of experience— then all he or she can do is present the self as an object. You will be told that to attain it you need to do certain things that will give you access to the self,

---

18. Chapter 12 presents self inquiry's signature discriminations.

like sitting in silence or surrendering the ego, an idea that was debunked in the last chapter.

Self inquiry is a complete multi-faceted teaching. It was not cobbled together by an inspired prophet or mystic in a few short months or years. Its scriptures contain apparent paradoxes that need to be resolved. The implied as well as the direct meanings of its statements need to be revealed. It uses simple but apt illustrations that need to be carefully set up if they are going to work. And all the arguments that make up the complete vision of non-duality, that is the context for all the teachings, need to be unfolded in a logical straightforward manner and brought to bear continually in the dialogue with the seeker. None of this can be accomplished by an individual without help.

## Listening, Reflecting, Contemplating

How does self inquiry work? The first stage is called hearing. However, you can hear something without actually taking it in, so *listening* is a better word. You listen carefully to the whole teaching and a vision of the subject, awareness, and its relationship to the objects develops in your mind. You can now say that you know you are whole and complete actionless awareness, but is it actually true? If you have been fortunate enough to have had epiphanies that confirm this knowledge, it adds weight to the vision of non-duality. Your teacher obviously knows who he or she is, but maybe he or she is just an exceptional or very lucky person and what is true for him or her may not be true for you. The knowledge at this stage is commonly called intellectual knowledge. In fact, all knowledge is intellectual because the intellect is the only instrument of knowledge we have. The problem lies not with an inferior kind of knowledge but with a lack of confidence in it.

The second stage is reflection. Reflection clears doubts. Reflection requires a simple lifestyle. If a doubt arises about who I am—and it does every minute or two, in the form of a particular fear or desire that happens to be disturbing me at the time—and I am about to work it out with reference to the knowledge and an urgent call comes from my broker, my mind will stop reflecting on who I am and start reflecting on the person with the money problem.

The doubt about who I am almost never comes in the form of the "Who am I?" question. If it comes in this form and it is more than just a clever spiritual parlor game that you play with your mind, it indicates a high degree of eligibility. But this question is actually with you all the time in the form of the thoughts "I want this. I do not want that. I like this. I do not like that." Desires and fears are proxies for self ignorance, so it is imperative that I question my likes and dislikes as they arise, trace them back to the source, and dismiss the source with the knowledge of who I am.

My mind says my house is getting too small. In fact, houses do not shrink. The things I put in them grow. Getting a bigger house will involve a lot of effort, time and money. So I reflect. "Why do I need a new house? Because it will give me peace of mind. Will it make my mind always peaceful? It will not. Once I have it I will also get all the worries associated with keeping it. Is acquiring and keeping a new house the only way to get a peaceful mind? No. Can I let go of this desire and get peace? Yes, I can. Is this not a much simpler and easier solution than going through the rigmarole of getting a new house? Yes, but will this stop future desires? It will not. Why? Because the desires are there to begin with because I believe that I am incomplete, not because I do not have a bigger house. Is it true? Self inquiry says it is not true that I am incomplete. Who is right, my desires or self inquiry? I will trust self inquiry, abandon my desire, and see if there is any fundamental change in who I am."

If you are unable to remain calm once you have renounced your fears and desires in favor of the knowledge that you are whole and complete, it means reflection was not enough and that contemplation is necessary. Certain thoughts, particularly the thought "I am incomplete," are nearly impervious to knowledge, even though taking a stand on the knowledge is the only way to root out duality. So I need to keep contemplating until I have completely assimilated the knowledge. Owning the knowledge converts it from indirect to direct knowledge and I can say confidently "I am whole and complete. Nothing can be added to me. Nothing can be subtracted from me. I am absolutely fine as I am."

The proof of the enlightenment pudding is in the eating. It is not just the belief that the self is whole and complete, or the verbal assertion that I am the self, nor is it the knowledge that the self is whole and complete. It is the pure, satisfied mind that comes when you have full confidence in the knowledge. Full confidence comes through the successful renunciation of desires and fears as they arise.

This does not mean that if I am enlightened I have to practice self knowledge forever. Enlightenment is freedom from dependence on objects. Knowledge is an object in awareness. The application of knowledge is also an object, something that needs to be done if freedom is the goal. Enlightenment is freedom from the doer. There has to be a doer to inquire and apply knowledge. So what is the use of knowledge and the practice of knowledge?

Every successful renunciation of the limited "I" notion, in favor of the whole and complete "I" notion, results in an increase in self confidence because the underlying tendency to think of oneself as small and inadequate is weakened. Eventually, the application of self knowledge breaks the back of the "I" notion altogether, and because knowledge is no longer necessary, it goes the way of ignorance, leaving me as I am. Or, it would be fair to say that I am the knowledge because knowledge is always true to its object.

So to attain enlightenment I need to disabuse myself of the experiential notion, understand that the pursuit of understanding is the correct path, find a qualified teacher—or let one find me—surrender to the means of knowledge and have faith in the teaching. Just as I need confidence in my eyes to reveal objects in the world, I need confidence in the means of self knowledge to reveal the self. If the eyes are defective, they may deliver information incorrectly but self inquiry is perfect, because the self is perfect. So perfect faith is required if the teachings are going to work as advertised.

The faith required by self inquiry, however, is not blind faith. It is temporary faith, pending the results of inquiry. Self inquiry is not a religious system that encourages you to believe in something you can never know, like a God in a heaven somewhere. It is a scientific method of investigation that destroys erroneous beliefs about the nature of reality and leaves you as you were before the belief clouded your relationship with the world and obscured your appreciation of who you are.

A belief may be in harmony with the truth or not. Belief is ignorance and implies doubt. Doubt is uncomfortable and leads to indecision and low self esteem. Beliefs need to be recognized as such and investigated. When a belief is investigated in terms of your own experience or in terms of the experience of others, i.e., self inquiry, it will be shown to be true or false and the insecurity created by the doubt will be removed.

When a belief is converted to knowledge through investigation or discarded because it is untrue, it has a profound effect on an individual's sense of well-being. The thought and feeling patterns that were put in place as a result of the belief disintegrate, leaving the mind free to enjoy life without prejudice.

Finally, what if I want to be free but have not realized that I have a knowledge problem and lack the requisite qualifications? Self inquiry not only has a complete methodology for how knowledge works, it also has effective programs—outlined in chapters 8–13—that help you acquire the kind of mind that is capable of assimilating the knowledge.

# CHAPTER FOUR

# Qualifications

In our democratic era it seems unfair that the Universal Declaration of Human Rights focuses so narrowly on political freedom and ignores the right to enlightenment. Should not the Galactic Congress of Sages issue a proclamation declaring inner freedom an inalienable right, empower world governments to grant it to all citizens, and establish a judiciary to seek redress when governments fail to deliver?

Democracy and great wealth have certainly affected the spiritual world; seeking enlightenment has become a mass phenomenon. The Dalai Lama, a famous enlightened being, is a media celebrity. Tens of thousands, perhaps more, spend large sums to have their brains rewired for enlightenment by India's most recent self proclaimed avatar. An enlightened master can earn a king's ransom from a month long intensive that involves nothing more than sitting in silence, a practice meant to induce enlightenment. Millions attend Oprah's webinar to discover the teachings of the West's guru du jour. If anyone anywhere can walk into a fast food joint for a quick lunch, why not purchase nirvana for the price of a Big Mac?

In a world of billions, the statement by an eighth century sage[19] that a human birth is difficult to obtain, seems to be a quaint relic from a bygone age.

---

19. Adi Shankaracharya

And the enlightenment qualifications he lists seem hopelessly outdated: good social position, a religious mentality, scriptural knowledge, "well earned merits of thousands of past lives," discrimination between the real and the apparent, the grace of God in the form of longing for freedom and an association with a perfected sage—among others.

If enlightenment is merely an experience of inner freedom, even psychotics and criminals qualify. Much of what is defined as psychosis in the West could conceivably be little more than the uninformed and clumsy reaction to unsolicited mystic experiences. Sinners regularly see the light and became saints. But enlightenment is not sainthood. It is the hard and fast knowledge that there is only one self and that the self, awareness, is everything that is—and that I am it. To gain this knowledge the individual needs more than a vague spiritual longing.

He or she needs to be a psychologically healthy human being. Unfortunately, Western psychology does not have a well considered definition of a healthy mind. It concentrates almost exclusively on pathology and tries to fix psychological problems with chemistry. Its failure to address the deeper needs of the soul and adequately treat the neuroses of middle class life drives many to religion and spirituality.

Self inquiry is not intended to heal neurotic egos. It works on a mind that consciously relates its suffering to a lack of understanding about the nature of reality, not to problems picked up in childhood and compounded by ill considered choices along the way. It investigates desires and values, for example, topics given short shrift by psychology. Its psychological program involves managing the likes and dislikes that compromise the ability of the mind to inquire into the nature of reality. It is not a discipline meant to make life work for an ego trying to find meaning in the world. Whether an individual has achieved his or her worldly goals or not, a mature person knows that seeking happiness in the world is a zero sum game.

The qualities listed below are not meant to be seen as ideals. Trying to live up to an abstraction creates conflict and becomes an additional problem that needs to be addressed before inquiry can bear fruit. In fact many of these qualities exist in some measure in most minds. Understanding them makes it easy to pinpoint areas that need work to prepare the mind for inquiry.

## An Open Mind

What is a healthy qualified mind? It is an open mind, one willing to question its assumptions about the meaning of life. An open mind knows that the conclusions the ego draws from experience are not always correct. Generally as we age, the mind becomes less and less open and its native purity is sullied by accumulated prejudices, beliefs and opinions. Even a mind awakened to the truth by an epiphany finds it difficult to stay open and inquiring once the epiphany wears off because it is just the everyday mind dressed up in mystic clothing. A truly open mind will inquire before, during and after any and all experiences, worldly or spiritual. If it thinks a mystic experience is the last word and stops asking questions, it will fail to convert its indirect self knowledge into direct knowledge. An open mind remains open irrespective of what happens, because it is awareness committed to seeking itself without judgments and conclusions. It simply tries to understand what happens as it actually is. It does not attempt to make reality jibe with its likes and dislikes.

Self inquiry is the knowledge distilled from the experience of countless self realized beings. Most of us believe we are unique, and assuming we have problems, we believe no one else is capable of devising solutions. We do not realize that the same being inhabits every body, that problems are universal and that workable solutions have been devised millennia ago. So even if we are told by the wise how to solve our problems, we reject the advice and keep experimenting until such time as we give up in despair and ask for help. But an open mind learns from the experience of others.

## A Reasonable Mind

A healthy mature mind is a reasonable mind, one not inclined to superstitions, opinions and beliefs. This is a particularly important qualification as the most outrageous and irrational beliefs are regularly passed off as truth in the spiritual world. The Buddha is reported to have said, "Believe nothing you have read or anything you have heard, even if I have said it, unless it corresponds to common sense and reason." Enlightenment is not a mystery. The self is not hidden away behind the mind as conventional wisdom has it. However, when something is not immediately available for perception, it is possible to speculate and fantasize. Awareness is self evident, simple and obvious if you know where and how to look. It does not contradict perception and inference. It makes perfect sense.

## A Discriminating Mind

Life is rarely what it seems to be. A discriminating mind intelligently avoids the petty dramas, conflicts and indulgences of daily life. To the discriminating person life is a tragicomedy to be acted to the hilt, no doubt, but of no lasting importance. "It is a tale told by an idiot, full of sound and fury, signifying nothing." A discriminating mind sees its likes and dislikes, memories, dreams, fears and desires for the transitory epiphenomena they are. It does not try to avoid action—action is unavoidable—but it acts for the right reasons. A discriminating mind realizes that action will not produce lasting freedom and avoids pursuits that will only momentarily free it from its concerns, preferring instead to inquire into the basis of its pursuits. It knows that life is a zero sum game because it sees duality playing out in everything: every gain entails a loss and every loss entails a gain. Because it appreciates the frustrating nature of samsara, expectations of object happiness do not unduly influence its determinations.

The definition of discrimination is "the settled conviction that the self alone is real and that objects are apparently real." Reality, awareness, is what exists in the past, present and future, before the past and after the future. It exists in and beyond the waking, dream, and deep sleep states of consciousness. Everything else—which is everything experienced—is apparently real or "not-self." With this definition in mind at all times, the discriminating mind turns its attention away from the world of objects and back to awareness over and over, until attention rests steadily on the self.

Knowing that life passes through you and that you do not pass through life is discrimination. Knowing that things happen to you, not by you, is discrimination. Liberation is discrimination, the knowledge that separates the real from the apparent. One need do nothing more than know the difference between the real and the apparent to free oneself of attachment to the apparent. Until discrimination is perfect, the ego will get entangled in appearances and suffer.

Objects do not stand alone. They depend on the self, but the self does not depend on them. To say that objects are apparently real does not mean that they are illusions. They do exist, albeit temporarily. It means that they depend on the subject, awareness. The self, the subject, stands alone. A rainbow, for example, exists but is apparently real because it relies on a conspiracy between the eyes and certain physical conditions. When the conditions that brought it into being dissolve—as they do—it ceases to exist. The practice of discrimination is a sure way out of samsara, provided it is supported by the following qualities.

## A Dispassionate Mind

A healthy mind is an objective, dispassionate mind, one willing to abandon sense indulgences, emotional passions and intellectual beliefs for the sake of peace. Inquiry works best in a peaceful mind, although it should be practiced at all times, particularly when the mind is disturbed. Every disturbance should be seen as a statement from the self that your attention is not where it should be. Born of the observation of the defects inherent in samsara, a dispassionate individual sins intelligently, walking the tightrope between attraction and aversion, indulgence and abstinence. When indulgence causes attachment, it withdraws the senses. When abstinence causes cravings that cannot be renounced, it judiciously allows contact with the objects until attachment develops. Both unfettered indulgence and fanatical abstinence produce emotional turbulence and hinder inquiry. A dispassionate mind is not an indifferent, cold mind. It enjoys an ironic, humorous, ho-hum indifference toward itself and the world. Usually this qualification is listed after discrimination because dispassion happens naturally when you understand samsaric pleasures fail to deliver what they purport to deliver.

## A Disciplined, Observant Mind

Successful self inquiry depends on many factors, not the least of which is a clear, still mind. Two basic sources of agitation hinder inquiry: the desire for a particular result and the depressed or angry reaction of the mind to unwanted results. It is impossible to withstand your desires without self understanding. They come from an unconscious source and enter the door of the conscious mind without permission. Control lies in your relationship to them. An immature person does not consider whether or not acting out a desire is desirable. He or she simply takes the desire or fear as a command and sets out to pursue or avoid the relevant object.

A disciplined mind is not a controlling mind. Just as you cannot directly control your desires, you cannot directly control your thoughts. A disciplined mind is an observing mind because observation produces understanding and knowledge is power. Thoughts have no intrinsic value, but the value added to the thoughts by a mind that does not know the truth may very well be a problem.

If you like somebody and ask them out and they reject your invitation, you feel hurt, although no hurt was intended; it was simply what reality had to offer at the time. But because it was an unsuitable result, you added the hurt. If you are not observant, you will blame the person or feel bad about yourself and miss an opportunity to discover the source of the pain. This will set you up to experience it again. Had you traced the hurt back to its source and discovered that it was connected to your identification with your desires, you would have lessened the likelihood of hurting yourself the next time. To strip your projections from the thoughts and see them as they are is the purpose of disciplined observation. A mind freed of its projections is capable of self inquiry.

Observation is not only useful to remove projections, it is also helpful for analysis of the content of thoughts. What you think about yourself and the world represents your knowledge or ignorance. Because the purpose of self inquiry is the removal of ignorance, it is important to know what you actually think and why you think what you think. A person caught up in samsara is more or less one with his or her thoughts. How can such a person evaluate his or her thinking, if the thoughts are not known?

Mental discipline implies restraint with reference to one's desires and fears. It is not always wise to act on every desire, even if it were possible. For instance, very rich and powerful people often destroy their lives because they have the wherewithal to satisfy all their desires, no matter how frivolous or inappropriate. To gain a mind capable of self realization, it is important to develop the habit of evaluating desires with reference to priorities. I want to lose weight and my neighbor brings over a big cheesecake. Desire arises and I want to eat it. Is it appropriate to satisfy this desire? Giving up gratuitous desires as they arise, with reference to the goal of achieving a quiet mind, is a necessary qualification for self realization. If you do not go with gratuitous desires eventually they will no longer disturb you.

Loose lips sink ships. Mental discipline also implies control of the senses. If you find that certain impulses cannot be released at the mental level, through observation and evaluation with reference to your priorities, the last line of defense is the sense organ level. For example, you have a distinct dislike of someone in your office. Every time you are in this person's presence, you have a big urge to express yourself. Perhaps you call it "being honest." As long as the feeling stays in your mind, you are OK karma-wise. If you are particularly egoistic and feel that you need to be "honest" with the person, there will be consequences. Perhaps he or she is tight with the boss. A month later you are out of a job. If you are out of a job, you cannot pay the mortgage. The bank forecloses and your wife takes up with the rich guy down the block. Your kids hate you for messing up their lives. If you thought your mind was unhappy before all this happened, think how it is going to feel once it happens. One's whole life can unravel from a very small incident. Karma has no sympathy. It does not care what you think. Think what you like, but it is wise to be careful what you do. Even if there are no obvious results in terms of your situation, you will feel agitated because injury in thought and word is also a violation of dharma.

Simply refusing to give in to the urge to project the mind into objects is the negative half of mental discipline. The positive half is turning the attention back to the self. Projections like anger, blame and criticism are never about the object. They are opportunities for self realization. Just as in a dream where all the co-workers in your dream office are your own dream mind, in non-dual reality all others are actually your self. So when you are angry, you are angry with yourself for a reason you do not understand. Convert the emotion into self inquiry. Ask yourself why you are angry with the object and if it is really true that the object is the problem. Ask why it matters that so and so is a jerk. Understand that if so and so is a jerk, you are the real jerk, because so and so is only in your mind.

In fact you have no control of the anger. Try to get angry when you are happy. Anger comes from an unconscious reservoir of unexamined beliefs and opinions. The object triggers something already in you. Once you have owned the anger, it is necessary to resolve it through continued inquiry into its source. The source of negative emotion is always the belief that you are small, separate, inadequate and incomplete. Ask yourself if it is true. The true you is never angry. Let the mind rest in this knowledge and the anger will disappear. Positive projections on objects should also be analyzed and traced back to the self. In this way positive and negative projections are resolved and the mind becomes objective and non-judgmental. When the mind has been cleared of most of its binding projections, it reflects awareness faithfully and the self is revealed in it.

## Self Duty

Good fences make good neighbors. Need is a fact of life. If you do not see that your needs are met in accordance with your self-duty, your mind will be agitated. Many people, particularly women, have been conditioned to take care of others' needs before they take care of their own. No particular virtue accrues to the one who takes care of others' needs, although much is made of it by society and religion. In fact, indiscriminate looking after others' needs, or your idea of their needs, not only hinders your growth, it hinders the recipient's growth because it keeps him or her from developing self reliance. If you have children, you have a duty to see that your obligations are fulfilled up to a point. If you have sullen and lazy adult children living in your home, eating your food and not paying rent, you have boundary issues and need to change the way you see yourself with reference to others.

One of the most egregious violations of this principle is envy, wanting to be like someone else, because it prevents you from appreciating yourself as you are. It is impossible to inquire successfully if you want to be different from what you are. You owe it to yourself to love yourself warts and all. One day a piston and a bolt were having a conversation. The piston was carrying on about its glamorous, dynamic life and deriding the bolt for its insignificance. "I make it all happen while you just sit there unnoticed, doing nothing," it said. That's true," said the lowly bolt, "but if I don't do my job you and this engine comes off the chassis, you will be out of a job."

To gain self realization, you need to respond appropriately to whatever life brings. Appropriate response to life is your duty to yourself. To ignore your duty to yourself poisons the mind with resentment and causes low self esteem. A resentful mind is not qualified for self knowledge.

## A Patient, Forbearing Mind

A mature mind is a patient, forbearing mind. Life often presents unpleasant and relatively intractable situations that will not resolve immediately. Your mother-in-law comes to visit and overstays her welcome. Your wife is particularly attached to her. Irritating the mother-in-law will cause problems with your wife, which can bring on further problems. So you patiently endure the situation, until she goes away. A forbearing mind is endowed with the capacity to tolerate sufferings and disappointments without struggling for redress or revenge. A mind that strives to right wrongs is constantly agitated. A mind that feels deprived or victimized is not qualified for self inquiry.

## A Balanced Mind

Equanimity is the peaceful state that ensues when the mind meditates consistently on the self and detaches itself over and over from sense stimuli, feelings and thoughts, as a result of a continuous examination of their defects.

# A Motivated Mind

A mature mind is a motivated mind. Everyone wants to be free, but not everyone has the burning desire that will generate the perseverance and determination required to overcome the surfeit of obstacles encountered on the path.

In fact, liberation is usually only one of several priorities for seekers. Most are satisfied with the idea of belonging to a community of like-minded souls and are realistic about their chances for enlightenment. One need not be the sharpest knife in the drawer to see that out of many seekers only a miniscule fraction of them realize who they are. The problem is further compounded by the fact that most of those claiming to be enlightened are so obviously controlled by their desires for love, fame, wealth, virtue and power that they give enlightenment a bad name.

If the teachers still pander to their desires, why should I subject myself to the discipline of self inquiry to get what I want? Why not just pursue samsaric ends directly? In fact, seekers are seekers because they are burdened with desires for security, pleasure and virtue. Finally, most teachers tout experiential enlightenment, because it does not require qualifications, not even burning desire. Somehow, one is meant to just hang out with an enlightened person and it will supposedly happen effortlessly by some kind of mystic osmosis. Were it made known what it actually takes for self realization, the spiritual world would shrink to the size of a pea overnight.

Furthermore, when spirituality becomes a middle class phenomenon, it takes on middle class characteristics. A middle class person is middling in his or her approach to life. He or she is afraid to test the limits and plumb the depths. Middle class life is essentially a virtuous life; the rules are followed and merit accrues. Merit is rewarded with security, a certain degree of comfort and a sense of virtue. Life may not be terribly fulfilling for the middle classes but the suffering is not terribly painful either, so the sacrifices required for freedom are usually not forthcoming.

Enlightenment, the realization that I am eternally free, is the culmination of human evolution. Everything is working against it. The one who pursues it with single pointed devotion is a salmon swimming upstream in the powerful river of life. The true seeker is someone who has actually lived to the fullest, tested every limit and realized without a shadow of a doubt that nothing here can satisfy the intense craving of the heart for freedom. The desire for freedom of one who takes to spirituality out of hurt, disappointment, the need for community or the romance of an alternative lifestyle will always be insufficient, although it can be cultivated by associating with realized souls.

When you near the end of your evolutionary journey, a raging desire to be free consumes you. It is not actually your personal desire; it is impersonal consciousness about to disabuse itself of the notion that it is something other than what it is. This burning desire, which is invariably uninformed—if you knew who you were you would not desire to be free—almost invariably formulates itself as a desire for experiential freedom. It will generate many intense and amazing epiphanies, but for it to bear fruit it needs to be converted into a desire for knowledge because only knowledge will extinguish it. And although you will not realize who you are without it, it needs to be accompanied in some measure by the qualities enumerated in this chapter.

## A Believing Mind

A mature mind is a believing mind. Knowledge requires a means and since perception and inference cannot reveal awareness, scripture and a teacher are required to reveal it. Inference and perception are operated by the ego, but the ego cannot operate scripture, as we mentioned in the last chapter. Scripture needs to be operated by a skilled teacher until the knowledge takes root. Just reading scripture and interpreting its words with your own understanding— or lack thereof—is not helpful. In fact the ego needs to be temporarily suspended for self knowledge to take place. This suspension is accomplished by faith in the teaching. Up to this point faith is placed in the ego to solve the existential riddle, but now it is transferred to the teaching and the teacher. When the teaching works, you either discover that the ego is like a shadow, wholly dependent on you, in which case it is not a problem, or the ego assimilates the vision of non-duality and stands alone with the self, as the self, or both.

Self inquiry requires faith, but not blind faith. If it did, there would be no need for an open mind, discrimination, dispassion and the other qualities listed above. You understand that if you could have set yourself free, you would have done so long ago and you temporarily agree that self knowledge can do the job. You accept scripture's contention that you are whole and complete actionless awareness and not the body-mind entity, even though you do not necessarily experience yourself as such. With this in mind at all times, you manage your mind accordingly, destroying any and all beliefs to the contrary, until such time as you realize the truth.

## A Devoted Mind

A mature mind is a devoted mind. Devotion is the patient willingness to apply oneself whole heartedly to the task at hand. You may be qualified in full measure and have circumstances conducive to liberation, but without devotion you will not see the inquiry—which may take years owing to the difficulty of dissolving the persistent dualistic orientation of the mind—through to the end.

## A Masculine Temperament

This quality is not gender related in so far as men can suffer from its absence and women can be blessed with it. It is a take-charge, seize-the-day attitude, the power to appreciate what has to be done and to do it without dithering. It does not conflict with the feminine quality of acceptance and surrender, nor with the wisdom to appreciate the futility of struggling in face of subconscious tendencies (samskaras) that cannot be easily dissolved by inquiry. In large part, spiritual growth depends on how quickly the inquirer sizes up subjective and objective problems and lays them to rest. Without this quality, the seeker will allow a resistant ego to have its way when it is not in the best interests of inquiry. It is the willingness to show a bit of tough love and resolutely stick to the inquiry. Life is short and every day that you do not move forward is a lost opportunity.

## The Teacher

In an age of instant gratification, sound bites and fast food, it is not surprising that many believe that a few minutes of deep breathing, concentrating on the space between the eyebrows, parroting a mantra, or sashaying through a visualization fantasy will produce enlightenment. On the other hand, because spirituality is totally unregulated, setting standards by which techniques, teachings and teachers can be objectively evaluated is impossible. So the situation is potentially dangerous, a further advertisement for a mature mind.

You need to be very clear about your true motivations, because the teacher you get depends on them. The post-World-War-II prosperity that led to the breakdown of the family has produced many love-starved seekers. A South Indian saint regularly hugs thousands a day, a sad commentary on the emotional health of the planet. If the desire for love is a strong motivation, caution is advised because needy people rarely enjoy good discrimination. It is important to love your teacher for the right reasons. Otherwise you will end up enlightenment-disappointed and love-disappointed.

Suspicion, the mirror opposite of neediness, is another unhealthy force operating in many seekers. A suspicious person has usually suffered abuse, real or imagined, at the hands of parents and others and often has a chip on the shoulder. This type is often highly intelligent, knows that everyone has an agenda, and is eager to discover it. But it is not always easy to figure out a teacher's true agenda because many teachers are self-deluded, their true motivations hidden behind a screen of pious concern for others or a flashy energy awakening practice. They make you feel good at first and when you are hooked, they dig in their claws.

This kind of seeker usually sits in the back and looks for flaws in the teacher and the teaching, unlike the love-starved emotional types who sit up front sucking up the energy as if it were a drug. They often end up loving a dead teacher, one of the greats of yesteryear. This approach avoids the pitfalls associated with unqualified teachers, but is ultimately unfulfilling because dead gurus cannot wield the means of knowledge and help with practical issues. This type often imagines that the guru is sending instructions from beyond the grave. But ex-parte instructions are unreliable because they invariably coincide with the seeker's spiritual desires, beliefs, prejudices and opinions. Loving an ideal has its joys, but it is a lonely and frustrating path. A radiantly enlightened person can sit at the same table with such a seeker and go unrecognized.

Seekers should view all teachers, gurus, meditation masters and their teachings unsentimentally. Claims of spiritual attainment should be taken with a grain of salt. The more a teacher self promotes, the longer the beard, the more extravagant the name, the slower the speech, the more grandiose the claims of special powers, the more your suspicions should be aroused. Suspending your critical faculties, though passing for devotion in certain circles, is dangerous. Enlightenment does not need advertisement. When you have assimilated life's lessons and sincerely long for liberation, the self will manifest a respectable purified teacher.

The potential for abuse is greatest when the teacher touts the "no ego, no thought" notion of enlightenment. If thinking is a problem in general, critical thought is definitely a problem for a guru, because it may be directed at him or her. When the teachings emphasize surrender, a red flag should go up. When enlightenment is presented as something you need to experience, the alarms should ring loudly.

There are many ways to deceive a person who does not know who they are. One of the most popular is the belief that you will get enlightened only when your karma is gone. The guru's job is to eat your karma. Therefore, you need a hungry guru. But karma does not stand in the way of the self; before you have karma you are the self. The self need only be revealed. Even if some karma has to be removed to prepare the mind for inquiry, nobody else could remove it, because it stands in your account. The guru can only remove the karma standing in his or her account, which will be considerable if he or she allows this notion of enlightenment to stand.

Perhaps the most common deception is the failure on the part of the teacher to elucidate clearly the qualifications for enlightenment—assuming that he or she understands their importance—permitting the seeker to entertain false hope about the likelihood of enlightenment.

The potential for abuse declines abruptly with a valid scriptural means of self knowledge, because it does not promise something you do not already have and it provides a way to check the words of the teacher for authenticity. It also encourages conditional surrender to the teaching, pending the outcome of your own investigation. A proper teacher will not promise to fix your life, because a means of self knowledge is not intended to fix your life. If your life is a mess, it is a mess because you are a mess. The means of knowledge will only make clear who you are and who you are not, assuming you are qualified to understand. When the teaching is assimilated, life takes care of itself. The teacher's authority should not rest only on personal experience but on how effectively he or she communicates the meaning of scripture. Additionally, the core teaching, discrimination, puts you in the driver's seat. In a proper lineage, the teacher sees his or her self as the servant of the student. He or she cannot teach unless you ask for knowledge, so you have equal power in the relationship.

Without self awareness, you are at the mercy of your conditioning. The most fundamental relationship imprint is parent-child. The parent has all the power, authority, experience and knowledge in the relationship and the child has virtually none. Ideally, as the child gains experience and knowledge, the gap narrows. When parity is achieved, the child is an adult. If you have not individuated when you begin seeking and you meet an authority figure like a spiritual master, you will unconsciously assume the role of a child. You will look up to the teacher, submit to his or her authority and quickly become dependent. If the teacher is not mature, you are putting the fox in charge of the chicken coop. He or she will be more than happy to be your parent, because it will be easier to achieve his or her agenda in this role. Usually teachers are not corrupt, but they are often at the mercy of their own unresolved conditioning, particularly the desire for fame, respect, power and love. This family paradigm is the default model for most teacher-student relationships and is contrary to the fundamental purpose of enlightenment. Freedom is freedom from your conditioning. It means you have nothing to work out and have no agenda. The ideal teaching style is friendship. Friendship is a spiritual archetype because an equal relationship obtains between friends. A friend may know more than you, but he or she does not make you feel as if he or she is doing you a favor by disclosing it. He or she happily shares, no strings attached.

The Zen Master Dogzen is reputed to have said, "Next to dharma, enlightenment is the most important thing in the world." When you focus exclusively on feelings associated with unresolved conditioning, you lose sight of the big picture. If a teacher can keep you high on "the energy" or distract you with a heavy load of service work, you will not ask questions. If you are wrapped up in your practice, the teacher can pursue his or her agenda away from prying eyes. Trust is good, knowledge is better. It is up to you to find out what goes on behind the scenes, if anything. You can only blame yourself when you discover that you are being exploited in some way. To avoid exploitation and disappointment, you must have a refined appreciation of dharma. A teacher who consciously appreciates dharma and follows it impeccably has a charismatic aura of sanctity, purity and grace. He or she has a clean and straightforward feel. His or her life is remarkable for its absence of conflict. He or she has no agenda. In other words he or she lives the teaching.

A teacher that immediately sets out to put you to work in his or her service has an agenda. Once it is known that you are compliant, demands for money, sexual favors etc. follow. The most common, unimaginative and irresistible agenda is the idea that you are helping others to enlightenment by helping the teacher get more people to enlighten. Ask yourself why the teacher wants more people to enlighten when he or she has you to enlighten. Invariably, you will be told that you are not ready, which will be true if you find yourself dealing with such a teacher. Find out how the teacher supports himself or herself. See the lifestyle. Is it five-star hotels, fancy cars and expensive jewelry? Bhagavan Rajneesh, who rechristened himself Osho to wiggle out of his bad karma, had ninety-three Rolls Royces and wanted one for every day of the year. How many are necessary to enlighten you?

Before you place your faith in a teacher, do your due diligence. Check the web for blogs and sites by disaffected students. Look for the scandal. Observe the students. What kind of people are they? Are they guarded and cliquish? Are they open and self-reliant? Do they act superior? Do they cower and simper in front of the teacher? Many teachers are power hungry bullies and obvious egomaniacs. Do the students think for themselves or do they only spout the party line? Do you have to learn a special language to fit in? Cults invariably have their own special lingo. Or do they speak normally?

Enlightenment is self knowledge. If a teacher claims that his or her enlightenment is experiential and that he or she can transmit it, the enlightenment will be temporary. Only energy can be transmitted, not enlightenment. Enlightenment is the knowledge "I am awareness." Awareness is not something you experience and develop; it is something you are. To realize who you are, a special means of knowledge needs to be worked on you by the teacher. Even if you are set free by the teachings of self inquiry, you are not necessarily qualified to teach. You need the disposition of a teacher and mastery of the means of knowledge.

## The Grace of God

In the last analysis, enlightenment is the self realizing the self. God is the self functioning as the total mind. God is entrusted with the task of looking after the lives of every conscious being. Your small life is not only important to you, it is important to the whole creation. You are here to make a contribution. If the world is somehow not ready for the enlightened you, your enlightenment will be postponed until the time that it is. But when the student is qualified, the teacher is qualified and God is amenable, enlightenment is inevitable.

# CHAPTER FIVE

# The Self

If the object of inquiry is beyond the scope of perception, it will be difficult to describe because language operates only in the world of experience. Therefore, we can never get a precise definition of consciousness from words. How can the limitless cause of existence be packed into words? Perception tells us that the universe is quite small, limited to what we can see with the eyes, hear with the ears, smell with the nose, taste with the tongue and touch with the skin. The invention of instruments that extend the range of the senses expands our notion of the scale of the universe and we now infer that it is infinite. When we try to infer the cause of the universe, both perception and inference break down and imagination takes over. We imagine someone or something so vast, grand and glorious that it cannot be experienced or described.

This imagination-fed belief leads to the conclusion that words are useless as far as enlightenment is concerned. It is responsible for the notion that consciousness is a mystery and will forever remain a mystery. It is a mystery if you do not know how to look for it, but once you are in on the secret, it is as accessible as the nose on your face. What if the cause of the universe is not out there somewhere in space or locked in the infinite past, but is in our own minds? What if you have unwittingly been tricked by perception into looking in the wrong place? Nobody says that love cannot be experienced and known, even though no words can describe it. In fact we do not need a word to describe the self, because it is self evident. But if it is not self evident to you, then words can be very helpful.

A finger pointing at the moon is not the moon. If attention goes in the direction indicated by the finger, the mind will experience and know the moon. If it is properly assimilated, the knowledge contained in a sentence or a group of sentences can destroy ignorance. The implied meaning of a sentence can also give knowledge. Self inquiry does not claim to describe the self, prove the existence of the self, or generate an experience of the self. It is not necessary because consciousness is always present and self evident. But if you allow its words to guide your investigation, they will reveal what is always revealed.

In the example of the snake and the rope, the weary traveler was ignorant of the rope. His ignorance caused him to misperceive it as a snake and fear to arise. Though he was never in danger, he believed he was. When the village elder used words to point out the actual nature of the perceived snake, it disappeared and his suffering ceased.

The self is not known for what it is because we have been fed a continuous diet of misinformed words about who we are. Our parents, their parents and their parent's parents all suffer the disease of self ignorance. Believing ignorance is wisdom, they compassionately pass it on to us. This web of uninformed belief and opinion stands in the way of a direct appreciation of our true nature and can only be removed by understanding.

Self ignorance is any statement, belief or opinion about my self that does not correspond to the truth: I am whole and complete ordinary actionless awareness. It can be neutralized by knowledge. In fact, the self is never completely unknown. The traveler's misperception took place at twilight. Had he come across the well at midday when the light was adequate, he would not have misperceived the rope. Had he stumbled upon it in the dead of night, no misperception would have happened. Twilight is a fitting symbol of the human condition. We have partial knowledge and partial ignorance of the nature of reality. This blend of ignorance and knowledge accounts for the many fortunate and unfortunate choices we make in life. Sometimes we get it right and sometimes not.

Because the self is uncomplicated, not a lot of elaborate words or combinations of words are required to indicate it. Both *consciousness* and *awareness* are good words but both need to be explained before we begin our inquiry.[20] *Consciousness, chit,* is perhaps the original word. *Awareness* seems to have gained currency sometime during the last one hundred years because the meaning of *consciousness* in English is quite different from the Sanskrit meaning. In English *consciousness* usually means subjective experience, the stream of phenomena incessantly playing in the mind. But the science of self inquiry says consciousness is completely free of gross and subtle phenomena.

Attention is consciousness but consciousness is not attention. We tend to think of consciousness as attention, consciousness of an object. Consciousness is not awareness or consciousness of anything specific, like a feeling or thought or a physical object. If you subtract the objects and activities that appear in it, you are left with simple, ordinary, uncontaminated, non-volitional, impersonal awareness.

It is important to understand that awareness is simple and ordinary because much of the discussion of the self, like the language associated with the word *God,* is couched in the language of hyperbole. The awareness that knows very subtle ideas, witnesses mystic experience and reveals the immaculate purity of love is the same awareness that knows the color of a sunset, the touch of a child or the smell of a rose. It is not a supreme or exalted awareness beyond the grasp of the mind. It is the ever present essence of the mind.

It is the non-physical "light" that makes experience possible. It is the container of experience and experience is the content. We exist quite happily in deep sleep without experience of objects, but we cannot experience anything without awareness, including the experience of sleep.

The continuous, effortless discrimination between consciousness and the phenomena appearing in it is enlightenment. For phenomena to appear and be

---

20. These words are synonyms and are used interchangeably in this text.

known, a subtle body is required.[21] The subtle body is insentient consciousness that seems to be sentient. It is called reflected consciousness—or awareness, if you prefer. When self ignorant people say "I" they mean the subtle body or the soul.

Identification with the subtle body causes suffering. All subjective phenomena appear in the light of pure awareness as it reflects on the subtle body: thoughts and feelings, desires, fears, beliefs, opinions, dreams, fantasies, knowledge etc. These phenomena are pure consciousness taking form and appearing as separate objects. They are not actually different from pure consciousness because consciousness is non-dual. However, they need to be distinguished from pure consciousness so that the individual, the self under the spell of self ignorance, can break his or her identification with and attachment to them. Liberation is freedom from attachment to subtle body phenomena. There is no need to break attachment to physical objects because physical objects exist only as sensations in consciousness. One is never attached to a house or a car—or even people—although it seems so. We are attached to what these things mean in our minds.

Pure consciousness is not the knower, knowledge or the object of knowledge. It is the factor that makes knowing possible. Sometimes it is called *knowing* but even this word is not completely adequate, since from its point of view there is nothing to know. Knowledge and ignorance are objects to it. It is the one who sees, not the perceived reflected objects. It is the witness. It is the eternal true "I," not the reflected apparent "I." If you believe that you change, you take yourself to be the reflected "I." If you do not know that you are pure consciousness, you will take the reflected "I" to be the only knower. In fact the reflected "I" cannot know anything, because it is inert. It is like a mirror in which objects appear. It is like the moon, borrowing light from the sun, the conscious "I." For the purpose of self inquiry, the reflected "I" should

---

21. In deference to Western readers, I use the words *mind* and *subtle body* more or less synonymously throughout the text, although subtle body is a more useful term. The subtle body is described in detail in the following chapter.

be considered "not-self" until the identification with the pure "I" is complete, in which case it will be known to be non-separate from you, pure awareness.

Pure consciousness, the self, is a partless whole. The words *partless whole* are significant because they imply that nothing can be done to make you whole. Enlightenment is not self improvement. A certain degree of integration of the centers in the mind[22] may be required before you can understand the nature of the "I," but once awareness becomes your primary identity, you can see clearly how all the apparent parts are actually one. This means that you can enjoy yourself without having to fix something that cannot be fixed. Partless means pure. A pure substance has no other substances in it.

The self is often referred to as bliss, but it is a bliss that cannot be experienced. Experiential bliss happens when the mind is temporarily unmodified. An unmodified mind illumined by awareness feels good. Sleep is blissful because the mind is unmodified.

The self is non-dual. The meaning of these words erases the belief that there are other selves and that perceived objects are different from the subject. Because of the belief that the self is the body, it is natural to conclude that there are other selves. But there are not two selves, a "me" and myself, although it often seems as if there were, which gives rise to the feeling of being disconnected. People routinely say, "I am just not myself today." Life is a problem when you feel disconnected from yourself, or see yourself as separate from everyone. Aided by the words that the self is non-dual we inquire and see if we actually are disconnected and separate. These words should also destroy the notion of doership. How can you do anything if you are everything that is?

To understand the meaning of non-dual, consider electricity's relationship to the appliances it powers. Light is a transformation of electricity when it comes in contact with a light bulb. Heat is a transformation of electricity when it comes in contact with a heater. Sound is a transformation of electricity when it comes in contact with a radio. Although it seems to be many because of its apparent association with billions of entities, awareness, like electricity, is

---

22. How to integrate the centers in the mind is explained in chapters 8-13.

one. The same awareness that enlivens an elephant enlivens a microbe. It does not swell to elephantine proportions to keep the elephant moving, nor does it shrink to insignificance to animate the microbe. It is that in which everything "lives and moves and has its being."

The self is the truth. Truth is what always remains the same. It is that which is desirable in every time and place and circumstance. What is more desirable than you? It is for your sake that you desire.

The self is that because of which a thing is what it is. The essence of fire is heat. Take the sweetness out of sugar and it is no longer sugar. Consciousness is the essence of everything because everything depends on it, but it is free of everything. When you realize your identity as consciousness, you stand free of everything.

Consciousness is limitless. It has no beginning and no end. It is out of time, eternal. It does not live or die because it is uncreated. When you see yourself this way, you have no fear of death and daily events have no impact. Consciousness, like water or air, has no particular form, but it can assume any form.

It illumines both the subjective world and the objective world. It is present in sleep. It never becomes unconscious. It is unrelated to everything, but nothing is unrelated to it. It cannot be an object of thought or feeling. It is the essence of the thinker and the feeler.

The self is not a doer. No action can take place without it, but it cannot act because it pervades everything, like space. Objects appear in space and activities take place in space, but space does not move from one place to another. All objects, including space, appear in awareness but they do not contaminate it.

Happiness is awareness, but awareness is not happiness. Awareness is not a person, but it is conscious and self satisfied. It is not self satisfied because it has achieved its goals. It has no goals. It is the goal of everything. Nothing can be added to it, nor can anything be subtracted from it.

It is self aware, self revealing. It cannot be illumined by any other light. Trying to know the self with the mind is like trying to see the sun with a flashlight.

It is self validating and self evident. The ego-mind continually seeks validation because it does not stand alone, but the self needs no validation. Because it is a partless whole, nothing can add to it or subtract from it.

# CHAPTER SIX

# Obstructions

### Extroversion of Mind

Assuming that I have a burning desire for liberation and the other requisite qualities, an understanding of the role of experience and the value of knowledge, and I am endowed with a clear understanding of the nature of consciousness, why is keeping my attention on the self—awareness inquiring into awareness—so difficult?

No matter how obviously separate I seem from the objects that I experience, and no matter how separate they seem from each other, nothing in creation stands alone. The body, for example, is actually an aggregate of common elements drawn from disparate sources, a shifting sand bar across which the elemental ocean ebbs and flows, its constituents changing from moment to moment. Where does it begin and the world end? If reality is non-dual, the barriers separating the mind from the body, the emotions from the mind, the individual from the self and the body from other bodies can only be the result of a misperception. Science assures us that we are living in a universe of predictable laws and forces that is evolving according to a vast cosmic plan. Religion insists that our purposeful world manifested from the mind of a just and disciplined divinity. Are these far-fetched views or a sensible description of reality?

In spite of their seeming disorder, things do fit together quite nicely. Unseen laws of cause and effect allow us to venture forth with a reasonable expectation that we will find what we seek. Water is never dry nor sugar sour. The sun goes up and comes down with frightening regularity. Because we can count on everything to follow its nature, we can search for happiness. How frustrating it would be to come here with five fully functioning knowledge-gathering senses only to discover that a perverse creator had neglected to provide sense stimuli. What a disappointment to be outfitted with an intellect in a world bereft of ideas. How cruel it would be to have been given a tender heart in a world without feelings.

Most of us are so busy chasing what we want and avoiding what we do not want, we do not have time to appreciate how skillfully we are put together and how neatly we dovetail into the universe. Rather than inquire into the nature of reality and who we are, we mindlessly steam down the tracks of life like a remote controlled locomotive headed for some imagined happy destination, looking neither left nor right.

From an individual's point of view, life is one long experience broken into many discrete experiences. Information comes in from the world through the senses and I react. After a seemingly endless procession of stimuli and an equally countless number of responses, the lights go out and I die. Although nothing can be done to change the mechanism of experience, even if it was desirable to do so, it is helpful to analyze the way it works because it impacts on the inquiry into the self.

The reflected awareness that bounces off the tiny mirror of the human intellect and makes perception possible casts such a small penumbra of light that it cannot reveal the complete cognitive process. It may reveal those parts of the chain of experience that are less subtle than it, but it cannot directly illumine the causal factors of which it is an effect. Modern psychology has developed a rudimentary understanding of this process, which the science of self inquiry does not contradict. But because it takes the ego to be the self and does not understand the actual relationship between consciousness and matter, it is of no help to our inquiry into the self.

Awareness, which is eternally self-existing, indivisible, apparently insubstantial and non-dual, transforms itself into the infinite diversity of names and forms that confront our senses. This is incomprehensible to the dualistic materialist mind. Yet, if the ancients are correct, this, or something akin to it, seems to be what happened. Quaint as it may seem, the ancient model explains how the five elements interact with the senses, and their relationship to consciousness, one that impacts significantly on the inquiry into the self.

At the expense of stating the obvious, something cannot come from nothing. If the universe has a beginning as science, common sense and scripture asserts, what came first, consciousness or matter? Even though consciousness is self evident, and all material objects, gross and subtle, are revealed in its light, yet none reveal it, material science believes that consciousness evolved out of matter. How this can happen is a definite mystery because matter is inert. The obvious conclusion, one that escapes minds whose sole means of knowledge is perception and inference, is that matter evolved out of consciousness.

Although the science of self inquiry says that matter ultimately evolves from consciousness, it passes through an intermediate or subtle stage. The material elements derive from the subtle elements, but where do the subtle elements come from? To find the answer we have to inquire a bit more. Just as a mighty oak exists potentially in a tiny acorn, the universe exists in an unmanifest or seed condition in consciousness. The seed state is comprised of three basic energies. When these energies, light (sattva), activity (rajas), and darkness or substance (tamas) are undifferentiated, there is no cosmos, a condition or state of perfect potential energy. When they differentiate, for whatever reason, the subtle and gross elements come into being and unfold the universe.

Our discussion of the cognitive process begins with the apparently mysterious statement that the sense organs arise from the elements. The five elements from the subtle to the gross are: space, air, fire, water, and earth. Their five corresponding properties give rise to the five perceptive senses whose instruments are: ears, skin, eyes, tongue and nose. For example, the property of space

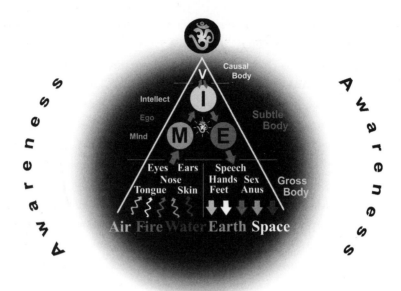

The self and the nineteen cosmic principles

is sound. The self, consciousness, the "unstruck sound," is beyond space and therefore soundless.

Although consciousness is non-dual, it has the power to appear as subject and object, cause and effect. Where duality exists, there is tension, continual vibration. Assuming infinite matter superimposed on limitless consciousness, would it be reckless to speculate that over trillions of years, one day, when the mix was just right, the first tiny ear emerged from the cosmic soup and gave consciousness the joy of listening to itself in the form of sound?

The property of fire is light. For example, the sun, a massive fire radiating light throughout the solar system, makes it possible for consciousness to evolve the organ of sight and its physical instrument, eyes, with which it can visually enjoy its creation. Air evolves the organ of touch and its physical instrument, the skin, allowing consciousness to calculate its proximity to itself in the form of physical objects and forces—heat and cold, for example. The power of taste relies on a tongue immersed in saliva, so water is said to be the source of the organ of taste. A dry tongue tastes nothing. Finally, earth, a composite of the three other elements, emits smells, which are transferred to consciousness through the nose. The sense instruments (eyes, ears, nose, tongue, and skin) are located on the physical body and composed of gross matter, but the sense organs are located in the subtle body and are formed from the light component of the macrocosmic mind.

The creation is consciousness's way to involve itself into the elements and eventually—when it tires of its game—to evolve back out of them. The elements evolve before the psyche/subtle body/soul, an idea that roughly coincides with the view of modern science. The idea that consciousness evolved the elements makes sense, if we assume that the universe was evolved so that consciousness could realize itself—even though it is never not realized—because it would need a field in which to garner experience and reap the knowledge necessary to set itself free. Why consciousness would do this when it is eternally free is unanswerable, because the intellect, that aspect of consciousness that knows, is an effect of pure consciousness. An effect cannot directly illumine its cause. It can only illumine objects on its own level of reality or those on a grosser level, although it can infer a cause and gain indirect knowledge.

The subtle body, illumined by consciousness and composed of the subtle components of the five elements, molds physical nature to serve its ends. If chemistry is destiny, a predominance of the subtle component of the earth element might lead to a practical nature, the predominance of fire to a passionate temperament, water to emotionality, and air to abstract thought. Moreover, a preponderance of a particular subtle element attracts the corresponding physical element into the body. The permutations and combinations of the elements and the varieties of environments and experience cause the immense variety of psyches and bodies comprising the creation. Animals and plants are rudimentary subtle bodies interacting with the elements. Air and fire predominate in hummingbirds, for example, while earth and water predominate in hippos.

The relationship between the psyche, the subtle body, and the material world, makes experience and knowledge possible. If the creation was exclusively material and conscious beings were absent, nothing would be known. For example, electricity is a form of energy. Though it is gross, a tungsten filament is nonetheless comprised of subtler particles: protons, neutrons, mesons, quarks and what not. When electricity flows into the filament, the energy excites subtle particles, which subsequently excite grosser particles, and light is produced. Similarly, when the subtle consciousness in the sense organ interacts with gross objects, knowledge, which might be called psychic light, is produced.

The elements evolve from subtle to gross. The most subtle element and first to evolve is space. Because it pervades everything, is unaffected by what it pervades and is intangible, it is often used as a symbol of consciousness. It is the invisible container of the other elements, and we infer its presence by listening to sound vibrations arising in it. Sound does not exist without space. The self, consciousness, is soundless because it is non-dual. Sound cannot be seen, felt, tasted, or smelled. The feeling of sound vibrations is due to the skin's contact with air that has been disturbed by sound. Air, the next element, can be heard by the ears and felt by the organ of touch. The smells in air come from earth particles carried by it, not from the air itself. Fire, the first element perceivable by the physical eyes, can be seen, heard and felt. Water, number four, can be seen, heard, touched and tasted. Finally, earth—the element from which the nose evolves—can be smelled, seen, tasted, felt and heard.

If five separate senses report five different stimuli in five separate theaters, why do not conscious beings enjoy five separate simultaneous experiences? Because consciousness evolved mind, an instrument that combines five unique perceptions involving myriad bits of information into one cogent perception.

On the way to the supermarket a car ran a stop sign and came hurtling at me. I screamed, slammed on the brakes and turned the wheel, narrowly avoiding an accident. Though such a situation had not previously happened, why did I react so swiftly and appropriately? A speeding object emits stimuli that strike my retina and are passed on to the mind, which is sitting behind the eyes. The mind sends a signal to my active organs and the accident is avoided. How did the mind know what to do?

In fact, the mind's command to the senses was the last step in a process taking place at an even deeper level. The mind did not unilaterally make the decision; it merely executed a command coming from a higher center, the intellect. The mind not only executes instructions coming down from intellect, but it sends the unified sense stimuli up to intellect for a decision on how to respond. Based on what does the intellect make its decision?

## The Causal Body

Imagine this situation. On the first day of creation a mountain shaped like a perfect cone thrust out of the earth and the first drop of rain struck the very tip of the mountain. In which direction would the drop flow? Because there is no precedent, each potential path is as likely as any other, so the drop slid down the south side and left an imperceptible little trail. After some time a second drop fell. What path would it take? High odds favor all paths, but marginally greater odds favor the south side. It followed tradition and etched the existing path a little deeper. After thousands of rain storms, other paths developed and the mountain sported canyons, ravines and gullies all around. And the original path became a great river valley.

We obviously cannot go back to the time when our psyches were perfectly clear like the consciousness of which they are a reflection, but let us pretend we can. On the day the first mountain sprung up, the first man strolled out of his cave and looked around. A few minutes later the first hungry bear wandered out from behind the first tree, spied the man and decided to have lunch. They grappled with each other for a while but the man got the upper hand when he grabbed a big rock and hit the bear so hard it died. And in life's first irony, the first man lunched on the world's first bear burger.

Was it a good or bad bear burger? Because it was his first burger experience he had no others with which to compare it, so he could not say. As the day progressed the bear experience replayed in his mind several times, gradually diminishing in intensity and frequency. When evening fell, it left his consciousness entirely and he dropped off to sleep.

On the second day the first man bumped into the first woman, one thing led to another and they made the first love, a delightful experience. When he fell asleep after dinner, the memory accompanied him and cooked up delicious dreams. The next few days saw many experiences, some good, some not so good. One morning, a week later, he woke up, ate his porridge, and looked out the entrance to his cave to see the world's second hungry bear looking in. Suddenly an exciting and emotional replay of the encounter with the first bear flashed in his consciousness and he understood what to expect if he ventured out.

Each experience, no matter how trivial, leaves a trace, like an elementary particle carving a track in a cloud chamber. The deep memory that saves experience, unlike intellect's facts-and-figures memory, is the causal body—the unconscious mind, which not only retains the essence of each experience, but also the subjective reactions to it: the feelings, emotions and thoughts arising in the mind during the experience.

What a blessing to have the knowledge from his experiences stored, out of his everyday consciousness, and able to appear when he needed it! He could get up in the morning, eat his porridge and venture out into the light of day without having the past intrude, very much like the first day. But as time passed he noticed a change. One day, as he was walking along without a care, he began to feel a little uncomfortable. It was a new feeling. Heretofore, he did not even know he had a mind; his attention was riveted on the pristine world outside. But now it became involved in this feeling. And then suddenly it made sense. A picture of the first woman appeared in his mind and the experience of their tryst vividly flooded his consciousness. Because the memory was so pleasurable and the first woman had run off with the second man, he became unhappy. He wandered about in this state for several days when, as luck would have it, he met the second woman of the world, one thing led to another and first man was happy once more.

After repeatedly cataloging the love experiences, the causal body realized it was running out of storage space and edited the extraneous details: the color of her hair, the cut of her garment and her name, saving only important facts like the big moment when the world stopped. As more experience flowed in, it merged the experiences of many different women into the essence of woman, compacted myriad episodes into the essence of love, and created a file marked high priority. Though the memories were meant to remain subconscious, the woman memory eventually took on a life of its own, popping into his conscious mind with disturbing regularity. Moreover, each repeated memory deepened the scar in the pristine landscape of his subconscious until it resembled the great river valley on the side of the first mountain after millions of years of wind and weather.

Now, sadly, when first man awoke, he had an agenda. Unable to sit blissfully in front of the cave enjoying the scenery as he had done before, he passed his days longing for a companion. Just as rain tends to flow down a mountain's deepest valleys, our hero's consciousness gushed wildly down the deep groove in the causal body, filling his conscious mind with desire.

His routine changed and he became increasingly indifferent to the practical details of life. Instead of enjoying random walks through the forest, staying home patching cracks in his cave or stocking winter stores, day and night he haunted the first bar, hoping to find love. The more he thought about a mate, the more he thought about a mate. His emotional state was recycled too. As he obsessed over the memory of love, his longing increased. And with each wave of longing the love channel in the causal body got deeper and deeper, flooding his mind with fantasies, tossing it hither and thither like a small boat in a storm.

Furthermore, he began to notice a strange connection between his all-consuming desire and the probability of meeting a first woman type. Were these the chance encounters they seemed? In the beginning, outer life seemed to be creating his inner reality, but now his cravings seemed to be influencing his destiny. Eventually he reached a point where his inner reality became as vivid and real as the outer reality.

We will leave first man and return to my drive to the supermarket. Although I had never been in an accident, I knew how to respond because the causal body activated the appropriate response. It can do this because it contains both the impressions of my personal experience and the impressions of the experience of all beings. When my personal experience proved insufficient, it selected a response from the collective memory and programmed me with that. In a fraction of a second the intellect, based on information retrieved from the causal body, determined danger, and passed on the information to the ego, whose identification with the gross body generated intense fear and caused the hands and feet to perform the appropriate action.

The five executive organs evolve from the active aspect of the macrocosmic mind and correspond to the five information gathering senses. They are: speech, hands, feet, genitals, and anus. Speech, which evolves from the active element in space, corresponds to the ears. Hands evolve from the active element in air and correspond to the skin. Feet, corresponding to the eyes, come from fire's active element and the genitals, born out of water's active element, correspond to the tongue. The earth element generates the anus which corresponds to the nose.

To round out our model, five vital airs—respiration, evacuation, circulation, assimilation and the power to initiate thought and to eject the subtle body from the physical body at the time of death—account for the autonomic processes that keep the physiological systems functioning.

The traces etched in the causal body by repeated experience are called *vasanas*,[23] impressions or tendencies, in Sanskrit. When they accumulate, vasanas become samskaras, deep grooves, and generate terrible internal pressure. Instead of waiting to see what comes, we try to make things happen that we think will give us relief. *Samskara* means *formation* and is similar to the psychological idea of a complex, an amalgam of subtle tendencies and proclivities that produce a particular mental-emotional condition.

The causal body determines the nature of the individual's experiences and the quality of those experiences, hence the word *causal*. No thought, feeling, emotion, memory, fantasy, dream, desire or idea appears in the subtle body that has not sprouted from a causal seed.

Whether life is a spontaneous reaction to external factors, a subjective compulsion to manipulate external factors based on the nature of the samskaras, or a combination of the two, attention is always riveted on what I want and on the aspect of the field that is meant to satisfy my wants.

Awareness, the self, is not directly involved in life processes. Just as the sun blesses earthly activities with its radiance, but does not participate in them, awareness simply illumines the gross, subtle and causal bodies. These bodies

---

23. The literal meaning is *fragrance*. Vasanas are the fragrance or subtle effects of our actions.

are actually inert but they seem to be alive and conscious because they are illumined by awareness. Although the self is present as the substance of the subtle body and the modifications in it, it is not known because the vasanas extrovert attention onto the subjective events taking place in awareness and the material objects resting in the field of awareness.

## Microcosmic Ignorance

Attention is riveted on the subtle and gross bodies because we do not appreciate the beauty of the self. Until the vasana for love developed, the first man was happy as he was. We cannot say he was enlightened, because he did not know he was awareness, but we can say that he was in his natural state: present and aware. As soon as he discovered the pleasure of love, he developed a craving for a love object. We can call him ignorant because he did not know that the pleasure he felt in love was just the pleasure of the contact of his attention with awareness, his self, when contact with the love object removed his desire. Whether we are born with tendencies from previous births, or whether we pick them up in this one, or both, they are caused by ignorance of our true nature.

Ignorance is the cause of the causal body. It has no beginning. In order to experience, perceptive instruments and their respective objects are required: the mind, intellect and senses, and the objects of perception. Before experience is possible, therefore, two events need to happen. The material universe needs to be projected and the perceptive instruments need to evolve. The interaction between them constitutes an experience and is the basis of time. Actually, time begins when the third perception/experience occurs. It is the interval between the first and the second, seen from the vantage point of the third. These two events, the projection of the universe and the evolution of the perceptive instruments, are the result of a preceding non-event or ignorance. Because ignorance is out of time it is beginningless.

Ignorance of the nature of awareness is called *maya* in Sanskrit. This does not mean that maya exists independently of awareness, but that it borrows whatever degree of reality it has from awareness, just as the snake borrows its reality from the rope. It is called ignorance or darkness because it has the power to apparently obscure awareness. Maya does not operate on the whole of the self but only on a small fraction of it, not that the self has fractions. For example, the power of the earth to produce clay pots only exists where clay exists. Although the self is a partless whole, the science of consciousness speaks in terms of parts to make it easier to understand the non-dual nature of the self, for someone accustomed to thinking in dualistic terms. With awareness as a substrate, maya creates the various objects of the world, just as an artist draws pictures on a blank canvas. It is an incredibly intelligent, dynamic power that produces such a convincing image that virtually everyone takes it to be real.

The creation that maya brings into being has a peculiar ontological status. It neither exists, nor ceases to exist. From the point of view of awareness it does not exist, but from our point of view it does exist. It is neither real nor unreal. It is real in the sense that it causes the world but it is unreal because it can be destroyed by self knowledge. Self inquiry is a means of knowledge that destroys maya. Maya causes the causal body, which in turn causes the subtle body

## The Subtle Body

The subtle body is composed of the instruments of experience: the ten senses, the five physiological systems, mind, intellect and ego. The ten organs are: eyes, ears, nose, tongue, skin, hands, feet, speech, anus and sex. The activities of the organs are controlled by the life force,[24] which is responsible for health and vitality. The reflection of awareness in the subtle body allows the senses to gather knowledge. In its causal form as rajas, it functions as the active or karmic organs—the last five. The life force also ejects wastes from the body. Thirdly, it transforms food into energy, which is distributed according to the need of each part. If walking, more goes to the legs, if cutting wood, more goes

---

24. Prana

to the arms. The life force also has the power to eject the subtle body from the gross body at the moment of death.

The subtle body is the instrument of perception. The points on the physical body where sense perceptions seem to occur are not the actual sense organs. For example, the eyes are only windows through which the power of vision shines. Perception is only possible when the mind is behind the sense organ. The eyes may report visual stimuli and the organ of sight may illumine them, but they have no meaning if the mind is occupied elsewhere—daydreaming, meditating or thinking, for instance. Experience shows that knowledge of events and gross objects does not arise when the mind is preoccupied.

Mind, a counterintuitive term, is the emotional center in the subtle body, the feeling function or "heart." It has several functions. It integrates sense stimuli into one cogent perception and acts as a conduit, passing the information to the intellect for a determination. It also receives instructions from the intellect and relays them to the active organs. In this capacity it is called emotion because it can induce movement.

Doubt is another subtle body function. The life that we take to be so real is actually a very cleverly constructed dream projected by ignorance on the screen of limitless awareness. Nothing is what it seems. Therefore, it is wise to doubt what you see with your eyes and feel with your heart, until you can determine what is real. Just like the senses, which are nervously fixated on the material world, the mind tunes into happenings in the emotional world, constantly monitoring its reaction to negative impulses from hostile minds and tender sympathies from kindred hearts. It also projects an array of positive and negative feelings: anger, jealousy, possessiveness, kindness, love, sympathy, affection, etc. Identification with and attachment to the mind is caused by self ignorance and is a primary obstacle to self knowledge and freedom.

Intellection is another subtle body function. The intellect gathers knowledge, remembers, analyzes, inquires into problems, and discriminates between the relative realities of various appearances. It is the most subtle and important aspect of the subtle body from the enlightenment perspective, because what we know or do not know about ourselves and the world determines whether or not we suffer.

## Ego and the Inner Enemies

The third aspect of the subtle body is the ego. When awareness seemingly forgets its limitless nature, it identifies with the subtle and gross bodies and concocts a secondary and limited identity based on its experiences—which it calls "I." The samskaras actually cause the mind-body-sense complex to act, but the ego thinks that it is causing action, so it takes itself to be a doer. When action produces results, it becomes an experiencer, suffering and enjoying accordingly. Faced with the apparent uncertainty of the unstructured oceanic reality of existence, it passionately clings to the belief that it is real. It also thinks that the world in which it pursues happiness is real. When self knowledge arises from inquiry, it destroys this "I," freeing the ever-free awareness from its apparent limitations. To more completely understand the phenomenon of the ego, let us trace its birth and development.

## The Separation

When ignorance apparently splits the non-dual self, it apparently becomes an individual. The first emotion it experiences is fear. Fear is a reasonable reaction to the separation because self ignorance has unwittingly removed the individual's only support. The longer it remains separate and tries to correct the separation by desire-prompted action, the more ignorance-reinforcing vasanas develop. The vasanas work out, attaching the ego to objects and polluting its contact with the world.

We deal with this non-specific existential fear by repressing and denying it. But fears and desires cannot be repressed. They come up again and again, because the causal body—often called the unconscious in the West—is not a musty basement where things can sit and rot, never to see the light of day. It is totally dynamic because it is illumined by awareness. Not to be outdone, the ego seeks another solution. It projects the fear. It does not realize that macrocosmic ignorance is to blame but holds itself responsible. So to rid itself of the guilt, it projects blame on anyone and anything. Blame is anger. Anger leads to attack, usually on another ego. Attack is a violation of dharma, causing it to feel guilty. Guilt engenders fear of punishment, which serves to reinforce the original sin or fear. And because it is in the dark about is nature, it takes these negative feelings as validations of its smallness, inadequacy and unworthiness, which in turn only serve to confirm its belief in duality.

## Desire

Desire is the painful but acceptable face of fear. The separation produces a sense of psychological poverty in the ego and generates a need to possess and enjoy gross and subtle objects: material possessions, situations, relationships, feelings, ideas and so forth. These desirable objects are meant to make the ego feel complete and erase its sense of limitation and inadequacy. In consumer oriented cultures, no belief probably commands as much sympathy and support as the idea that we are needy, wanting creatures.

The idea that desire is an inherently unworkable and self-defeating game plan has always been a hard sell. Yet, no matter how you wish to see it, wanting is suffering. Still, the ego fanatically worships desire, which it sees as a straight-forward way to resolve its sense of limitation and inadequacy. That the world is in constant flux is the fly in the ointment of this approach, however. Even if the ego gets what it wants, the object eventually ceases to be attractive because new desires surface. Or, the relationship between the desirer and the desired breaks down, as relationships are wont to do. Were the ego to continually get what it wants when it wants it, the feeling of poverty would not disappear because it is produced by ignorance, an unexamined belief about who it really is.

## Inner Conflict

As if the picture painted so far were not grim enough, when the self is unknown and the causal body is chock full of the kind of samskaras mentioned above, over time a structural distortion takes place in the subtle body that becomes a secondary source of conflict.

Each limb of the subtle body has its own agenda and functions in its own way. The mind deals with emotional issues, the intellect with thoughts, and the ego with desire and action. In a healthy subtle body these three centers work together for a common goal.

When ignorance is operating, the mind entertains a belief that its feelings are more important than thoughts or actions. It insists that spontaneous emotion will bring happiness, passionately seeks love, and is prone to sentimentality. It effortlessly becomes embroiled in the emotional world where it uses its impressive arsenal of emotions, guilt and what not, to get what it wants. A subtle body dominated by the mind views the intellect and reality-based advice as an attack on the value of feelings.

Intellect dominates the subtle body when a strong conviction that happiness can be attained through careful analysis, inquiry, logic and reason obtains. Intellectuals live mainly in their heads and often view the emotional side of their natures with suspicion. When ignorance operates, the intellect contributes to inner disharmony by questioning ego's every desire and action, leaving its self esteem in tatters. When it should be offering impartial counsel, it often plays handmaiden to mind, providing self-serving rationalizations and justifications for its negative feelings, or cooking up grandiose schemes to please a needy ego.

The greater the sense of separation from the self, the more one's actions are motivated by guilt, fear, anger and desire. Because it is unaware of its identity as the self, ego develops a relentless and single-pointed drive for success, continually faces the prospect of failure, and constantly wars with the world and those parts of itself that seem to limit its freedom. Its inflations and deflations, grandiosity and low self-esteem render it unfit as a stabilizing factor in the psychic economy. Like the mind and intellect, ego is subject to the vagaries of power. It may support the mind one minute or attack it the next. Often it is so pig-headed it willfully ignores the intellect's good advice and goes against helpful feelings.

Intense and consistent pressure over time from the samskaras compromises the subtle body's perfect geometry and contorts the personality, until it is incapable of living in a peaceful, dignified and meditative manner. Depressing as this discussion of the primary obstacles to self realization may seem, it is important to enjoy a realistic understanding of the challenges we face when we try to cultivate the balanced, open and dispassionate mind that is required for self realization.

# CHAPTER SEVEN

# Inquiry into Karma and Dharma

### There Is No Doer

Anything that changes is karma. All activities are karma. Thinking is karma. Feeling is karma. Breathing is karma. It is something that either happens or is produced by an act of will. Karma has both seen and unseen results.

You can create with karma. You can destroy something that is already in existence with karma. You can modify something by cleansing or purifying it, or you can go from one place to another by karma. You can undo the effects of an action with karma.

In reality there is no karma. It only exists in the mind of individuals. It is the result of likes and dislikes, attachment to pleasing things and the desire to avoid upsetting situations. It comes from the belief that getting something or avoiding something will improve my existential lot. Because this belief is untrue, karma is sourced in ignorance. I am forced to act because I do not know who I am.

If enlightenment is self knowledge, what does karma have to do with it? Because reality is non-dual, karma and the self are intimately connected. Since everyone thinks the self acts, it is necessary to investigate karma to see if it is actually involved in action. If it is not involved in action, you are not a doer. If you understand that you are not a doer, your life will be happy and peaceful.

## The Factors Involved in Action

The basis of action is the body-mind-sense complex, because the instruments of action and perception are located in it. Every perception requires a physical location. The body is the place where subtle body phenomena—desire, aversion, happiness, sorrow and knowledge—express. Desire manifests as efforts to satisfy it. Aversion manifests as actions intended to avoid things. The perceptive instruments are located in the body and deliver information that produces pleasure and pain. Because the body is only matter in various permutations and combinations, the science of self inquiry refers to it as "the five elements."

The second requirement for action is a conscious being. The conscious being initiates action and takes responsibility for it. It is called the ego or the doer. It does actions so that it can enjoy the results. When it receives results, which it does constantly because life is nothing but the results of past actions, it is called an enjoyer, even if the results are unwanted.

The third factor is the means of action: the five perceptive organs, the five active organs, the mind that desires the result and the intellect that decides to perform the action. Together these are called the subtle body or the inner instrument. The ten organs correspond to the ten instruments. The instruments are in the physical body and the organs are in the subtle body.

The fourth factor is *prana*, or energy. Without energy none of these activities are possible. There are five energy systems: respiration, evacuation, circulation, digestion and the power that reverses the physiological functions.

The fifth factor is the macrocosmic subtle and gross bodies, the whole of existence. It is the field in which individual subtle and gross bodies operate. It is made of gross and subtle matter and the myriad forces that control the behavior of the subtle bodies and the elements. These forces or laws are called *dharmas*. Everything in the field behaves logically and impersonally. This fact makes the physical, psychological and metaphysical sciences possible. On the level of the senses, eyes do what eyes do, ears do what ears do and the nose does what noses do. It is the same for everyone.

If all these factors are required to produce karma, how can the self, non-dual awareness, be an actor? If it could make itself incomplete, it might complete itself by action, but it is a partless whole. If it was limited in space, like an individual body, it could go to someplace it was not. But, like space, it pervades every atom of the universe. If it was impure, it could purify itself, but it is not made of parts. When an individual says, "I am doing, thinking, feeling, remembering, dreaming etc.," he or she is deluded. Why? Because the doer—the ego—cannot be the doer, as it is only one of the five factors required for an action. For the same reason none of the other factors qualify as a doer. If none of these five is the doer, who is the doer? There is no doer. Duality, which makes action possible, is only a belief that has no basis in reality.

If this logic escapes you, and you still insist that you are a doer, consider this: an action is not conscious and therefore has no faculty of choice. It takes a conscious agent to perform an action. So action depends on a doer, but the doer does not depend on action. He or she is there prior to any action. If he or she is there prior to action, he or she is free of action.

To be free of action means that with reference to any situation you can act or you need not act. It is useful to know this because it frees the doer of the belief that no choice is involved in action. Many feel they have no choice concerning their actions. They believe they have to do this or that. They imagine dire consequences if they fail to fulfill their desires through action. Such beliefs cause suffering and prevent growth. Discretion is always possible with reference to action.

## Knowledge Causes Karma

You come in the kitchen and see a stack of dirty dishes sitting in the sink. Before you wash them, a long series of actions have taken place. First, awareness in the form of attention flows out through the eyes and envelops the sink. This produces the thought, "There are some dirty dishes. I will wash them." To wash the dishes, hands are required. But hands cannot move themselves. They require energy. I need to breathe and blood needs to circulate through my body. Where does the energy come from? It does not manufacture itself. And it is not conscious, so it cannot think the thought that caused the action. The thought supplies the energy. Therefore, whatever actions take place, in so far as they are real, are a product of knowledge. But thought is not conscious either. Where does it get the energy to move the organs? The thought came from the causal body. But the causal body is inert too. It is only capable of producing thought because it is illumined by awareness, another reason you are not a doer. If any doing is taking place, consciousness illuming the causal body is the doer. "The Lord within doeth the works."

If, as you read this, you find yourself saying "so what?" or "I already know that" or "it makes sense," you need to reflect deeply on this knowledge. In a sense, you need to stop making sense. Yes, this idea—and others in this book—can be taken only as information, but to do so would be a mistake. Knowledge is not mere information. It has the power to transform your life, because it is non-separate from the truth. The truth liberates. Reflection is required to convert information to knowledge. When the significance of self knowledge is understood, there is a transformation, a qualitative shift in your vision. You are no longer constrained by a suffering, desiring, egocentric view of reality. Your limited awareness merges into impersonal awareness and you see what is. The vision of non-duality is enlightenment.

It is true that reflection takes considerable effort, but once the information is converted to knowledge by reflection, no further effort is required. You can relax and enjoy, because knowledge has a powerful action of its own. Yes, you will have to reflect again when your vasanas produce another disturbance in your mind. However, if you can cultivate a vasana for reflection, your life will move forward more or less effortlessly. Eventually you gain complete confidence in the knowledge; you "become" the knowledge, reflection is no longer required, and your spiritual seeking ends.

It is not completely correct to say that knowledge causes the transformation, although it seems to. Knowledge removes the ignorance and the mind, freed of its sense of limitation, conforms to the truth of who we are. When this happens, suffering ceases. It should be understood that it is neither necessary nor desirable to wait for this to happen. It can be consciously induced by the moment to moment practice of self knowledge. The practice of knowledge assumes that the seeker does not dismiss knowledge as merely an intellectual pastime, but fully appreciates its power to enlighten and transform.

So knowledge not only causes karma, it causes liberation. Knowledge itself is just knowledge, what cannot be negated. But the object of knowledge and the degree of assimilation determines the effect. In the case of the dirty dishes, the transformation caused by the knowledge was purely in terms of the removal of food. The vision of the one washing them remained the same. But self knowledge changes the very relationship of the mind to the self. It shows the mind that it is non-separate from its source.

## Action in Inaction and Inaction in Action

Life is never what it seems. For instance, you are standing at the shore of the ocean watching a large boat that left the pier twenty minutes ago and moving directly away from you. When it gets to a certain point, it seems to be standing still, even though it is moving rapidly through the water. Even though nothing seems to be happening, something is happening. It is common for spiritual people to misunderstand the teaching "I am not the doer." Often they "drop out" and stop doing what has to be done, to their detriment. But "I am not the doer" does not mean that the ego can attain enlightenment by not doing. Even when you are sitting still, you are acting. A wise person sees action in inaction and does what has to be done.

At the same time he or she understands that nothing is happening. Things seem to be happening because we identify with our ever changing instruments of experience. If you look at the moon on a cloudy, windy night it seems to be racing across the sky, even though it is relatively stationary. Although you are sitting still in your compartment, you seem to be moving when the train on an adjacent track pulls out of the station.

Movement, change, is apparent, not real. When you look at reality through the lens of time, it seems to change. An eon is essentially stationary from the point of view of an individual lifespan, but a millisecond passes in a flash. One minute of excruciating torture seems like an eternity, while a minute at an exciting movie goes unnoticed. Time, like space, is an artificial distinction superimposed on awareness in an attempt to structure a reality that has no form. If we analyze a conscious being in terms of time, nothing actually happens throughout its life, although it seems to. I look out at my decrepit eighty-year-old body today just as I did when I looked out at my vibrant youthful body at eight. The mind still cranks out emotions, the intellect continues to think, and the energy systems continue to function, albeit in a limited capacity, but they leave no mark on me. If they leave no trace, can they be said to be real? The best we can do is to say that they are apparently real.

If the self is not the doer and the ego is not the doer and the field is not the doer, there is no doer. Awareness shines on the field and all the objects in it seem to dance. Action apparently happens, but it is not caused by anybody.

If you know this, you act without thinking that you are acting. Seeing, you do not see. The eyes, blessed by the presence of awareness, see. Hearing, you do not hear. Walking, you do not walk. Thinking, you do not think. If you were the thinker/feeler you would be able to predict and control your thoughts and emotions, but you have no idea what they will be. They arise automatically out of the causal body and appear in the subtle body without permission.

When you do not know that you are whole and complete, you identify with the desires and fears that appear in the subtle body and do actions you think will make you feel complete. This creates tendencies that predispose you to action. So you become an ego, a doer. It is the tendencies, not you, that actually cause action. You can neutralize some of your tendencies, but you cannot totally eliminate them because there is an inviolable cause and effect relationship between an action and its result; vasanas are produced. So you cannot refrain from action.

As awareness, you can accept karma because the self is ultimately responsible for action, if such a thing exists, even though it does not actually do anything. It is like the person who says he did ninety miles an hour sitting in the back seat of a car. Yes, he did ninety, but he did not do anything because he was sitting still all the time. If you look at the self from the standpoint of the body, it is a doer, but from its own viewpoint it is purely a witnessing presence. In the presence of awareness, actions seem to happen. You can say fire burns, but does it? It is the nature of fire to burn. If you put your finger in a fire it will be burned, but the fire does not follow you around like a mosquito waiting for a chance to burn you, because it is not conscious. Although the self is conscious, it has no personal will. It cannot act, because there is nothing other than it.

## Karma and Dharma

If you cannot see inaction in action and still take yourself to be a doer, it pays to understand as much as you can about action. Because the results of action are uncertain, you might be tempted to believe that if you refrain from action, you will not get bad karma. Although the non-performance of an action does not create unhealthy tendencies, it creates a vacuum that may be filled with wrong actions, which do create negative tendencies. When you fail to do what is right, it will not be long before you will find yourself doing something wrong, because it is impossible to remain inactive.

Therefore it is necessary to do the right thing. The right thing differs from one situation to the next, assuming that dharma, universal values, is not contravened. Universal values are abstractions that are always in play on a higher level. Non-injury is an example of a fundamental dharmic principle. But what does non-injury mean? How am I to interpret this value? My wife and I have different opinions with regard to the value of her mother. She wants her mother to come and live with us but I do not. I am definitely not going to attack her with a knife to get my way, but should I say something hurtful to win the argument? There is a universal value for truthfulness and I will definitely not lie to rob my rich friend of his money. But what do I say when he badly wants me to go fishing on the weekend and I have nothing to do, but I do not want to fish? Should I hurt his feelings with the truth, or tell a white lie and spare them?

Common sense should be enough to tell you what to do and what not to do, assuming your goal is clear, but many do wrong things even though they know what is right. A thief knows that stealing is wrong or he would not use stealth, nor would he care if someone takes his belongings. He knows what he wants and the risks involved. Even if he knows that he loses peace of mind, he will keep stealing if his value for peace is not as great as his value for security. When you fail to do the right thing, the mind is disturbed and inquiry is necessary.

We cannot escape the consequences of our actions because free will and the law of karma go together. Free will presupposes a set of values that determine which actions we do. I can steal, or I can give money to charity. I can hurt or I can heal. I can tell a lie or I can tell the truth. Once choice is there, what values inform it? What is the right choice and what is the wrong choice?

I am never sure of the outcome of my actions, but the appropriateness of my actions depends on my knowledge of the laws operating the field into which my actions are offered. Just as everything in the field that is not endowed with the faculty of choice follows its nature, humans have a built-in appreciation of right and wrong. Even without the knowledge of gravity, a baby monkey knows that it will fall to the ground if it lets go of its mother while she is swinging through the trees.

Dharma, the moral order, is the control system that greases the wheels of life and free will exists within it. Without it, people would act without considering others and life would be completely chaotic. Because dharma is created by the self, it is not separate from the self. By following dharma, my small life blends seamlessly into the whole.

If I choose an action in keeping with or against the law of dharma, the impact will be appropriate. If I violate the law I will suffer and if not, not. If an object is dropped from a certain height, it will fall at a predetermined rate. There is no way to escape natural law, unlike man-made laws. You can always purchase a radar detector and avoid arrest when speeding, but you cannot avoid the result of an action that is against a natural law. If you have any doubt, stick your finger in a flame.

The law of karma depends on the law of dharma and is connected to one's sense of doership. Free will can be a blessing, if dharma is taken into account, because it allows human beings to create new karma or exhaust karma. All other beings can only experience the karma that results from their programming, but they cannot change their circumstances at will. The freedom to create or destroy karma means that I can improve my lot, materially and spiritually.

Sometimes an individual feels so spiritually incomplete that he or she suffers an uncontrollable desire for objects, like love, money or status. Or the sense of incompleteness creates so much anxiety it leads to mind-numbing habits—drugs, alcohol, cigarettes, junk food and excessive sex, for example. In the first instance, the mind is too distracted by its cravings to be sensitive to dharma and to interpret it correctly and in the second, it is too dull. Consequently, such people's lives fall completely into the hands of karma, an unfortunate situation because freedom is the core value of everyone. If you feel that you are stuck in a particular situation, running on habits, striving hard to keep life interesting or reacting emotionally to everything that happens, your life is controlled by karma. To be controlled by karma when you are actually the ruler of karma is painful.

As long as you only take the doer into account and ignore all the other factors, you will be bound by karma. You will be a slave to your likes and dislikes and you will feel like you are a doer. "I am a doer" is a very heavy, uncomfortable thought, entailing endless duties, obligations and responsibilities. The lion's share of our sense of existential exhaustion does not stem from the many activities we perform. They happen automatically because awareness illumines the body-mind-sense complex. It stems from the weight of doership.

When you understand that doing is not possible without the contribution of all the factors in the field, you no longer take full responsibility for what happens or does not happen, and the weight of doership is lifted. Karma only stands in the way of enlightenment when it is dictated solely by an individual's likes and dislikes. It can also be dictated by dharma, by what is right and what is wrong. If conformity with dharma is the standard for action, likes and dislikes are neutralized. Neutralized likes and dislikes are an indirect means for enlightenment, because a mind that is free of them naturally turns inward and contemplates the self. Conformity with dharma means that when you are confronted with a situation that involves a choice between what you want personally and the demands of the situation, you sacrifice what you want for the sake of the situation. It is an appreciation of the debt you owe to the total.

When your likes and dislikes motivate your actions, you will experience anger, frustration, depression, resignation and so forth because they will often put you in conflict with dharma. But when you take dharma into account, you are in harmony with the self, since dharma is the self operating the creation. This is why there is a sense of satisfaction when you do the right thing.

On one level, dharma is the eternal web of universal psychological and moral forces that make up the whole of existence. It is rooted in the universal mutual expectation of individuals. What I want or do not want from others is the same as what others want or do not want from me. Everyone wants to be treated with love and respect, for example. Nobody wants to be injured. Most of us, particularly spiritually inclined individuals, respect these forces automatically. We do not lie, cheat, steal or injure others because our desires and fears are not so strong that they cause us to break the rules.

But on an everyday level, we do not always follow dharma. Dharma, on the day to day level, could be defined as making the appropriate response to the situations life presents to us. I play a number of roles to accomplish my goals. My values determine my goals and my goals determine which responses are appropriate. If my goal is freedom, certain actions will facilitate the realization of my goal and certain others will not. The actions that do facilitate it are right and the ones that do not are wrong—for me. For instance, when I get home from work I can sit down and meditate, or I can have a beer. Drinking beer is certainly not morally wrong, but it does make my mind dull. A dull mind is incapable of inquiry. I can switch on the TV and watch the news, or I can study scripture. Watching the news is not contrary to any universal norm and I will not be punished for it, although it will not be an appropriate action, considering my goal, because it will reinforce my media habit. A well informed person makes a good citizen, but an informed person is not an enlightened person.

Scriptural knowledge, on the other hand, facilitates inquiry. So karma is only opposed to enlightenment when it is used solely for the purpose of fulfilling likes and dislikes.

Allowing dharma to guide your actions and accepting the law of karma indicates a high degree of maturity. When you keep dharma in mind, suffering is kept to a minimum. True, following dharma does not guarantee the result you envisage. Achieving specific results often requires many actions done in a particular sequence, in environments with many variables. It is easy to omit a particular action or to be ignorant of important but hidden factors that are necessary to bring about the desired result. Or the action may be done incorrectly and produce an undesirable result. But if you know you are the self, it will not matter if you do not get what you want, because the result of any action is always a satisfied self and the self is never dissatisfied.

Accepting the law of karma can help you take responsibility for your life, although it can also be used to avoid responsibility. It means that nobody else is responsible for the results you are suffering or enjoying. What comes to you comes because of your past actions. The trump card in the karma game is the fact that you are always free to interpret what happens, even particularly unpleasant things, in a helpful way. You can see yourself as an emotionally disturbed person, or not. It is completely up to you. If you blame your horoscope or your upbringing for your suffering, you are misusing the law of karma.

There are few better ways to rid oneself of the sense of doership than surrendering to dharma. When I accept dharma as my guiding light, I need only know what it is. This is not difficult, because dharma is built in. I instinctively know what is right, although if I have a doubt I should consult scripture. A seeker of freedom should consider following dharma a sacred duty. This relegates likes and dislikes to the background. They eventually fall off, leaving the mind contemplative and inquiry-worthy. And it will be easy to relinquish doership, in this case the idea that "I" am following dharma. This will lead to the realization that dharma is me, but I am free of dharma. The universal dharma of a seeker of enlightenment is a pure mind. So he or she need only consider whether or not a particular type of thinking leading to a particular course of action disturbs the mind.

To define happiness solely in terms of satisfying desires is not morally wrong. But it causes emotional turmoil and produces intermittent feelings of joy and sorrow, because the results are not up to the doer. An individual who defines happiness in terms of objects will not be able to easily surrender his or her likes and dislikes. Letting dharma decide will seem like a loss of freedom and freedom is a human being's highest value. But when someone conforms to the demands of the situation, assuming the situation does not require a transgression of dharma, he or she serves the self because the situation is the self. Every situation is an opportunity provided by the self to purify the mind. When you connect to the self through service of the total, it causes joy.

Holding out for what you want at the expense of the situation is an inappropriate response and will not lead to your happiness, or the happiness of others. If the police arrest you, it is not appropriate to resist, even though arrest is something you do not want. It will not make the police, who are also the self, happy because it will hinder their ability to perform their duties properly. When they perform their duties properly they connect with the self and feel happy. Is your happiness more important than theirs? When you resist, you compound the negative consequences.

When you do the right thing, the law of karma, the law of dharma, and your action become one, creating an experience of peace. If you can gain peace by accommodating dharma and exhaust an ego-centric tendency in the process, you are that much closer to a pure mind. If you do this day in and day out, it will gradually neutralize your likes and dislikes. It will also create a vasana for peace, which will motivate you to further accommodate yourself to dharma. There are very few more sublime feelings than the feeling that you are in harmony with everything.

If you do not accommodate to dharma, your personality will become fixed and rigid, your life will become predictable and boring—or full of conflict—and you will be incapable of self inquiry. But if you connect to the self through dharma, the burden of doership is lifted and your personality will become fresh and flexible. You will see that your life is just the self serving the total. You will be led to where you need to be and life will present you with many varied and interesting opportunities for growth.

## Three Kinds of Karma

All life forms, excluding humans, do not have karmas, because there is no sense of doership in their actions. They are simply awareness expressing itself in conjunction with the macrocosmic vasanas. *Agami* karmas are the actions an individual willfully performs, under the spell of ignorance, with a sense of doership. They leave positive and negative impressions in the causal body that fructify in the future. This kind of karma is destroyed by self knowledge because self knowledge cancels the doer. In this sense the enlightened are like animals with reference to karma.

The store of positive and negative impressions accumulated over time and standing in an individual's karmic account, waiting to fructify, is called *sanchita* karma. It keeps the doer doing and is the cause of rebirth. It too is destroyed by the assimilated knowledge "I am limitless awareness."

The results of previous actions that fructify in this life and which can be exhausted only by either suffering or enjoying them, are called *prarabdha* karmas. The prarabdha karma determines the form of body and the type of environment that is most suitable for the prarabdha to work out. Whether the environment is pleasant or unpleasant is determined by the nature of the karmas working out. When the prarabdha karma is exhausted, the body dies. Self knowledge also cancels this kind of karma. The body does not die when the self is realized; the self dies to the notion that it is the body. This closes the individual's karmic account and karma has no place to deposit itself. If a person lives a long life, does many actions, and suffers and enjoys the results of those actions in a dream and then wakes up, do the dream actions and their results have any effect in the waking state?

The law of karma and the three types of karmas explain the variety and diversity found in human life. Some people are happy and some are not. The same individual is sometimes happy and sometimes sad, depending on the type of karma at play. Even in animal and plant life, these diversities are evident.

Just as a man who views himself in a distorted mirror knows that he is free from the limitations of the distorted image, a self realized soul also knows that he is not bound by the limitations of the body and mind.

## Karma, Vasanas and Reincarnation

From the self's point of view there is no karma, no vasanas and no reincarnation because nothing ever happened. But this is not how I see it. I think I was born and I think I will die. I do actions here for the results and I expect to enjoy the results. What if I am a seeker of freedom, understand the work that has to be done, do all the appropriate work to significantly reduce my vasana load, notice that my mind is becoming contemplative and then drop dead short of my realization? Will not a lot of effort be wasted?

Nobody questions the idea of heredity today, yet the idea of reincarnation has yet to gain widespread acceptance in Western societies, even though both explain how experience transcends death. Heredity describes how certain physical tendencies in one generation reincarnate, i.e. return to flesh. Microbiology has discovered that these tendencies, which are the result of an ancestor's experience, are stored in a very subtle part of the body's cells, the DNA, and passed on to the succeeding generations. The science of the self accepts the DNA theory, expands it to include the subtle body, and asks one more question: what programs the DNA? If it is not conscious, it cannot program itself. The obvious answer is that consciousness in conjunction with the macrocosmic samskaras programs it.

Materialists think there is only one life and do not take the subtle body into account because they think it is the result of biochemical processes. According to them, when the physical body disintegrates, the psyche, a chemical by-product, apparently just dissolves into thin air, never to be seen again. The ideas found in religion do not pretend to be scientific. At death we meet up with God, who sends us to heaven or hell depending on the nature of our past deeds, minus the physical body. Even in this scenario, fanciful as it is, the subtle body, the soul, does not miraculously dematerialize when the physical body gives up the ghost.

In the case of genetics, what actually survives death? It is not the physical body. It is the parent's physical traits, reduced to tendencies and stored in the DNA, that are combined when the sperm fertilizes the egg. The tendencies immediately begin to imprint on the body of the new individual and determine its physical characteristics. DNA is just a materialist's description of the vasanas.

Science tells us that matter is energy and energy cannot be created or destroyed. Evidently the DNA, which is a kind of subtle matter, is neither created nor destroyed at the time of death. If everything is energy and energy cannot be created or destroyed, and there is such a thing as a subtle body, then why would not this fundamental fact apply to the subtle body? If it does apply, then why is it not possible for the subtle body—the soul, or what is commonly referred to as the self—to transmigrate? The science of self inquiry says that the subtle body is subtle matter and is subject to the same laws that physical matter is subject to. In fact, the material world evolves out of subtle matter.[25]

You may wish to argue that the soul is not matter. But if it is not matter, how did it evolve out of matter, since by definition matter is not conscious? It seems more reasonable to assume that matter is an insentient form of consciousness, subject to the laws that consciousness imposes on the creation.

Before we attempt to explain reincarnation, we need to know that the gross, subtle and causal bodies are not specific to particular individuals; they are the structure that consciousness gives to itself when it appears as an embodied being. In other words, there is only one soul or individual, an "everyman," not an infinite variety of unique souls. It only seems as if each gross, subtle and causal body is unique. This is because of the infinite possibilities of experience that come into play when consciousness associates with ignorance and creates multiplicity.

It is important to understand this because conventional wisdom, which upon inquiry turns out not to be wisdom at all, has it that the personality reincarnates. This argument hinges on the meaning of the word *personality*. Is the personality something that is conscious, eternal and unique to every individual, and therefore transcends birth and death, or is it the result of the interaction of the vasanas with the environment? If it is conscious, eternal and unique, then why do you not remember who you were in preceding lives? If it

---

25. See chapter 6 for a reasonably detailed discussion of how creation evolves.

was conscious and eternal, human beings would not quest for identity in this life.

Rather than pursue this argument further, let us explain the idea of reincarnation according to the science of self knowledge, keeping in mind that it is only a secondary teaching for individuals who are not yet prepared for the complete vision of non-duality.

When the prarabdha karma for a particular birth ends, the subtle body is separated from its physical sheath. Where does it go? When the fertilized egg that will become a new body is established in the uterine wall, the causal body, which contains the template for the subtle body, and the samskaras, which carry tendencies abstracted from previous lives, imprint themselves on the cells of the developing fetus.[26] The memory, which is a function of intellect, a subtle body function, is scrubbed clean during this process and accounts for the fact that an individual does not remember who he or she was in the previous birth or births. When the samskaras have been imprinted on the new subtle body, they immediately begin to interact with the environment and a new personality develops, which the individual takes to be "me." That nothing in samsara remains the same accounts for the fact that the new environment—the parents and their karmic situation—will be different from the previous birth and cause a unique personality to emerge. But the vasana for spiritual work that developed in the past life will fructify in the next birth and bless the next iteration of you, with an inclination for self realization.

If you want to bring the self into it, reincarnation only makes sense if you believe that the dream of existence is the self trying to wake up from a sleep it is pretending to sleep.

---

26. Contrary to the popular belief, the individual does not choose his or her parents or the next birth. The *samskaras* choose on the basis of the similarity of the child's *samskaras* and the parent's ability to fulfill them. How they choose is a complicated topic.

# CHAPTER EIGHT

# Inquiry into Practice

All actions only produce limited results or bring about the gain of something that the doer does not have. But the self is limitless and not an object. Even millions of actions by a limited entity will not produce limitlessness. That we are limited with reference to action may lead to the conclusion that abandoning action will produce freedom. If freedom is the nature of the self, the cessation of action cannot produce enlightenment, for the same reason that action will not: the self is beyond the world of action. Furthermore, if the cessation of action is enlightenment, we would all be enlightened, because who has not slept? As long as we live, we are doing something. Awareness shines on the causal body; desires and fears spring up and are automatically acted out. No choice is involved concerning action in general; discretion only applies to the type of action performed and the state of mind motivating it.

A spiritually undeveloped person works for worldly results, but a seeker of freedom works for a pure subtle body, because a pure mind is necessary for self inquiry and self inquiry is a means for self knowledge. An individual can gain a pure subtle body irrespective of the type of results he or she reaps. Both good and bad karma facilitate purity if the seeker has the right understanding.

Unless the subtle body is peaceful and discriminating, the knowledge that is tantamount to freedom, "I am limitless, non-dual, actionless awareness," will not take place, nor will it be assimilated and retained, even if it does take place.

Pure means partless. Nothing in existence can be completely purified. The three bodies, for example, are made of parts. The causal body is a storehouse of many helpful and unhelpful tendencies which may be dormant or active, tendencies. Because the causal body is an aggregate of tendencies, the subtle body is also an aggregate of thoughts and feelings. The physical body is comprised of many parts and processes. Purification of the physical body is certainly helpful, in so far as the sensations it produces impact on the subtle body, but physical purification has no effect on the tendencies that produce functional or dysfunctional psychological fixations. When self inquiry encourages purification, it does not mean that the mind should be completely vasana free. It means that binding vasanas should be neutralized so that they do not obstruct discrimination.

Usually qualified seekers possess common sense and do not need major lifestyle changes. However, a simple lifestyle is required to insulate the mind from unnecessary distractions. Spiritual practice purifies the causal body so that meditation is deep and spontaneous, making self inquiry reasonably effortless. However, the causal body cannot be purified directly by karma, because it is subtler than the doer and karma. A purified causal body is relatively free of the projecting and veiling energies that hinder self inquiry.[27]

The subtle body can be purified either directly or indirectly. A peak experience or epiphany that puts the mind in contact with the self is an example of direct purification. It can occur by the practice of spiritual techniques, through contact with spiritually powerful persons, or as a result of traumas. It causes spiritual energy to flow like a powerful river and spontaneously purge vasana-generated thoughts and emotions, leaving the subtle body still and clear, a spotless mirror in which the light of consciousness can be experienced and identified. Epiphanies, often unsolicited and the source of great inspiration

---

27. An extensive discussion of these factors can be found in chapter 10.

and faith, eventually wear off because unhelpful vasanas inevitably extrovert the mind once again.

Moment to moment application of self knowledge to the phenomena arising in the subtle body purifies the causal body directly because it prevents the vasanas from recycling. The inquirer observes desires and fears as they arise and neutralizes them, with the understanding that the result of any action will not permanently erase the sense of incompleteness that produced them in the first place. Action reinforces ignorance unless it is done with the right understanding. Or the inquirer can simply apply the knowledge "I am whole and complete, actionless awareness," assuming the meaning has been assimilated through careful reflection. The argument that renunciation is painful is contradicted by experience. This practice produces an immediate clearing of the mind, a feeling of lightness of being, not to mention joy. It also reduces the pressure of the vasanas because a desire or fear that is renounced destroys the existing vasana and does not produce another vasana.

A program of conscious living that utilizes knowledge-based techniques, designed to change or remove vasanas, indirectly purifies the mind. Unhelpful vasanas dominate the mind pictured below on the left, extroverting the attention factor and creating a disturbance that obscures the self. The mind on the right, however, is free of the agitating effects of binding vasanas. The

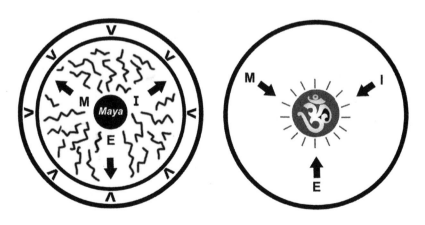

Samsara (Extroversion)                    Yoga (Meditation)

mind, intellect and ego are turned inward and are in a state of constant self awareness.

The causal body can be your friend or your enemy. It does not make a judgment concerning the nature of the experience it recycles. Vasanas can be either helpful or unhelpful. Whether a tendency is helpful or unhelpful depends on whether the action that it generates is in harmony with dharma[28] and whether the mind absorbs the rebound of the action with equanimity. This is not to say that only actions that make the mind feel good in the near term are helpful. Many actions make the mind temporarily feel good, but produce binding vasanas. Conversely, an action that causes suffering is not necessarily unhelpful, because it illumines a problem area. When you try to stop smoking, for example, the mind becomes agitated, even though not smoking is a very helpful non-activity. Abstaining from a bad habit requires considerable discipline and should be considered an action. It will also produce an abstinence vasana which is always useful. In general, however, actions that bring long term happiness, peace and satisfaction are helpful, and those that consistently roil the mind with negative emotions are unhelpful.

It is erroneously believed that the best way to purify likes and dislikes is to perform selfless action. Doing charitable acts for an ideal, others or God, is generally considered selfless action. Aside from the fact that there is only one self and action cannot be performed without it, or by it for that matter, people do selfless action because it makes them feel good. The causal body registers this motivation and creates a vasana for selfless action that can bind just as tightly as so-called self centered actions, not that feeling good is necessarily a problem, although it can be, assuming you are seeking liberation. The issue is not the nature of the action, but whether dharma and one's disposition are taken into account and whether the mind becomes settled in the long run.

Dharma is the self, operating in the dream of maya. It is the web of physical, psychological and moral laws that sustain the cosmos. If an action, thought or feeling violates dharma, it will produce agitation. If not, not. An action that violates dharma need not be illegal or immoral; it may simply involve doing

---

28. A detailed discussion of dharma can be found in chapter 7.

something that conflicts with one's disposition or works against self inquiry. Many avoid actions that violate dharma, but fritter away years doing meaningless work or idly pursuing trivial amusements. Such actions do not produce helpful vasanas nor do they reduce the vasana load.

Individuals cannot be faulted for not knowing they are limitless, but many do not even know who they are in a relative sense. Or if they do, often they do not like who they are. Or they have an excessively flattering view of themselves. We even see people who believe they have the wrong gender and do actions to change it, not realizing that the body is just meat and gender is a state of mind. Most of what a person thinks is wrong with himself or herself is not wrong at all. Yes, if you find yourself molesting little children or robbing banks you need work, but most negative self judgments are irrational projections brought on by lack of self knowledge.

It is common for an individual who is dissatisfied with his or her personality to try to become like someone he or she particularly admires or envies, and to build the tendencies that result in a new personality. This is dangerous, because in this case the undesirable traits are not being subjected to rational inquiry, where they could be accepted or abandoned. Instead, they get buried under the assumed traits and create a conflicted inauthentic person. It is common for religious and spiritual people to imitate Christ or the Buddha, or some other apparently great being, or to attempt to live up to a spiritual ideal. Aside from the fact that most of our spiritual idols are simply abstractions generated out of our own sense of inadequacy, not everyone is blessed with exceptional intelligence, determination and talent, and those that are owe the presence of these qualities to the grace of God, not their own efforts. Irrespective of how plain and ordinary you find yourself, you have a role to play or you would not be here. Therefore, it is wise to accept yourself as you are.

A desire-prompted activity that produces a favorable result generates an attraction vasana. A desire-prompted activity that generates an unwanted result produces an aversion vasana. Identifying with subtle actions like thoughts and feelings also produces vasanas. If an experience happens and the mind remains non-attached, a memory is produced, but not a vasana. Vasanas are just tendencies to repeat subtle and gross actions. If the word *vasana* is intimidating, think of them as likes and dislikes in this context. You become aware of your tendencies when they appear in the subtle body as your preferences. The practical psychology of the science of self inquiry involves managing likes and dislikes.

If a like or dislike appears in the mind and the self acknowledges it, does not identify with it, repress it, or act it out, the tendency for it to reappear is lessened. Therefore, it is possible to ameliorate unhelpful tendencies to a significant degree. It is also possible to pick up and cultivate new tendencies and to transform existing tendencies.

The vasanas are the building blocks of the psyche. As the individual proceeds through his or her life, he or she has the opportunity to have many experiences and develop many tendencies. Similar tendencies cluster together and reinforce each other. As the subtle and gross actions associated with them play out, these patterns are reinforced. Eventually they crystallize into fixations. These fixations become the individual's disposition or conditioning. The more they are repeated, the more predictable the response to life. At some point, the individual no longer consciously responds, but merely reacts to what happens. Unexamined negative fixations quickly become compulsions or addictions.

When we say that unhelpful tendencies need to be eliminated for self inquiry to work, we mean that the tendencies that produce unhealthy emotions need to be dissolved with understanding. For example, many people feel sorry for themselves because certain unhappy things happened in the past. Perhaps they were neglected or abused as children. The more they indulge in the thought that they are victims, the more depressed or angry they become. The more anger they feel, the stronger their sense of injustice becomes and the more they tend to get involved in unpleasant encounters with others. Even if the tendency does not produce conflicts with others, it causes inner conflict. To neutralize this kind of tendency, one needs to ask if he or she is actually a victim without reference to what happened, real or imagined, in the past. An individual's story often takes on a life of its own and has little or nothing to do with what is actually going on in the present. It is quite possible to construct a false self on the basis of imagined hurts and injustices. Even if there are legitimate grounds for complaint, anger and resentment are not helpful and need to be eliminated for inquiry to bear fruit.

In fact, self inquiry is not suitable for treating psychological dysfunction, other than mild neuroses. It is a means of liberation for otherwise reasonably healthy individuals who are highly motivated to know who they really are. A large smorgasbord of therapies is available these days to deal with psychological problems.

In any case, the motivation behind an action determines whether or not a vasana is created. A person developed colon cancer and needed an operation. The doctor cut the abdomen to remove the cancer and caused the patient's death. Though the operation was unsuccessful, the doctor was lauded for a noble attempt to save a life. Another man walking down a dark alley after the bars closed was accosted by a mugger who thrust a knife in his abdomen, killing him instantly. The robber was vilified and sent to prison for life. In both cases the cause of death was the same, a knife to the gut, but the killers suffered quite different fates. Were the action itself inherently evil, the doctor would be cooling his heels in prison; were it inherently good, the mugger would have gone scot-free. Actions in themselves are neither spiritual nor unspiritual, helpful nor unhelpful, good nor bad. If the motivating attitude is the critical ingredient in the production of helpful or unhelpful tendencies, it stands to reason that changing the nature of the attitude will have an effect on the tendency.

To change our attitudes, we need to pay attention to what we think and feel and square our thoughts and feelings with the truth. Altering behavior without changing the underlying attitude that caused it does not result in purification and spiritual growth. The dry drunk, an alcoholic who quits drinking but retains the psychology of a drunk, is a case in point. The following attitudes enhance agitating samskaras: fear, desire, attachment, pain, guilt, dishonesty, obsession, compulsion, pride, vanity, cruelty, envy, jealousy, anger, lust, fantasy, delusion, depression, selfishness, excessive concern for results and many others. Or if you want to look at it from another angle, anytime there is significant agitation in the subtle body, a negative idea is working out.

A non-binding attitude produces a non-binding vasana or exhausts an existing vasana. Non-binding attitudes are: kindness, compassion, forgiveness, acceptance, dispassion, non-attachment and joy. Non-binding attitudes neutralize binding likes and dislikes, purify the causal body, and make the subtle body meditation-worthy. A meditative subtle body, one turned toward the self, is the instrument for self inquiry. Do not think, however, that inquiry can be practiced only when the mind is calm and clear. An agitated mind is a sign that inquiry is needed. If you can figure out how to dismiss agitation with inquiry, you can quickly change your life for the better.

Spiritual practice means working with these subtle tendencies and adjusting our attitudes. The science of self inquiry offers five proven techniques to prepare the mind: action yoga, devotional yoga, knowledge yoga, the yoga of the three energies and meditation. The word *yoga*, in this context, means technique. Action or karma yoga purifies the ego, devotional yoga purifies the heart, knowledge yoga purifies the intellect and the yoga of the three energies purifies all three, including the gross body.[29] Meditation, discussed in chapter 13, is an advanced yoga because it only works when supported by the other yogas.

The yogas neutralize the likes and dislikes and correct structural distortions in the subtle body. A purified subtle body displays a stable geometry, like an isosceles triangle. No longer under intense pressure from unhelpful tendencies, its centers turn inward, yoke[30] together, and meditate naturally on the self. When the causal body has been purified and anxiety for results abandoned, the mind rests comfortably and joyfully in the present, taking what comes with equanimity. The three centers respect each other's turf and present a unified front to a changing and uncertain world. In a purified subtle body, the intellect, skilled in non-dual thought, cheerfully presents a dispassionate

---

29. There is no mention in the Vedas of devotional yoga as a separate path although devotion is a common topic. This is so because devotion is necessary for success in any pursuit. Furthermore, the rituals that are commonly thought of as devotion are actually karmas, actions. However, devotion has a positive transformational effect on the subtle body and can be looked upon as a separate technique. The "three energies yoga" can fall under the topic of karma as well. The Vedas only deal with two basic topics, action and knowledge.

30. The word *yoga* also means "to yoke" or join together. In psychological terms it indicates a state of inner integration.

and discriminating view to the ego and the mind, whose clarity is regularly compromised by excessive passion and emotion. Refusing to unduly push its own agenda, it counsels a balanced response in all situations, and in highly-evolved persons, turns its formidable power of observation and analysis on itself, ferreting out poorly-conceived plans, incorrect analyses, and emotion-dominated conclusions. If it is blessed with self knowledge, it continually reflects on the self, dissolving conflicts on the spot as life unfolds.

In the best of all possible inner worlds, the mind, ordinarily handmaiden to a needy and selfish ego, resists egoic desires, loves purely and refuses to disturb subtle body equilibrium with petty conceits, insecurities and ill-conceived sentiments, all the while offering emotional support to the intellect's non-dual reflections. A well-balanced, satisfied emotional self is an essential condition for self inquiry.

The tendency to operate exclusively from the emotional center is not conducive to subtle body harmony, and causes much suffering. Because unhealthy emotions are the result of incorrect views about oneself and reality, during initial phases of unrestrained ego-motivated devotion the inquirer should take extra pains to develop discrimination and dispassion. Even if the emotions are largely positive, it is spiritually undesirable to romanticize feelings at the expense of knowledge, a common tendency these days.

The third limb of a purified subtle body, the ego, should be strong and confident, not necessarily because it has successfully negotiated life, but because it has the courage to follow its spiritual inclinations and practice self inquiry. A mature ego, mindful of its dependence on subjective and objective factors, will refuse to play inner politics. It will promote inner harmony by carefully heeding the intellect's impartial counsel and respecting the mind's feelings and intuitions.

## Karma Yoga

Karma yoga is a powerful way to reduce the extroversion of the mind by exhausting vasanas, so that attention flows toward the self. Attention flowing to the self is self inquiry. Contact of the attention with the self is called *yoga*, union with the self or experience of the self.

In reality, the self cannot be experienced as an object as it is commonly believed, because the experiencer, the individual, is already the self. How can you experience what you are, if you are always experiencing what you are? This means that it is possible to realize the self without the help of discrete self experiences, or epiphanies. It does not mean, however, that indirect self experience is unhelpful. Self knowledge can also come directly from words, contrary to the modern spiritual world's fascination with silence and the prevailing ill informed belief that it cannot.

It is possible for a highly purified individual with a clear idea of the nature of the self to gain self knowledge in silence, but sitting in silence is far from a guarantee of enlightenment because silence is not opposed to ignorance. If silence means the absence of sound, it is not conscious and does not realize that you are ignorant of who you are. If silence means a pure mind, the self can be recognized for what it is. The knowledge of the self that appears in the mirror of a pure mind destroys the belief that the self is an object, which is how it seems experientially, and duality collapses, assuming the meditator understands that ignorance is the problem. Duality is a belief, not an experiential fact, although it seems quite real. Experience can be extremely helpful, in so far as it can give rise to knowledge or corroborate previously gained knowledge. Therefore, an inquirer should practice the yogas to purify the mind.

It is the god given right of everyone to act. And it is obvious that actions have results. Actions have results because reality is non-dual awareness. This means that the doer of action is conscious and the field in which actions are done is consciousness. It is the desire of everyone that his or her actions should produce the intended result. But this does not always happen. Sometimes we get what we want. Sometimes we get what we do not want. Sometimes we get what we once wanted when we no longer want it. Sometimes we get something that we neither wanted nor did not want. Whatever the case, it is never clear when we act what the result will be and when it will come. And it is very clear, spiritually materialistic beliefs like those embodied in *The Secret* notwithstanding, that just wanting something will not produce the desired object.

Nor will simply performing the appropriate actions produce the desired result. Millions buy lottery tickets, but only one person wins. If the results of action were up to the desirer of results, then everyone would have everything he or she wanted.

What determines the results of our actions? First, the wanter-doer needs to see that his or her actions are appropriate and timely. If I want a new tire for my car and go to the ice cream parlor, I will not get what I want. If I go to the tire store at midnight, I will not get what I want. If I go to the tire store during business hours and neglect to bring my wallet, I will not get what I want. Yet, even appropriate and timely actions are not enough. By far the most significant factor is the nature of the field in which I offer my actions. If a huge fire in the Amazon burned down all the rubber trees, the tire manufacturer would be unable to ship tires to my local tire store and I would be unable to get what I want, even if I fulfilled all other requirements.

Assuming that the action is appropriate and timely, the nature of the field determines the result. If this is true, then anxiety about the result is gratuitous. Yet the wanter-doer inevitably worries about whether or not the desired result will materialize before, during and after the action is performed. This anxiety is not only wasted energy, it is spiritually unwise because attention, which should be fully engaged in the skillful performance of the action, is dissipated by the concern for the result. Because it is so obsessed with an imagined result, a child on a trip to an amusement park says: "Are we having fun yet, mommy?" How many job assignments have been hopelessly botched because of performance anxiety? A person suffers through school to get a job, gets a demanding job to support a family, produces the family to enjoy retirement with, and worries about death throughout retirement. At every stage the fullness of the self is unappreciated because of an unhealthy anxiety about the future.

If my actions are appropriate and timely, why do I not always get what I want? Life is vast. It includes everything in existence from the gross elements, the whole cosmos, to the subtle bodies of every existent life form. This field is presided over by limitless pure consciousness in the form of the macrocosmic causal body, or God, if you prefer a religious term. God has non-dual vision. Non-dual vision means that everything in the creation is of equal value to everything else from God's point of view; the whole of existence sinks or swims together. To God, a beggar in the slums of Bombay is as important as the President of the United States. The parasite living in the lymph system of an individual is as important as the individual itself.

God is both the substance of the creation and the intelligence that creates, maintains and destroys all creation's forms. Through the law of karma, it takes care of everything animate and inanimate. So, when an individual wants something, God needs to determine whether or not the desired object will serve the total. If it serves the total in some way, the individual is more likely to get what he or she wants. If not, not. In fact, there are no hard and fast rules, because the mind of God is inscrutable and because the number of variables in the field is virtually infinite. The only certainty? The results of actions are not up to individuals.

What are the needs of the total? The basic need of all life forms is sustenance and reproduction. So God has to look out for all the material needs of the conscious beings. When it comes to human beings, who have intellect and are endowed with free will, other needs, particularly the need for freedom, need to be fulfilled. Plants and animals have no conscious interest in freedom because they do not know that they are bound. If there is evolution and lower life forms become higher life forms, then the lower life forms will develop a desire for freedom when they evolve intellect, and can understand what bondage and freedom are. But human beings have a built in desire for freedom, because they are partially conscious of their innermost nature, consciousness.

Consciousness was never bound. It is always free. We can tell that freedom is natural to human beings, because they always attempt to remove any and all limitations to their well-being. And when a human being is happy, he or she does not try to become unhappy. He or she clings to the happiness, tooth and nail. Fundamentally, all human pursuits can be reduced to the desire for freedom. Finally, we need to know that an individual's desire for freedom is just God trying to free itself from the ill-considered belief that it is bound. If this is true, then God is responsible for looking out for the spiritual welfare of human beings, as well as their material welfare. Therefore, when an individual acts, God needs to consider not only the impact of that action on the welfare of the total, but on the spiritual welfare of the individual; not that

God is a big person like us, who has to make daily choices to keep his or her creation going.

More often than not, what we want is not what we need spiritually. We erroneously believe that security, pleasure or virtue will make us happy. Sometimes it is important that we feel materially secure, for example, before we seek freedom, so God may give us material wealth. Sometimes we will seek freedom only when we are insecure materially, so God provides insecurity. Sometimes falling in love is good for us spiritually, sometimes it is not. Sometimes character flaws cause us to seek God and sometimes a good character prevents us from seeking the truth, so God shapes the character that is best suited for our growth. Often an accident or a serious illness, the will of God, kick starts self inquiry.

God is that factor that understands the flow of our little lives from start to finish and how they impact on the whole. And since our liberation does not take place outside of the context of the whole of existence, how it impacts on the total is also meaningful. Since God is not a big person eighty feet tall who can appear physically, display its credentials, and command us to accept its words as truth, it can teach us who we are only through the results of our actions and the odd epiphany, assuming we are willing to listen. What a pity that our attachments make us exceptionally resistant to the lessons life so graciously tries to teach us.

Karma yoga is an attitude we need to cultivate toward action and its results, if we want a pure mind. It is based on the fact that God, the field of life, is the giver of the results of action, not the doer of action. It is an attitude of gratitude. What do I have to feel grateful for?

Life itself is a great gift. No individual consciously decided to come here. We all appeared one fine day, and it is obvious that we had nothing to do with the creation into which we were so unceremoniously thrust. Not only can we not claim authorship, we cannot claim ownership of one single thing. Mom donated an egg and dad donated a sperm to get the ball rolling. Every nutrient that formed our bodies came from our mother's body and she was a thief too; she appropriated everything in her body from God's body, the earth. Plants and animals sacrificed their lives for her; she only supplied the space in which life could happen, not that she had any choice once she decided to copulate during her fertile period. She cannot even say that she was responsible for the desire to copulate; it just happened.

When we popped out of the womb our eyes opened, the breath started automatically and an amazing world appeared, a benign cornucopia of experience fit for a king. To say that we were as helpless and dumb as a loaf of bread would not be an exaggeration. Mom held us and beamed love into our eyes. Dad went to work the next day to get the money to see us through the next twenty plus years. After a while, the brain started thinking on its own and good old mom and pop commenced to fill it with knowledge. Unfortunately, a lot of what they thought was knowledge was actually ignorance, but they cannot be faulted because their hearts were in the right place.

Karma yoga is an acknowledgement of the great debt we owe the world. Everything we do is a contribution to a world that keeps giving till the day we die. To be human is a privilege, not a right. And with it comes responsibility. God, awareness operating the creation, is no fool. It does not ask much, only that we respond appropriately to life's demands. If we do not respond appropriately, God, who operates the law of karma, delivers unwanted results. Most of us have a long list of reasons why life has failed to give us what we want. These grievances show up constantly as a whining, complaining attitude.

Action yoga is a change of attitude toward life and its doings. It does not destroy the ego, remove it from daily life or condemn it to specific religious activities. It corrects the ego's relationship to the body and the world. In the short run, however, because of a perceived threat to its sense of importance, the ego may cause disturbances that hinder meditation and self inquiry. But because karma yoga causes friction, it is an excellent way to coax the ego out from behind its wall of self serving rationalizations and deceptions.

How does karma yoga work? First, all actions, even the most insignificant, should be dedicated to the self. I offer my work—whatever it is at any moment—as worship in the temple of life. As seeker of truth I worship the truth, and want my life to be in harmony with it. If the concept of worship is too difficult, think of karma yoga as a contribution or a participation in life. Everything else contributes selflessly to make the universe what it is, why not me? Nothing, except the self, sits on the sidelines as a witness, so why not actively participate? Furthermore, why would the active organs—hands and legs, for example—evolve, if consciousness did not intend for us to make a contribution?

In any case, before acting I need to examine my motives. For example, I want a new automobile. Will an automobile make it easier to pursue my spiritual path? If the present vehicle will not get me to work reliably, and I need work to support myself and take care of obligations so I have time for meditation, the purchase of a vehicle is justified. This technique calls for great integrity, because the ego is not above cooking up spiritual ideas to justify unspiritual impulses.

Next I need to clear my negative emotions. Acting from a negative state of mind produces negative tendencies. Actions dedicated to causes and ideals, especially those fuelled by a sense of injustice or unexamined motives, do not qualify as action yoga, nor do capricious motivations like the desire for luxury or status, because they conflict with spiritual values, agitate the mind and re-inforce unhelpful tendencies.

Then I lovingly dedicate my actions and their results to God. Leaving the results to God means that I need no longer worry about them. Karma yoga removes stress. When the mind is stressed work tends to be sloppy and inefficient, reducing the likelihood of a favorable result. Letting go of stress means letting go of fears and desires concerning what I want.

Maintaining the karma yoga attitude is a full time discipline because we are always initiating actions. Dedication at the onset of an activity should be balanced by an attitude of gratitude when results, positive or negative, accrue. Each life experience, no matter how trivial, is a previous action fructifying and provides an excellent opportunity to practice gratitude, even when unwanted results manifest. For example, a man took a flight from New York to San Francisco that was forced to make an emergency landing in Oakland, causing him to miss an important appointment and lose a valuable contract. He could either be upset he did not receive the intended result, or be happy to be alive. Taking what comes as a gift neutralizes likes and dislikes. Since likes and dislikes are the cornerstone of ego, purifying them purifies ego and makes the mind peaceful. Unhealthy attitudes are easy to identify in a peaceful mind. Most unhealthy attitudes are unconscious and cannot survive the light of inquiry.

Karma yoga does not mean that I do not do actions for the results, only that I understand that the results are not up to me. This understanding is the basis of dispassion and allows me to take whatever comes as a gift. As a seeker of truth, my number one goal is to understand the nature of reality, not to obtain a particular object or situation. Unwanted as well as wanted results contain valuable messages. Karma yoga, the foundation of self inquiry, is beautiful because I need not journey far afield to prepare myself for enlightenment; my daily life is my spiritual practice.

# Love

Non-dual love is the realization of oneness with the self. Because the self is everything that is, non-dual love is unconditional love of everyone and everything.

The most fundamental expression of our sense of separation from the self is the craving for love. And the most common expression of the need for love is the desire for relationship. A relationship is meant to erase the craving for love and bring happiness. Can relationships solve the happiness issue?

## Special Relationships

Our conditioning appears as likes and dislikes, the result of pleasant and unpleasant experiences. Guided by likes and dislikes, the self's non-discriminating love flows toward an object. This phenomenon is called falling in love and is thought by worldly people to be the result of some kind of special chemistry.

But what is it, actually? When we are lonely, we fantasize about love objects in line with our likes and dislikes. When the mind obsessively dwells on an object, the desire for it increases. Desire is suffering and suffering is unnatural, so we would like to get rid of it. When a real life approximation of the fantasy appears, the desire for completeness temporarily disappears, the mind becomes still and the bliss of the self floods the heart. The feelings that arise when the mind is free of desire are called love. So far, so good. But there is one small catch.

The bliss seems to be coming from the love object, when it is actually coming from the self. Consequently, the mind becomes attached to the love object. Unfortunately, the love object did not create the sense of longing that produced the desire in the first place, so falling in love with the object is not a lasting solution to the problem of separation. Even if the love object can be tied down with marriage, children or another way, the desire for completeness does not go away once the relationship is in place; it simply changes into a desire for something else. It does not go away, because it is born out of ignorance of the self, whose nature is, ironically, non-dual love.

For a relationship to succeed, the participants should have accurate information about themselves and each other. To gather information effectively the mind should be clear, alert, focused, observant and panoramic. But being in love is so exciting and pleasurable, that the mind focuses solely on the feeling of love. To its detriment, it unconsciously excludes information about the qualities in the love object and difficult karmic factors that might threaten its enjoyment. The intensity of the pleasure associated with this feeling is directly proportional to the degree of attachment to the fantasy. And the degree of attachment to the fantasy is related to the intensity and frequency of the desire for love. The desire for love is a consequence of self ignorance, because the self is love. In other words, romantic love is the self loving itself but pretending that it loves someone else. And although the ego believes that it loves the object, it is actually in love with the feeling of love.

As less attractive aspects of the respective personalities surface in unguarded moments to challenge their fantasies, the lovers need to continually update their romantic notions about each other. When the love object exhibits behavior that contradicts the fantasy, confusion, doubt and ambivalence arise. Furthermore, because dependence on objects limits one's innate sense of freedom, an unconscious aversion to the love object may develop.

If it was known that love was the nature of the self, the anxiety associated with getting and keeping love would disappear. It is virtually impossible to keep the illusion of romantic love alive for long because the needs of both people, the relationship of each to his or her needs, and the context in which the love is happening are all constantly changing.

In the world of object oriented love, likes and dislikes seem to be a reasonable basis for a relationship. A man falls in love with a woman because she is attractive and has a beautiful, sexy body. She falls in love with him because he is handsome and successful. They take out a thirty-year mortgage on a lovely home and produce three darling children. Maintaining such a life is stressful. To cope with the stress, he starts drinking and watching sports on TV and she overeats and smokes. Slowly their attraction to each other is no longer the basis of the relationship and they are forced to define it differently, usually as a kind of duty or obligation. As the love slowly dissipates they begin to quarrel. Even if they manage to patch things up for the sake of the children, new desires and fears come into play, forcing them to continually react and adjust. Eventually, the desire for freedom trumps the desire for love and the relationship terminates, leaving them with a negative view of relationships, the opposite gender, or indeed, romantic love itself. If nothing is discovered about the way likes and dislikes operate to condition the love, they may think they chose the wrong person, blow life back into the romantic fantasy, and set out to remove the loneliness inspired by ignorance of the self by repeating the same experiment again with someone else.

## The Soul Mate

The soul mate is an apparently superior option to the notion of romantic love. Because relationships based on physical and emotional likes and dislikes are so insecure, a relationship based on spiritual factors is meant to produce the emotional stability and intimacy lacking in ordinary relationships.

Spiritual relationship can be equally problematic, however, because the value of spiritual qualities, like worldly qualities, is also based on ever changing likes and dislikes. A quality that I particularly admire in someone one day may not be as important to me later. Or that quality may disappear from the love object as he or she changes. I may be attracted to someone because of their sunny disposition. But what happens when my significant other suffers a series of misfortunes and becomes cranky and morose?

Additionally, spiritual qualities do not exist in a vacuum, but are conditioned by their opposites. For every transcendent urge there is a powerful need to cling to security and pleasure. Behind every generous impulse, a selfish tendency lurks. Every attraction to the light is balanced by a fascination with the dark. When you sign on to a relationship with a saint, understand that you get a sinner in the bargain.

Conflict in relationships between people with worldly values is difficult to resolve because both, no matter how far apart they are on the issue in play at the moment, are essentially right. They have, or believe they have, come to their respective points of view honestly. And there is no court of appeals to which the conflict can be presented for adjudication. Furthermore, because they have no value for self awareness and spiritual growth, conflicts tend to be suppressed rather than resolved and the relationship slowly becomes unworkable.

If both individuals value the quest for truth more than they value each other, the relationship might succeed because of a willingness to sacrifice selfish impulses—unreasonable demands for love, for example—for the sake of the truth. But the soul mate idea is still an object-oriented solution to the problem of incompleteness. And as we know, object-oriented solutions to spiritual problems invariably lose relevance and fail.

## Marriage

Marriage seems to have lost some of its luster since the idea of relationships appeared in the sixties. Marriage has always been stressful, but post-war material prosperity put a strain on the idea of lifetime commitment. At some point, the idea that desires need to be instantly gratified gained currency. Mechanics could no longer be bothered to take apart a carburetor to find the offending part, for example. They simply swapped it for a new one. Likewise, husbands and wives were reduced to the status of replacement parts.

However dismal the statistics on traditional marriage, it is not clear that the relationship solution produces more happiness than marriage in the long run. And although it is impossible to know how many traditional marriages succeed, many who stuck by their wedding vows found deep and lasting emotional satisfaction, albeit after many ups and downs. Commitment to an ideal engenders growth. This is not to say that the committed love of another is a satisfactory answer to the deeper need for unconditioned freedom that is the cry of every human heart. But it need not stand in the way. It might become a platform from which one could evolve spiritually.

## A Different Kind of Marriage

Vedic spiritual culture offers an interesting variant of the marriage idea. According to the Vedas, the purpose of life is self realization. The realization that I am whole and complete frees my love from its dependence on objects and it flows into everyone and everything.

If the goal of life is not object defined emotional security but inner freedom, how does the biological urge to mate and produce offspring fit? The Vedas ask humans to serially assume and relinquish four limited identities as they pass through four stages of life. These are: student, householder, seeker and renunciate.

During the student phase the individual learns moral values, the karma yoga attitude and the idea that the ultimate purpose of life is fulfillment through self realization. The second phase is family life. To raise a family, it is necessary to mate. Mating involves emotional excitement and pleasure, which causes attachment. Attachment is generally called love. When children arrive, a second major attachment appears. To raise a family, money is required. To get money, work is necessary. Work and money constitute a third attachment. In fact, the householder phase is an ocean of attachments. An inability to cope with the attachments of the householder phase is probably the primary cause of the tendency for the failure of marriage in desire-oriented societies.

But the Vedic model offers a powerful tool for dealing with attachment. In the first place, marriage is not considered an end in itself. It is just one of the four stations on the road to liberation. So on the wedding day, the respective spouses understand that it need not continue after the children are married and have assumed their place in society. If marriage is no longer necessary in late middle age, attachment to the idea of marriage will not be as strong as it would be if the individuals felt committed for life. Simply agreeing to this possibility in the beginning removes considerable stress from the marriage and makes it possible to emerge from marriage more or less psychologically intact.

Secondly, marriage is a spiritual duty, not a hormone inspired right. It is meant to honor the natural order of creation by producing offspring. As such, it provides an impersonal framework for individuals to work out their core samskaras—love, work, children, and security—together.

The basic vehicle used to negotiate the tricky currents of married life is the karma yoga attitude, unfolded in the last chapter. If you take the beliefs, emotions, attitudes, opinions and actions of your spouse as the self helping you to discover what you need to work on, marriage can provide an excellent opportunity for spiritual growth. Western societies are desire-oriented societies. As long as you play by the rules, you have a right to pursue happiness as you see fit. While this approach has certain benefits, it has a downside; the needs of others, if they are considered at all, are not valued as highly as one's own. Although it is necessary for the individual to take care of his or herself, everything in life comes through others. So it is wise to properly value others, particularly one's spouse. Desire-prompted, rights-oriented societies are afflicted with many social ills, probably because others are not properly esteemed.

The Vedic model, which is responsible for the relative stability of marriage in India, is a duty-based approach; the idea being that happiness lies in fulfilling one's duties and obligations to the family, caste, occupation and religion first and to one's personal needs second. Not only is such a view conducive to social harmony, it neutralizes likes and dislikes and makes it possible to eventually fulfill the primary duty to one's self—freedom through self realization.

So the primary gift that the society gives a young person about to enter the householder phase is the understanding that the results of his or her actions are not under his or her control and are meant to be taken as grace. In short, the society cultivates a value for devotion to God, non-attachment and gratitude for what one has. Armed with these tools, it is possible to enter marriage and emerge relatively unscathed. When life has no purpose other than the gratification of an individual's needs for security and object-oriented love, the ego rules and conflict is inevitable.

Success in duty oriented relationships does not depend on the widely unrealistic expectation that each partner is responsible for the other's happiness, only that both serve the relationship as defined in the scriptures and endorsed by the society. The wife plays the wife role and the husband plays the husband role. When individuals are freed of the burden of unrealistic expectations, real love can flower.

If true love happens in the context of a duty-oriented marriage and the participants view love relationships as means to an end and not the end itself, both will be well prepared when the next stage of life dawns, whether or not they enter it as a couple. When you understand how to love through service to others, life transitions are easy to face.

The next stage is the conscious search for the self. Mystics of all times have made this journey in search of the self. During this phase, the seeker experiences the self through contact with great souls and various spiritual practices. This provides a clear idea of the goal and the desire to realize the self becomes a burning ambition.

In the final stage, the love that motivated the search is invested in a life of meditation and inquiry. The renunciate dies to the world and to the idea of doership. He or she realizes that the self is free of action, that there is only one self and that he or she is it. To formulate it in terms of love, I discover I am love.

## Converting Emotion into Devotion

Discounting the ego, the subtle body has two wings, the intellect and the heart. The intellect is subtler than the heart. As the intellect, I can understand what the mind is feeling, but the mind can never understand what I am thinking. The heart, the emotional sheath, is sandwiched between the intellect and the body. The intellect is situated between the heart and the causal body. Materialists think that consciousness, in the form of energy, flows from the world through the senses to the mind, up to the intellect and on to the self. Actually, it flows from the self through the causal body down to the intellect, then to the heart and finally through the senses into the world. I do not see the world because it is there; the world is there because I see it.[31] This is important to understand if you want to gain control of your emotions because emotions are triggered by thoughts. To be fair, it is easy to miss the connection because the stimulus response mechanism is subtle and fleeting. Tendencies sprout in the causal body, a thought appears in the intellect, and an emotion is instantly generated.

Thoughts not in harmony with the nature of reality cause negative emotions. For example, my wife leaves me and I get angry or depressed. On the surface, this seems to be a logical reaction. But is it? In the first place, is she my wife? Is there a document backed by the full force of the law that defines her as my possession? Even if there is, a higher law—free will—declares that everyone is free to do what they like, including to break unjust laws. Additionally, is there a rule that compels me to look for happiness in a relationship? There are many other paths to fulfillment. Furthermore, it is a fact that a situation obtaining now will not exist later. Even if she stays with me, one of us will die one day. I knew this when I married her. What use is my grief?

The more refined is my appreciation of the dharmic matrix of things and beings, the less stress I will experience. Although it need not do so, desiring things can easily put me at odds with dharma. When desire is thwarted, anger arises. Anger is difficult to maintain and eventually collapses into depression. Depression creates confusion, the arch enemy of discrimination. When discrimination deserts me, I have lost my best friend and life becomes a mess, because I can no longer find my place in the natural order.

The most common emotion-producing thought is the idea that I should have what I want, when I want it. The next most common emotion-causing thought is the idea that once I get what I want, it should continue to supply happiness for as long as I want it to. Neither of these thoughts is helpful, because reality does not care what you want. It knows what you need based on your place in the matrix. It is not going to alter the natural order just to suit your gratuitous desires. So the reason for unhelpful emotions is attachment to irrational beliefs, nothing else.

---

31. The realization of this fact is the essence of enlightenment.

If my thoughts are rooted in the knowledge that I am whole and complete, that I am what I want and that my nature is love, I will not have negative emotions. I will feel a deep and abiding sense of emotional satisfaction.

## Spiritual Practice and Psychological Work

At a certain point, it becomes clear that objective solutions to the love problem do not work and I realize that I suffer because I do not love myself. I observe that I always seem to be working against my own happiness. If I eat too much, not only am I guilty of taking more than my share, which causes guilt because it is a form of theft, but I unduly stress the body and eventually cause health problems. If I loved myself would I do this? If I smoke or drink excessively, which I do to please myself, I inflict suffering on my body in the name of pleasure. If I waste time socializing mindlessly, I prohibit myself from doing more meaningful things. If I actually loved myself, would I do this? If I lie to obtain love, I will suffer guilt and anxiety, another indication that I do not love myself. All self insulting actions—addictions and compulsions, for example—are signs of low self esteem.

If my self esteem is low, I have a psychological problem and need therapy. Seeking help means that I love myself. Therapy can provide tools to work on myself and give me confidence. Psychotherapy does not qualify as a means of liberation, however, because it takes the ego to be the self. But it can be an important step, because I need a reasonably healthy ego before I am capable of questioning my view of myself as an ego and opening up to the idea that I have a greater identity. Once I have evolved beyond the desire for object-oriented love, am free of psychological problems and want liberation, I am suited for an emotional upgrade—the yoga of devotion.

## Devotion

Devotion is intense love of the self with attachment. It is either dual or non-dual, object centered or objectless. Non-dual, objectless love is the nature of the self. If I want to be emotionally happy, I should love the self. But self love is abstract, because I cannot see the self. If, however, I understand that everything I perceive is awareness in a gross or subtle form, then reality abounds with altars to which I can offer devotion.

Meditation on the silence is a form of devotion. Contemplation on the words of the scripture is a form of devotion. Serving the world by responding appropriately to its demands is devotion. If you do not love the world and everything in it, you lack gratitude, one of the purest forms of devotion. You should love it because it has given you everything you have.

Devotion is awareness paying attention to itself. In terms of an individual caught in the dualistic snare of the apparent reality, it is a technique that gets your feelings flowing in the direction of the self, instead of toward transient objects. When you take the apparent reality to be real, you do not know that you are what you are devoted to. You know there is something more than what you see and you have a certain degree of love and respect for it, even though it is not clear what it is. So you become devoted to selective objects that remind you of it. Symbols can take us to the self, because the self is always present. When we worship a symbol, the self works through the symbol to provide the experiences and insights necessary to draw us ever closer to it, both in love and understanding. If the symbol is a word like awareness, devoted contemplation on its meaning will reveal awareness. This is possible because that to which the word refers is always present as the essence of the devotee. Symbols also work because nothing that exists is actually separate from the self, reality being what it is. So even though you think that God is someone or something other than the symbol, the symbol is actually God too.

God is the most common symbol of the self. Whatever idea of God you have exists solely by the grace of awareness. If you are not aware, how can you worship God? If your concept of God is less inclusive than formless awareness, it does not matter because the self knows that you are actually worshipping it. If you believe that God is somewhere else, it is fine because awareness is everywhere, so when your prayers reach God, they reach awareness. In fact, awareness caused you to think of worshipping God in the first place. It is there before you even wake up in the morning. If the idea of God is distasteful because of its association with the negative aspects of a particular religion, any object that invokes the self in the form of love can be used to get love flowing.

Prayer, congregational worship, study of scripture and the lives of great saints are equally effective practices. Another good technique is to strip every object of its secular projection and instill it with a divine aura. See your body as God's temple, your home as the house of God, your family as God's family. Consider every spoken word the name of God and every activity, spiritual or otherwise, service to God. Bending, lying or kneeling should be seen as prostration to God and all lights as symbols of self. One should see sleep as meditation and eating as God eating God. In this manner, every object and activity gradually loses its worldly associations and becomes a living symbol of the divine.

When you see a mountain, see it as a symbol of your self. Mountains are good self symbols, because they are relatively eternal. They rise above everything and provide an unsurpassed view. The self is the highest part of our being, jutting above the plains and valleys of our body-mind territory affording us unlimited vision. They are unmoving, like the self. It cannot move because it is non-dual. They are silent like the self, "the unstruck sound." When you see a river, see it as your self. Like the self, rivers give life, nourishing everything with which they come in contact. See the sky as the limitless self.

If you wish to personify the self, see to it that your god or goddess is compassionate, conscious, peaceful and beautiful. Installing these qualities in the symbol is an indirect way of invoking and recognizing them in your self. A human being is a good symbol of the self. When you love a human, it is the self shining in the human that you love. Nonetheless, humans, like everything else, are "cast in the image of God," i.e., they are awareness in a form. If awareness is non-dual and it is the cause of the creation, the creation cannot be anything other than awareness because an effect is just the cause in a form. Ignorance makes it seem as if forms stand alone, but they do not; they are only awareness. Is a wave separate from the ocean?

The love light that is awareness shines with particular brilliance in human beings because they are endowed with intellect and are capable of knowing who they are. The worship of humans is an essential step on the devotional path because the worshipper is a human being. By loving others you love yourself. The worship of others does not mean that you value others more than you value yourself. It means that you see no difference between them and you. Worship is being there for yourself and others when you are needed. See the request as the self asking for worship. Refusal to give is refusal to love yourself, because there are no others. Loving others is a valuable practice because conflicts with others are a major source of agitation. Eventually this practice destroys duality and results in self realization, the understanding that there are no others.

To the materialist part of the mind, projecting divinity into objects seems to be irrational, but the practice is good psychology. Just as an actress becomes the person she portrays by totally identifying with every aspect of the character's life, the devotee discovers identity with the self through intense identification with the symbol. The more you love your symbol, the more likely it is to produce a vision of the self. Having experienced the beauty of the self, it is impossible not to fall deeper in love and become passionately attached. Because worldly beauties pale in the presence of the self, attachments to other things automatically fall away.

India is the world's number one spiritual superpower because the truth is so deeply embedded in the culture. The self, which is not available for objectification, has been kept alive by a remarkably sophisticated devotional culture. It is not the intention of the author to suggest that other religions are devotionally inferior. Only that to my knowledge, no other religious culture has developed a more effective way to lead the devotee from the form to the formless, not that liberation is the stated goal of any religion, except Vedic religion and its most famous derivative, Buddhism. To show how this works, let us unfold the meaning of one of Indian culture's most beloved deities.

It would be fair to say that Ganesh, the elephant God, the remover of obstacles, is the most popular deity in the Hindu pantheon and the easiest to decode. If you wish, take him as a charming, bizarre cartoon, ask him to remove the obstacles to the satisfaction of your desires, and leave it at that. If you want to go deeper you can use his divine form to enter the shining world of the self.

Ganesh has a fat human body and the head of an elephant. How he got the elephant head and what it means is revealed in the following story. Shiva, his father, had been meditating on the top of a holy mountain for many years, when suddenly he was overcome by a desire to make love with his wife. He had been away for so long that he decided to knock before entering his house. A chubby young boy answered the door. He did not know that the boy was his son because he had gone off shortly after the boy was conceived. The boy in turn had never seen his father, so he took the man at the door to be a stranger.

Ganesh, the remover of obstacles

'What do you want?" he asked Shiva.

"Step aside," Shiva said, "I want to see Parvati."

"You'll have to wait," said Ganesh, "I'll ask her if she is willing to receive visitors."

"I said get out of my way," Shiva replied with considerable irritation.

"I said you'll have to wait," replied Ganesh protectively. "I do not know who you think you are, but you certainly are lacking in manners."

At this Shiva, who was known to have a short temper, brandished his sword and shouted, "Get out of my way, you fat little dwarf or I'll cut off your head."

"Over my dead body," said Ganesh digging in his heels.

Shiva swung his sword and cut off his son's head, just as his wife arrived at the door.

"What have you done, you beast!" she screamed looking at the dead body of her son. "You fix this right away or you will never see the inside of my bedroom again."

Realizing that his chances of getting what he wanted were fast approaching zero—there were no relationships in those days, divorce was out of the question, and Shiva was too virtuous to visit prostitutes—Shiva said, "You do one thing, dear. Run out and bring the first creature you see that has a head."

When she got to the street, she saw an elephant coming her way. She led the elephant to Shiva, who cut off its head and stuck it on the body of Ganesh. He immediately revived, Parvati was thrilled to have her son back, and Shiva was invited in.

A Freudian psychologist might have a field day with the oedipal implications of this myth, but it is not a psychological statement. The boy Ganesh represents any human being who does not know who he is. A boy is an undeveloped adult. In fact, he is the son of Shiva, which is to say, the self. The word *Shiva* means *that which is auspicious at every time, place and circumstance.* Is anything more auspicious than you? Ganesh does not know this, however, because his understanding is limited. He is just a boy, spiritually speaking. Elephants are symbols of intelligence and memory. When Ganesh confronts Shiva, his own innermost self, he is relieved of his limited understanding. The elephant head represents the Vedas, the knowledge of the self. The self is the source of our intelligence. The message of the Vedas—I am limitless, non-dual awareness—needs to be assimilated in one form or another if we want liberation.

The name *Ganesh* refers to the self. *Gana* means *planet* and *Isha* means *the ruler.* He is the ruler of the planets. The thoughts in our minds predictably revolve around the awareness, just as planets revolve around their sun. Without this controlling power, our thoughts would spin out of control and purposeful work would be impossible. Awareness illumines the mind like the sun illumines the moon. If awareness is withdrawn from the mind, as it is in deep sleep, the mind dies.

Ganesh has only one tusk. This means that the self is non-dual. Shiva was entreated by the gods to give out the Vedas because the world was suffering for want of self knowledge. He agreed to teach them, with the stipulation that he would not repeat a single word. Ganesh agreed and duly took up his pen. In the middle of Shiva's discourse his pen ran out of ink. Fearing that he would miss something important while he refilled the pen, he broke off his tusk and continued to write. This means that the words of the Vedas destroy dualistic views. It is necessary to subject your mind to the complete means of self knowledge, because every doubt about who you are needs to be removed. The broken tusk is a symbol of enlightenment.

Ganesh's full round belly symbolizes non-duality. The self is whole and complete, always full. Nothing can be added to you or subtracted from you. As the self, you are always satisfied.

Ganesh rides on a rat or has a small mouse worshipping at his feet. Rodents are symbols of desire. They have so much desire, they are continually active. Desire is synonymous with the ego. Because it feels limited, inadequate and incomplete, the ego endlessly desires to complete itself by obtaining things in this world. Desires control people who do not know who they are, but they do not control the enlightened. The enlightened are non-doers. You can only attain the status of a non-doer and rule your ratlike mind, if you realize that you are whole and complete.

Ganesh's four arms symbolize the emotional/feeling function, the intellect or thinking function, the ego or "I" sense and the causal body.

In his upper left hand, he holds an open lotus. The lotus is a symbol of enlightenment because it closes in the night, a symbol of spiritual ignorance, and opens in the day, a symbol of self knowledge.

His upper right hand carries an axe that represents discrimination. Discrimination is the power to distinguish what is real from what is apparently real. The self alone is real, meaning enduring. Its forms are apparently real. Enlightenment is discrimination, knowing what is real and what is apparently real.

His lower right hand is the gesture of fearlessness and is inscribed with an om. Om is a symbol of the self as unfolded in the Mandukya Upanishad. It represents awareness as the fourth and invariable factor in the three states of consciousness: waking, dreaming and deep sleep.

In the lower left hand, Ganesh holds a big bowl of sweets. This means that the self is bliss, the sweetest thing. There is nothing dearer or sweeter than one's self.

Ganesh sports a beautiful golden crown, symbolizing dominion, power, and overlordship. The self has dominion over everything, in so far as it is the source of everything. It is omnipotent and rules the world.

Devotional practice works for the following reason. When a devotee approaches a deity, he or she typically wants something, the solution to a problem, for instance. When approaching someone who has something we want, we assume a humble, anticipatory state of mind. And when we lay out our problem, the mind is temporarily freed of it. And in that problem-free moment, the peace and bliss of the self floods into the heart. We assume that this feeling of peace and bliss comes from some unknown source, or the deity in front of us, but in reality the deity was only a key that unlocked the door to the self.

## Karma Yoga as Devotion

Often individuals with a dualistic orientation take to devotional practice as an alternative to real life. They hope that they will be blessed by God with some kind of experience that will give them true happiness. So they neglect their relationship with the world and lose themselves in devotional practice. If you find yourself caught up in the worship of a God that you cannot see, at the expense of doing what is to be done in the real world, you cannot progress spiritually. So to set the God in you free from its apparent limitations, you need to engage every situation that life presents in a devotional spirit.

## Devotional Dispositions

The science of self inquiry separates devotion into two categories: primary and secondary. Primary devotion is non-dual; the self and the devotee are known to be non-separate. Secondary devotion is dualistic, a communion between the devotee and the object of devotion. It is conditioned by the instrument of worship, the subtle body. The subtle body is the human "heart" or "soul." Because everything is conditioned by sattva, rajas and tamas, there are three types of secondary devotion.

When tamas, ignorance, predominates, a primitive style of devotion develops because a sleepy dark energy envelops the devotee's heart. God is not known directly because the mind is too dull. God is not an ever present living reality but it is a blind belief to be worshipped fearfully and slavishly. Tamasic devotees are prone to believe in magic, ghosts, evil spirits, poltergeists, demons and devils. This type of devotee loves ritual and favors literal interpretation of scripture. He or she believes in heaven and hell and is obsessed with sin.

Ignorance loves organization and swells the ranks of cults and religious institutions. Because thinking for oneself is considered a form of disobedience, the tamasic devotee is easily manipulated by corrupt priests and will thoughtlessly surrender to powerful spiritual personalities. To question or attack this kind of faith is to gain an enemy for life. Religious history is replete with examples of the many excesses, like the Inquisition, caused by this narrow state of mind. On the other hand, this type of faith tends to be rock solid and allows the devotee to withstand not only the small pinpricks of life but her major crises too. The conviction that an external God exists is steady, deep and heartfelt.

Rajas, the projecting power, keeps the mind and emotions perpetually disturbed and acts like an opaque moving screen, effectively concealing the self and blocking the flow of love from within. The rajasic devotee's sense of dissatisfaction works against developing a steady stream of love for the self. This type of devotion is narcissistic and the devotee is not above bargaining with God for power, position and wealth. The perennial theory of abundance appeals to this type of devotee. Rajasic devotion tends to be status and image conscious, views devotion as evidence of spiritual virtue, and is not above using it to impress others. Scratch the surface of this mentality and you will find a person more interested in presenting a devotional front to the world than a devotional heart to God. Unlike the steady dependability of the dark type, the active devotee will change religions, beliefs, teachers and practices at the drop of a hat.

Rajasic devotion, unlike the sleepy innocence of tamasic mother-father God worship, is passionate. For rajasic devotion to evolve into sattvic devotion, the devotee must be convinced that God, not the goods of this world, is the true goal of life. Once committed to union with God through love, this devotee becomes a spiritual dynamo and makes rapid progress.

Sattva, the third strand in the psychic rope and the highest of the three lower stages of devotion, is rooted in awareness, *sat*. It is the most secure foundation for a devotional life because the sattvic heart is a clean mirror, capable of accurately reflecting God's image; to see the self is to love the self. Sattvic devotees are blessed with curiosity, intelligence, discrimination and powerful epiphanies. But because the veil separating the devotee from the self is so thin, the devotee may become spiritually conceited and suffer attachment to purity, goodness, beauty and knowledge, golden chains difficult to break if devotion is to flower into primary devotion, the fourth and final stage.

Formulating devotion in terms of personality types can be misleading if we fail to understand that the ultimate purpose of devotion is the dissolution in love of our limited identity into our limitless identity. Love destroys the fear that sets up the apparent boundaries between each of us and our true nature. Rather than develop an identity based on the predominant quality, it is better to use knowledge of the three energies to assess and transform rajasic and tamasic tendencies into sattva, because all tendencies exist in everyone.

If you are begging God for something other than God, it means your vasanas are rajasic. It is fine to ask God for the things you are too incompetent or lazy to acquire on your own, but you need to know that God may refuse your request because it is not in your best interest. And even if it is in your interest, God has to work through the law of karma to deliver the results you want. Because the availability of objects that you might want is limited, or you would not be praying for them, and the desires of others vying for the same result—who are just as important in God's eyes—are virtually limitless, you will have to wait your turn. This will not be a happy situation because rajas is the mother of impatience.

Nobody asks God for air because air is not in short supply. If your heart is pure, you will have the good sense to ask God for something that is readily available. Because God is readily available as the self of the devotee and self realization is the fulfillment of all desires, a sattvic prayer would be: "Reveal yourself to me."

Secondary devotion leads to primary devotion. Sattva is the springboard for non-dual devotion. Primary devotion will not develop when the heart is tamasic. Rajas is the way out of tamas. Tamasic devotees believe in God, but are too lazy to actually seek God. If the tamasic devotee becomes devotionally proactive and takes up a rigorous practice, it will generate epiphanies and insights. Eventually, as the devotee experiences the self more and more, sattva develops and the desire for self knowledge arises. The desire for self knowledge is the highest form of devotion because self realization is the purpose of human life. The more the self is experienced, the firmer the self knowledge becomes. Knowledge of the self is indirect self knowledge, but inquiry will convert it to direct self knowledge, the hard and fast understanding that my nature and the nature of everything is non-dual love.

The notion that devotion and knowledge are separate paths leading to the same goal is based on the idea that individuals with an emotional nature should follow the devotional path exclusively, while intellectual types should pursue the path of knowledge. But every human is endowed with a heart and a mind, so for the sake of getting one's thoughts and feelings on the same page, all devotees should cultivate both love and understanding. As love of the self grows, the desire to know the self increases. And as knowledge of the self, based on scripture and direct experience, grows, love of the self grows.

Self realization is not possible without devotion because the self can only be realized when the head and the heart are single-pointedly absorbed in it. Because self absorption is hindered by binding vasanas, a seeker should employ all necessary weapons to purify extroversion. When binding vasanas are rendered non-binding, devotion comes naturally because attention flows back to its source. Emotion is just attention under the influence of likes and dislikes directed at objects. Emotion moves you toward certain experiences and away from others. So the purpose of devotional practice, working with emotions, is the transformation of emotion into devotion.

The transformation of emotion into devotion requires sustained and persistent commitment to the practice of non-attachment. Serious devotional progress is impossible unless the devotee converts attachment to objects into attachment to the self. True renunciation, non-attachment, means that the devotee is willing to abandon craving for the fruits of action, self limiting concepts, and attachment to the belief that objects are the source of love.

Contrary to popular opinion, renunciation confers power, understanding and love on the devotee. For example, people willingly sacrifice less attractive objects for more attractive ones. When someone addicted to sensuous pleasure discovers the subtler pleasures of the mind, physical objects lose their luster. And when a devotee finds the state of love that is the innermost self, the small personal loves that captivate the heart pale. As the practice of letting go grows, love grows.

When we strip away the shallow cravings for romance and excitement that are the hallmark of the unenlightened, we discover that our deepest need is the desire to love and be loved. Nothing is more attractive than love, realizing oneness with someone or something. When the real object of our desire is unknown, we chase object love, but when we wake up to the self, we understand that we only ever loved the self. We see that our small daily loves are merely faint reflections of the love that is our nature, the love that pervades every atom of the universe. Devotional practice directs our attention to the true object of our affections.

## Devotional Conversion Identities

Each of us has built-in psychological templates that can be put to good devotional use. Everyone feels bound to certain things in this life. Bondage to objects causes a feeling of helplessness. As long as the body lasts, we will be tied to it in one way or another. Who is not chained to physical passions, indentured to selfish feelings, and painfully shackled to unforgiving thoughts? The more we strive for freedom, rail against injustice, and court empowerment, the more we acknowledge our bondage to the apparently real.

To convert feelings of powerlessness into a positive devotional force, the devotee should surrender his or her life to God and become a faithful executor of God's will. In addition to loyalty and respect, this practice develops a quiet mind and keen discrimination, qualities necessary to distinguish God's voice from the many self serving ego voices playing in the mind. Practiced faithfully, this devotional mood reduces ego inflations and empowers the inner self.

If thinking of yourself as a servant of God is not your cup of tea and you can love someone with deep feeling and commitment, you might see God as your spouse. The bond between the husband and wife is the model for this devotional identity, because there are few sweeter, embracing as it does all expressions of love including sexual intimacy—which should be seen as a symbol of ecstatic union with God. If you can love in this way, direct a stream, preferably the whole stream, of your love to God.

If you have a sattvic temperament, you may wish to see God as a confidante, one with whom your innermost secrets can be shared. This devotional stance involves cultivating a diffident sacrificial attitude towards God, your dearest friend. It should be developed to the point where the devotee suffers moments of separation and continually craves God, either in the form of a deep experience or through communion with other devotees.

Perhaps the most natural devotional identity is the child, because people naturally identify with undeveloped parts of the psyche. It is based on the universal experience of parental love. Parents, our physical source, make nice symbols for God, our spiritual source. This devotional mood asks the devotee to love God with the unsuspecting trust of a child, acknowledging and accepting his or her state of total helplessness, ignorance, dependence and attachment.

Similar to the servant mentality, this identity is an imperfect vehicle for self realization because it does not encourage the pursuit of self knowledge, leaving the devotee vulnerable to exploitation and manipulation by primitive unconscious forces and unscrupulous religious figures. Ultimately, love begets knowledge because the intellect develops curiosity for what the heart loves, but this devotional stance is at best a preliminary step in the long march home.

Anyone who has felt the need to protect and nurture small helpless creatures will find the parent of God identity appealing. Children, because of their purity, innocence and guileless bliss, make excellent symbols of God. A devotee who cultivates a love of God as a child shines with maternal or paternal splendor. Because it encourages identification with a mature part of the psyche, this attitude heals negative views towards parents and authority figures and encourages the devotee to abandon his or her inner child and attain spiritual maturity.

Identifying oneself as the parent of God helps the devotee overcome ideas of power, fear and punishment often associated with God. It calls into question the concept of mindless obedience, an enemy of discrimination. It also roots out primitive religious concepts of devotional unworthiness associated with God's glory, majesty and grandeur. Unlike children, parents are not generally moved to awe in the presence of the child. Because they cannot beg from the child, this identity helps to negate the tendency to ask favors of God and to complain about one's lot, like Job.

A selfless lover, eager to gratify his or her beloved, is the intriguing model for the passionate lover. But passionate love of God is often considered the most advanced devotional stance. It is difficult to maintain because of the difficulty in generating deep and consistent epiphanies. It is also difficult to break owing to excessive attachment, brought on by the experience of extreme joy in the presence of God.

When love of God, the innermost self, is passionate, the devotee sees God as divinely beautiful and loves with an affection verging on the erotic. In this style of love, all conventions, reservations and personal views are cast aside and the devotee feels a gargantuan craving for the embrace of God—the realization of the self. Just as lovers often do not know which body is which, the devotee, in union with the self, experiences the sweetest bliss and sees no distinctions between himself or herself and God. When the devotee returns to samsaric consciousness, love in absence develops. When love in absence is mastered, the need for a love object disappears and the heart is free.

Based on the fact that true love comes only from within, the passionate lover is a sophisticated method for sublimating intense desire into a high devotional state of mind. It can be successfully practiced by virtuous celibate individuals or married souls in mature non-possessive relationships. Unlike love born of rajas, passionate love of God derives from the sattvic element and aims to gratify God, the object of one's affections, not the devotee.

The state of mind and the emotions produced by the direct immediate realization of the presence of God, the deity in the heart, may include loss of consciousness and suspension of animation as if one were asleep, erratic breathing, perspiration, shaking of the limbs and other symptoms of intense emotion. When the devotee is not connected, he or she may feel helpless, anxious and depressed, and view God as a fickle, inconsiderate and unfaithful lover prone to selfishness.

The forbidden lover operates on the assumption that the more love is obstructed, the more it intensifies and converts feelings of secrecy and shame associated with love into a positive devotional force. Love of God often awakens in the most unlikely and inconvenient circumstances. When a declaration of love for God would invite ridicule, condemnation and persecution, taking God as a forbidden lover is sensible. Devoid of outer signs, the forbidden lover is a stealth psychology through which devotion grows by inner yearning, silent repetition of the holy name, and meditation. This mood is tailor made for devotees who need to protect their spirituality from unspiritual spouses and cynical friends.

Because ultimately it spells the end of the ego, devotional practice sometimes generates strong resistance. In general, however, the more devotional one's relationship to God and the world, the less negativity is experienced. Occasionally, however, negative tendencies are persistent and refuse to yield to devotion. Taking a negative attitude toward negativity, thinking of oneself as a sinner, for example, is not wise because negativity is reinforced, discrimination is destroyed, and spiritual practice derailed. Taking a negative attitude toward the world is a karmic disaster. If the purpose of devotional practice is to produce an unbroken flow of thought and feeling toward God, allowing periods of negativity to break the flow is devotionally unwise. Therefore, though our offerings are ugly and inappropriate, we should place them squarely on the altar.

Rather than abandon my practice when I am angry, I need to castigate God for denying me the courage to overcome my weaknesses. Rather than turn my back, why not blame the Lord for turning His or Her back on me? With a little imagination and a bit of help from a dysfunctional conditioning, a devotee can dump any kind of negativity at the feet of the Beloved, a practice that protects his or her self and the world. When it is given to God, it does not recycle, but dissolves like clouds in God's vast inner heaven, filling the heart with love.

A touching example of a negative relationship with God is provided by a commentary on a verse in the Narada Bhakti Sutra by H. Poddar. "When a child begins to toddle, it often stumbles and falls. Hearing the cry, the mother runs to help but the child becomes angry with the mother for assuming that it might need help, even though she was not at fault, and chides her to make her feel guilty. 'Why did you leave me alone? See what happens when you leave me,' it says. Then it decides to punish her. 'I'll never talk to you,' it wails. 'I'll never sit on your lap again!' To appease its anger the mother tries to take it in her arms, but it evades her and runs away weeping. It does so because it recognizes its power over her and hers over it. She is everything to the child and the child is totally dependent on her. There is no discrimination. The child can express anything without fear, including all its negativity. The dependent devotee makes God the object of passion, anger and pride."

## Primary Devotion

Love of God is the last stage in the evolution of the soul. It is not liberation, however, because the devotee still takes God to be an object, someone or something other than his or herself. Unconditional love of God has been achieved, but non-dual understanding has not happened.

Since time immemorial, an intense debate has been going on in the spiritual world about the issue of the identity of God and man. On one hand, the dualists say that man is not God and can never become God. They say that the best we can do is to learn to love God unconditionally and turn our lives over to God completely, accepting everything that happens as the will of God. "Why would you want to become God," they say? "If you become God, you do not enjoy the experience of God. It is much better to experience God than to become God."

"If you knew the nature of God you would not say such things," the non-dualists reply. "Becoming God is not a problem because God includes the world of experience. So when you become God you do not lose your experience of God, you gain a greater identity. You do lose something, but it is something that you will be happy to lose—the belief that you are separate. When you see yourself as separate, you are dependent on God for everything. This does not free you from your desires and fears. You have to rely on God to fulfill them and you must suffer while you wait. The very fact that you pray to God means that you are tormented by your desires, beliefs and opinions.

When you become God, you lose your sense of separateness, incompleteness and inadequacy. Your mind is perfectly calm and happy. You do not need to accept anything, because whatever you have or do not have at each and every moment, is seen as God. You need not strive to make yourself better, because you are fine as you are."

To which the dualists reply, "Why is complete dependence on God a problem? We are like babies and have to do nothing because our Mother-Father God takes care of our every need. We remain blissful all the time and our minds remain perfectly calm because we accept everything that happens as the grace of God. You say you are one with God, but you did not create the universe."

The non-dualists reply, "What universe? We see only eternal, unborn, non-dual awareness everywhere. There is no creation. It is a belief you have unwittingly accepted because you take yourself to be the body. Besides, we do not say that we are one with God. We say that there is no duality, so the notion that you and God are not the same is just a fantasy. It is all God."

Is there actually a difference between these two points of view? If faith in God never wavers, then the effect of dualistic devotion on the individual is the same as the effect of the non-dual realization "I am God." Dualism and non-dualism are simply two different languages that express the same vision.

But the dual and non-dual views are not identical. The idea of separation is a problem, no matter what religious or philosophical arguments we use to support it. It is a problem because it is not fundamentally in harmony with the nature of reality. Without non-dual understanding, it is impossible to maintain faith continuously, not that faith is an issue when you know who you are.

It so happens that even people whose love of God is perfect and who surrender to life as it is, still have one doubt: who or what is God? Most resign themselves to it and rest in the belief that the creature cannot know the Creator. But it is not the limited mind that knows God. It is God that knows God. And with or without understanding, love of God is a great and satisfying love, so on that account too it is possible not to pursue the path of love to the end.

How can this doubt be resolved? When someone experiences God, they are actually experiencing the self as an object. The experience is a great pleasure and attachment quickly develops. The more you love, the more you desire to understand what you love. So devotion to God leads to inquiry and inquiry, if it is diligently pursued, leads to the understanding that God is everything that exists. Because I exist, I cannot be anything but God, i.e., consciousness. Is it not strange that one of the world's most dualistic religions worships a man who proclaimed the non-dual nature of reality, "I and my Father are one?"

At some point during your experience of God, you realize that your nature and God's nature are non-different. It is not that you actually become awareness, because you are already awareness. There is no other option. The becoming is simply a recognition of your nature. You understand that God is a projection born out of the belief that the world must have a cause. But the world is not an effect of consciousness. It is consciousness, just as a ring is not an effect of gold or a wave is not different from the ocean. You understand that you are not great, because you are apparently associated with everything that is. Nor are you insignificant, because you are apparently associated with the tiniest unicellular organism. You realize, "I am that in which everything lives and moves and has its being." Without me nothing exists, nor is anything separate from me.

This understanding/experience is known as supreme devotion, unconditional love. It is the recognition that the essence of every transaction in the world is love and that the subject and the object, appearances to the contrary notwithstanding, are non-separate. It is the understanding that allows Christ at the height of his torment to say, "Father, forgive them. They know not what they do."

# CHAPTER TEN

# The Assimilation of Experience

## The Ropes

Experience requires two factors: a conscious subject and an object. Consciousness, of which our personal everyday consciousness is a pale reflection, is radiant light. It is not physical light. Light, however, is a fitting symbol for consciousness because it illumines physical objects just as consciousness illumines physical light and subtle objects, the inner world of thoughts and feelings.

Consciousness is self luminous. It does not require another principle to illumine it. If a light is shining in a room, it is not necessary to turn on a second light to see it because it is illumined by its own light. Consciousness is like a limitless light bulb that was never created, that shines endlessly without being connected to a source of electricity. It was shining before the universe came into being and it will continue to shine effortlessly once the universe has packed up and gone away. No object can reveal this light because it is subtler than all objects. It is easily known, however, because it is self revealing.

The creation is an object from the standpoint of consciousness. Experience takes place in the creation and consciousness is free of experience. There are a number of theories about how the creation came into being but there is no reasonable way to determine if they are true. It is apparently here. It is known. And it is the field in which we pursue happiness.

Animals and plants do not seek happiness, because they do not have intellects. Without an intellect, it is impossible to evaluate one experience with reference to another or with reference to other standards. If pleasure happens, it is accepted. If pain happens it is accepted. Because they do not enjoy free will, the idea that pain can be eliminated does not occur to them. Humans experience pleasure and pain too, but they can do something about it because they are self aware; they can think. That pleasure is the natural state is indicated by this fact: when pain comes we immediately seek ways to eliminate it, but when pleasure comes, we cling to it tooth and nail.

If experience was under our conscious control, everyone would be happy all the time. However, we are not completely helpless with reference to what happens, because we have been blessed with the ability to think. We can make inferences, choose between alternatives, and interpret experience with reference to various values. If we want to be happy, it is possible to understand all the subtle and gross factors operating in the field of existence, apart from our own actions, that impact on our experience.

Although it is non-dual, the vast field of existence can be divided into three levels for the purpose of understanding: causal, subtle and gross. Human beings experience on the subtle and gross levels of existence. The causal level causes experience, cannot be experienced, and is known by inference.

Our thoughts and feelings, memories, dreams, beliefs, opinions, fears and desires, etc. take place in the subtle body. The senses provide access to the gross level, the objects outside. Experience is not only a transaction between a given subtle body and the physical world; it is a transaction between subtle bodies as well. Consciousness shines incessantly on the subtle body and illumines what is happening in it, making knowledge of ourselves possible.

There is probably not a human alive that does not want the continuous, radiant, charismatic experience of unalloyed happiness. Assuming it is possible, what factors are in play that help or hinder this experience?

The Subtle Body is sandwiched between the self and the world. It is the instrument through which the self, consciousness or awareness, observes itself as the world. It functions as intellect—the discriminating function; as mind—the feeling function and as the location of ego or "I" sense. These functions are conditioned by a fourth factor, the *chitta*,[33] the causal body. Much more than a memory, the chitta is the most powerful function of consciousness. It retains both the essence of experience and the individual's interpretations of it, in the form of samskaras. It controls the lives of every being in existence. It causes desire and karma.

As mentioned in chapter 2, the chitta as unfolded in Vedic science is composed of three energies. These energies affect all the beings, objects, forces and processes on the gross and subtle levels. They are called ropes because they bind conscious beings to gross and subtle objects. They are called *sattva, rajas* and *tamas*, and need to be understood if you want to consistently experience radiant, charismatic, unalloyed happiness.

Because our culture suffers from a lack of understanding of the self and the causal body we need special terms, even though these energies are known to everyone. They do not describe esoteric mystical states, although they impact on them and the interpretation of them. As we unfold the meaning of these words you will see that they accurately describe the quality and texture of everyday experience. Although some of our words accurately describe aspects of these energies, no English words convey their complete meaning.

Only when they are identified, can we cease to identify with them. Identification with rajas and tamas stands in the way of happiness, whether or not we are committed to seeking enlightenment. A human being may have a preponderance of a particular energy at a particular time, but energy does not define the self, because the self is free of energy. Once the three energies are identified and controlled, there is virtually no limit to the experience of radiant happiness.

The root of the word *sattva* is *sat*. Sat is radiant self aware consciousness. In its most subtle manifest form, consciousness is called sattva. Sattva is consciousness, but consciousness is not sattva. Sattva makes knowledge possible.

---

33. Literally, "mind stuff."

Nothing in the creation happens without knowledge. If the subtle body, the apparently conscious being—me—was one hundred percent sattvic, I would experience radiant, unalloyed happiness all the time. I would be charismatic and attract many people. Life would flow with unspeakable ease. When I feel present, wise, happy and free of desire, my subtle body is under the influence of sattva. When a creative idea makes perfect sense, a thought is completely appropriate for a given situation, and attention is fully present to deal with what comes, sattva rules the subtle body. Unfortunately, everything in the chitta is impermanent. Therefore, sattva must give way to tamas and rajas.

Rajas, the projecting power, often called the mode of passion, is the second of the chitta's three fundamental qualities. On the macrocosmic level, it makes things happen. To create, action is necessary. You need knowledge, you need a substance, and you need the power to shape the substance according to your idea. If the physical universe is the result of a Big Bang, as inference seems to suggest, some power is causing the matter to travel away from its point of origin at astronomical speeds. On the individual level, rajas is a spiking, agitating, extroverting energy. It makes you move physically, emotionally and intellectually. It is desire and the emotional agitations that desire morphs into, when it is unfulfilled: anger, anxiety, frustration, hatred and aggression. It is responsible for the feeling that there is never enough of what one wants and too much of what one does not want. It is responsible for obsessions about what might happen. It causes the mind to hop uncontrollably from one thought to another and limits the attention span to a few minutes, sometimes a few seconds. Attention deficit disorder is a mind completely dominated by rajas.

When it emerges from the chitta and appears in the subtle body, as it inevitably does, it takes over from sattva and happiness disappears. When the mind is under its influence, inquiry is very difficult. A detailed description of the effects of rajas on the subtle body can be found in the following section, entitled "Enlightenment and the Assimilation of Experience." The point is, however, that rajas—desire—is the enemy of happiness. In fact, the statement "I want" means "I am not happy." The best one can hope for in this state is intense, fleeting moments of joy. The obvious conclusion: if you want to be happy, you can wait for the next period of sattva or you can transform rajas into sattva.

The upside of rajas: it is a great motivator. If one's goals are clear and the environment is conducive, success comes quickly for those in whom this type of energy is predominant.

To say that desire is the enemy of happiness does not mean that happiness is only possible when desire is completely eliminated. To transform the mind into a pure vehicle for self inquiry, the desire for object happiness should be sublimated into the desire for self realization. Whatever desire remains, need only conform to dharma. When a rajasic person's self esteem is particularly low, it may produce strong desires that result in violations of dharma and cause conflict. Desire need only be reduced until the actions it engenders will not conflict with dharma.

The third strand of the chitta is tamas. On the macrocosmic level it is substance, matter. It is inert and insentient. It has no power to act or think. On the individual level it is the body and a very uncomfortable state of mind. Tamas means cloudy. When it emerges from the causal body and replaces rajas or sattva, it conceals the subtle body under a heavy, dark cloud. It is dullness, torpor and sloth, the morning after a night of revelry or a twelve-hour shift, for example. It keeps you from seeing what is, as it is. It twists what you do see into what you want to see. A detailed description of the effect of tamas on the subtle body can also be found in the following section.

The experience of radiant, unalloyed happiness is not possible when the mind is tamasic. The best an individual can hope for in this state is dull sense pleasures. The obvious conclusion: if you want to be happy you can wait for sattva to take over the mind and provide a few moments of happiness or you can transform tamas into sattva. The means for creating a predominately sattvic mind and therefore radiantly happy life are explained at the end of the following section.

## Enlightenment and the Assimilation of Experience

Experience is an unbroken series of inner and outer events and the reaction or response to them. The reaction of animals to experience is totally programmed. Humans have the upper hand in the evolutionary game because they have the power to think. They can study their experience and extract knowledge from it, freeing them to some degree from their programming.

Spiritual growth is accomplished through the proper assimilation of experience. Just as partially digested food inhibits the efficient functioning of the body, partially or improperly assimilated experience compromises the development of the soul. Because consciousness illumines the body-mind entity, it is propelled along its life track to its ultimate destination: the realization of its non-separation from everything. As long as the meaning of life's experiences is unknown to it, the soul is little more than an animal and cannot fulfill its destiny.

Like an animal, a human infant unknowingly lives out its subconscious tendencies. It grows physically, but it does not evolve. It has no control over the direction of its life because it has insufficient experience and knowledge to make informed choices. Once its intellect develops and it assimilates certain values, it can evaluate its experiences and begin to evolve.

The longer an experience remains unassimilated, the more problems it causes. Let us say that you are a woman whose father was an alcoholic and abused your mother, so that she fell into a lifelong depression and was unable to raise you and your siblings properly. Because you were the eldest, you ended up parenting your younger brothers and sisters. You did it because you had no choice. You developed a deep resentment toward your father for robbing your childhood and a deep sympathy for your poor victimized mother. In reality, she was not blameless, because she never stood up to her husband; she actually enabled his alcoholism in subtle ways. Nonetheless, you saw her as a martyr and loved her for it. Your father died, but your hatred lived on. You believed a grave injustice had been done and it colored your feelings toward men in general.

One day, a nice man wanted to marry you and in the excitement of first love, you agreed. You married, but as time went on certain things your husband said or did reminded you of your father. This brought up old feelings of resentment and rage. You began to pick quarrels with him for no reason. Your fears slowly got the best of you and you incorrectly imagined that these small things he shared with your father—a certain inflection in his voice when he was stressed, for example—revealed a selfish and abusive nature. You accused him of "changing" and said he did not really love you, which was not true. Your relationship deteriorated and your children started to become neurotic. You confided in one of your divorced women friends who came from a similar background and was holding a grudge against her ex. She showed so much concern for your plight that you fell in love with her, left your husband, abandoned your children and became gay. But after a while your new identity did not work, because you loved her for the wrong reason: she was not a man. Had your mother been the abuser, you may have hated women and loved men. We can make this story go on and on for fifty years or more, each tragic event unfolding out of the preceding event like clockwork, until it becomes impossible to work back to the beginning and discover the reason for the suffering and heal the wound.

Experience does not interpret or assimilate itself. The intellect interprets experience. It sits behind the mind and evaluates what happens. There is nothing wrong with it. This is what it is supposed to do. If experience conforms to the soul's desire, the intellect gives the thumbs up and positive feeling arise. If life delivers experience contrary to the soul's desire, the intellect gives the thumbs down and negative feelings arise. How it interprets experience depends on acquired knowledge and ignorance plus three factors that are normally beyond its control. Two of these factors inhibit its ability to discriminate and one facilitates it. The factors over which the intellect has limited control are rajas, tamas and sattva.

How do rajas affect the assimilation of experience? If the individual's values are materialistic and the mind is predominately rajasic, the intellect uses its power to design and execute strategies to accomplish worldly goals. If the values are spiritual, it evaluates progress with reference to its idea of purity or enlightenment. A rajasic intellect is not concerned with the truth of experience, only in whether or not what is experienced relates to the fulfillment of the soul's desires.

Whether the goals are worldly or spiritual, and whether or not they are realized, rajas is a source of frustration because everything gained is inevitably lost. An object gained causes attachment and an object lost produces grief,

neither of which is conducive to happiness. Rather than accept the impermanence of life as a fact and be satisfied with what is, rajas causes the soul to
continually seek fulfillment in new experiences. Even though the individual
knows better, rajas can cause such a lack of discrimination that the individual
will consistently repeat actions that produce suffering. Rajas often generates
so many actions in such a short time that the intellect can never determine
which action was responsible for a given result, thus preventing it from learning from its experiences.

When a pleasurable experience ends, rajas brings disappointment because
it wants the pleasure to continue, even though the intellect knows that pleasure is fleeting. If an experience is mediocre, it wants it to be better. If it is bad,
it should end instantly and not happen again. If experience repeats itself over
and over, as it does owing to conditioning, rajas causes boredom and produces
a strong desire for variety. More-better-different is its holy mantra. It produces
an endlessly active, time-constrained life of loose ends, a life of shoulds and
should nots.

A person under the influence of rajas feels that nothing is ever completed.
No matter how much is accomplished, the list of things to do never shrinks. It
is a closet, garage, basement and attic overflowing with a confusing assortment
of neglected and unused objects. It is a late tax return, a forgotten appointment, an unreturned call, a frantic search for one's keys. Rajas's aggressive,
extroverted thrusts are inevitably accompanied by tiredness and insomnia.
Because it cannot sit still, it is often referred to as the monkey mind in spiritual literature.

Assimilation of experience takes place only when the mind is present.
Therefore, when rajas dominates the subtle body, the innate wisdom of the
self, much less common sense knowledge, is not available to help the intellect
accurately determine the nature of experience and resolve doubts about it. A
resolved experience leaves attention fully present, so that it is able to engage
the next experience without prejudice. Because life is an unending procession
of experiences, it is important to lay each experience to rest as quickly as possible, preferably as it happens. A successful inquirer processes experience as it
happens.

Unresolved experience, however, subliminally drains attention. Difficulty focusing on what needs to be done and avoidance of what should or should not be done are signs that the mind is excessively rajasic. Two holy men were walking along the Ganges when they heard cries for help from a bather who had been swept away by the current. One of them dove in, rescued the naked woman, and carried her to the shore in his arms. They continued on for several hours and eventually stopped to rest. The one who had observed his friend rescue the woman was agitated and said, "What kind of a holy man are you? You violated your vows never to touch a woman. You carried her naked out of the water and left her on the river bank!" The other sadhu said, "What you say is true, but I left her there. You seem to have carried her for the last three hours."

As unresolved experience accumulates, the individual suffers uncomfortable existential constipation. He or she feels overwhelmed, stressed and unable to keep up with life's demands. Growth rarely comes through the easy attainment of desires, but an extroverted person is also denied the growth-enhancing benefits of assimilated unwanted experiences.

Tamas, the veiling power, inhibits the assimilation of experience as efficiently as rajas, but for different reasons. Under its influence, the subtle body, though seemingly quiet, is actually dull. Efficient evaluation of experience requires mental clarity, but when a torpid veil covers the subtle body, perception is distorted and assimilation is compromised. When the intellect is dull, it has difficulty connecting the results of its actions with the thoughts motivating them, causing uncertainty with respect to what has to be done and what should not be done. When the subtle body is predominately dull, you are negotiating the ocean of samsara in a rudderless ship. "Where should I go? What should I do? What's going on? I don't know. I do not want to know" are some signature thoughts.

A tamasic mind is a lazy mind; it prefers to run off conditioned patterns. Unlike rajas, it hates the new. Because creative thinking takes so much energy, the tamasic mind does not value inquiry. Therefore, it cannot gain control of events and is forced to continually revisit negative situations. Consequently, tamas is responsible for the feelings of helplessness that cause deep and lasting depressions. Tamas solves problems by denying them. When unwanted karma happens, it teams up with rajas to lay the blame elsewhere.

When it is balanced by appropriate amounts of sattva and rajas, tamas helps the psyche function smoothly. It clings to what is good and provides the patience necessary to ground ideas in reality. Finally, it is responsible for sleep. Insufficient tamas results in sleep deprivation, a major source of suffering, because the body and mind need rest.

The undigested experiential backlog caused by a tamasic mind causes the ego to dither and procrastinate. If you have a rajasic lifestyle and find yourself feeling constantly exhausted, know that rajas is causing tamas. When tamas is particularly heavy, even small daily duties, like brushing teeth, combing hair, or taking out the garbage seem like gargantuan undertakings. Neglect is tamasic and is responsible in large part for the rampant emotional dysfunction seen in materialistic societies. Parents become so caught up in their own lives that children are neglected. Unloved children quickly develop low self esteem and are unable to properly fulfill their roles in society.

Rajas projects and tamas obscures, but sattva reveals things as they are. When sattva is present, the intellect is clear and experience is seen for what it is. Unlike rajas and tamas, sattva is an indirect means of enlightenment, because it reveals the self.

In the diagram on the next page, the self, awareness, shines on each of the three energies in the causal body. Its light, reflected on the subtle body, produces three distinct conditions. If I desire to experience the self, and the subtle body is the instrument of experience, it stands to reason that I would want to have a sattvic causal body. In fact the chitta, the substance of the causal body, is consciousness and reflects consciousness accurately. But if it is burdened with tamasic and rajasic tendencies the reflection will be distorted and inquiry will not bear fruit. If the causal body is dominated by rajasic tendencies, the self appears as dynamic energy, not radiant light. If the causal body is tamasic, I will have no idea of the self whatsoever. The conclusion is obvious: if I want to experience the self as it is, I should cultivate a sattvic mind. Experience of the self is not enlightenment, but it can lead to enlightenment if the intellect can assimilate the knowledge—"I am awareness"—that arises when the attention is turned within and the mind is sattvic.

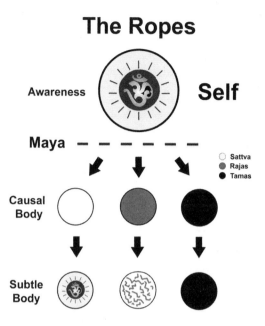

Irrespective of its value for enlightenment, a predominately sattvic mind is a happy creative mind. Unenlightened but happy worldly people owe their happiness to sattva, which they evolved unconsciously because they impeccably follow dharma.

Because reality is non-dual consciousness, the mind is consciousness. To gain a predominately sattvic mind, one capable of discrimination and the easy assimilation of experience, the proportions of rajas and tamas relative to sattva need to be manipulated. Enough rajas needs to be retained for motivational purposes and enough tamas kept to ground one's ideas in reality. But the lion's share of the mind should be sattvic. A predominately sattvic mind will gain success in any field, worldly or spiritual, because it can discriminate properly. Faulty discrimination causes unskillful and inappropriate actions.

When rajas dominates the mind, desire interprets experience. When tamas dominates, fear interprets experience. Both obscure the truth. When sattva dominates, truth interprets experience.

Finally, these three energies are called *gunas*, or ropes, because they bind the soul, the indweller in the body, to habitual thoughts, feelings and actions. Each binds in a different way. Rajas binds by longing and attachment. Craving for things and attachment to things pressures you to become a doer and ties you up with karma. Furthermore, desire makes rule breaking tempting. If you push against the rules, the rules push back. Continual reaction to events is bondage.

Tamas binds by ignorance and its effects. When you are dull you cannot think clearly, so you are uncertain about what needs to be done and you tend to opt not to do what you should do or to do what you should not do. In the best of all possible worlds you would not be penalized for not doing something, however life is not the best of all possible worlds. If you do not respond to life appropriately, you are blessed with suffering. Try not paying taxes or the mortgage and see what happens. Furthermore, when you are lazy you are prone to cutting corners, which does not make you a friend of dharma.

Although sattva is a necessary stepping stone to self realization, it binds through attachment to pleasure and happiness. When the mind is sattvic, you feel good. When you feel good, there is a strong tendency to identify with the feeling. Actually, there is only one "I" and it does not feel good or bad, but when it is apparently ignorant of its nature, it thinks it is an enjoyer. The pleasure that one feels is always associated with an object and objects are experienced in the mind, so when rajas or tamas takes over, the pleasure disappears. By identifying with happiness, you are asking for unhappiness.

Sattva also binds by attachment to knowledge. Because sattva is responsible for knowledge and because knowledge is necessary for survival, it is easy to become attached to what you know or do not know. It so happens that the "I"—consciousness—is not a knower. It illumines the knower, knowledge and the objects of knowledge. It illumines the absence of knowledge. Therefore, attachment to sattva, not sattva itself, stands in the way of self knowledge.

We believe that we consciously interpret our experiences, but actually rajasic, tamasic and sattvic values do the interpreting. For a worldly person, someone who takes the dream of experience to be real and pursues happiness in it, a sattvic mind is a guarantor of success, such as it is. This is so because only true knowledge bears the desired fruit, assuming a conducive field of action.

A sattvic mind is an inquiring, open mind. Every mind is controlled by a secular or sacred belief system. Imprinting starts in childhood when the intellect begins to function. By the time the individual realizes that he or she could have just as well been conditioned to a different view of reality, it is almost too late to change, the power of the vasanas being what they are. When rajas or tamas dominate the mind, epiphanies and scripture are interpreted according to conditioned beliefs, opinions, prejudices, fears, desires and fantasies. Misunderstood and misapplied knowledge causes suffering. Only when the mind is clear can it grasp the import of the teachings.

No one is experience-free. Life is experience and experience is fickle. One moment it is conducive to happiness and the next it is not. Freedom, the conscious or unconscious goal of everyone, is freedom from attachment to uninformed interpretation of experience, not experience itself—although the quality of experience can be altered by manipulating the gunas/vasanas with knowledge. When self knowledge dawns in a sattvic mind, it is a perfect means to evaluate and process experience. Unexamined experience no longer accumulates, because it is processed on the spot, allowing the mind to remain unmodified and bask in the light shining on it from within. Self knowledge removes doubt about the nature of the world because it reveals things as they are. When things are known as they are, the desire to have them be different subsides, freeing the mind from its need to have experience conform to its likes and dislikes, and eliminating emotional suffering. Self knowledge is the knowledge that you are what you seek. It ultimately destroys desire because it is clear that the bliss you seek in objects, you already have as the self. It also eliminates fear, because the vision of non-duality means that there is no other.

If we go back to the example of the woman with the alcoholic father, we see how failure to resolve her childhood experience resulted in a lifetime of suffering. Of course, it is not possible for a child to see what is actually happening as it unfolds, and to have the wisdom to lay it to rest. Even as an adult— she is not actually an adult because she has not grown out of her childhood pattern—she is incapable of understanding the reasons for her suffering. Her hatred has kept her narrowly focused on her ego, and she has not been able to develop a realistic view of the complex impersonal factors involved in her situation. What would be a realistic view and how would it lead to resolution and forgiveness?

People would not be who they are if they could help it; we would all be the gods and goddesses we want to be. We are victims of our ignorance of the truth. When you do not understand that you are one with everyone and everything, a profound fear suffuses your being. No one is immune to this existential fear, except the enlightened. It hides the self, stealing your intelligence and compassion. Fear is reactive, not responsive. If you are walking along a street at night and suddenly there is a power outage, your first emotion is fear. You are in the dark and confused. You do not know what to do. This causes you to imagine dangers that are not present. Your heart races and you want to be free of the dark. To respond with compassion you need to be free of fear.

Nobody is born wise. Everyone who comes to earth is in the dark about who they are. Consequently, fear and desire run their lives. When you are motivated by negative impulses, dysfunctional behavior is the norm. If we look dispassionately at the lives of the woman's parents, we inevitably discover that their parents and their parent's parents were also governed by fear and desire. The chain of dysfunction goes right back to the day the Big Bang blew out the lights and plunged humankind into darkness.

Christian doctrine calls this blackout original sin. In Vedic culture it is called maya, the non-apprehension of reality and the subsequent misapprehensions that arise from it. It is original in the sense that it precedes the existence of all beings. When you are fearful you want to protect yourself, so you lash out at real and imagined threats. You abuse yourself and others, like the father in the previous story. Or you hide and neglect yourself and your duties like the mother. Had the woman been informed that her psychology was a replica of her parent's psychology, she would deny it. In her mind she sees herself a blameless victim, which, in a sense, she is. She may be a victim—who is not?—but it does no good to see yourself as one. To take this stance is to deny your true nature. When projection and denial operate, delusion is not far behind.

It is not a secret that psychological dysfunction is carefully handed down from generation to generation. Conditioning means that you do not have any choice. It happens when you are not aware. If this is true, how reasonable is it to blame your parents, your teachers, religion, society or the government for your problems? Everyone is in the same boat; we all suffer the seemingly incurable disease of ignorance. How logical is it to take what happens personally? This does not make abuse or other bad actions right, but right and wrong have nothing to do with it. Right action, thought and speech are not possible when fear and desire control your life.

How we think about a problem may be only part of the problem, or it may be the whole problem. To successfully resolve conditioned patterns, it is very helpful to depersonalize them. It is virtually impossible for materialists to develop an impersonal view of suffering, because materialists are dualists. They see the ego as the only self and take it to be incomplete and inadequate. They believe that everyone is unique and is therefore special. For them, everything that happens is personal. "Us and them" is a dualist mentality. Dualists need enemies to define themselves. They think it is a dog eat dog world and the sooner we realize it, the better. Tolerance, compassion, dispassion, accommodation and forgiveness are seen by them to be weak, unrealistic and foolish values.

This orientation is unhelpful for solving problems. Projected into society, it begets culture wars; into politics, gridlock; into religion, the Crusades and the Inquisition; into international relations, war. Because her orientation was dualistic, the woman in our example reacted with anger, resentment and hatred. She cast herself as a victim and her father as a victimizer, a typical dualistic concept. As long as she accepts a personal world view, her suffering will persist.

There is perhaps no more eloquent example of non-dual vision than Christ's statement under torture on the cross, "Forgive them; they know not what they do." There are no evil people, only ignorant people. Ignorance causes unhealthy behavior. Another of Christ's pronouncements speaks to this issue,

"Hate the sin, not the sinner." The sinner is just the self under the spell of self ignorance. He or she is worthy of love.

The vision of non-duality is built into the sattvic mind because it is non-separate from the self. The self is not unique. It is the same in everyone. It binds everything into one whole. Any problematic experience can be quickly laid to rest when this vision is applied. Therefore, cultivate sattva in the form of inquiry into the nature of reality.

## How Can I Get a Pure Mind?

Radiant, charismatic, unalloyed happiness is consciousness reflecting in the clear lake of a pure mind. The auras depicted around the heads of saints symbolize this kind of mind. Although the light of consciousness falls on a dull mind as well, it produces virtually no happiness because it is absorbed by dense tamasic clouds, which prevent it from reaching the soul. The passionate mind is illumined too, but it derives little benefit. Its incessant cascade of tightly packed thoughts creates an opaque moving screen that prevents the light from illumining the soul. Cut off from its radiant source, it slowly suffers death by animation. Unfortunately, there is no easy fix when the mind is dominated by these two unhelpful energies. But it is possible to create a predominately sattvic mind, one that delivers the more or less constant experience of radiant happiness, one that can efficiently process experience.

First, pay close attention to the mind and recognize the energy in play at the moment. Rajas and tamas, by their very nature, are inimical to self study. Rajas diverts attention into the world, when it should be focused within. Tamas conceals the intellect behind a dark cloud, making observation difficult. To further complicate matters, the ego resists every effort at self study because it is attached to the way it sees things. It thinks that its life is like the famous Chinese ball puzzle: remove one piece and the whole thing falls apart. Often it is helpful for the ego to hit bottom, but it will do anything to avoid this possibility.

Life is not a Chinese ball puzzle. What you have and what you do does not make you who you are. Granted, certain minimal possessions and activities are necessary to sustain life, but a significant fraction of our things and doings are completely gratuitous. Less is more on the path of self inquiry. A simple lifestyle is necessary if inquiry is going to work. Nobody is holding a gun to my head and insisting that I stay up till two am watching my fifty-four inch hi-definition TV. No one forces me to buy a big house with a three-car garage on credit, eat in fancy restaurants, and send my kids to Ivy League schools. No law compels me to vacation in Europe or to smoke cigarettes.

It is not easy to accept the fact that I am living a life that is not what my heart wants, that I have cleverly convinced myself that bondage is superior to freedom. It is painful to listen to my mind intone a steady rajasic chant of "have tos," "supposed tos," "shoulds" and "musts." It is dispiriting to listen to its continuous tamasic dirge: "I can't, I won't, I don't want" and "I'm not good enough."

Inquiry begins when we look into the excuses we make to avoid simplifying our lives. There is never a good reason not to do what is right for your happiness. Ask what your life would look like if you do the right thing. Tamas will try to scare you, "Could be dangerous. The planets are not favorable. No new projects till Mars transits Aries in 2010!" Or rajas will say, "I've got to finish this project right now, but I'll get to the spiritual stuff in the spring." Or it will convince you that your present problem is much bigger than it is and suggest you ask God for help. You pray in earnest, but your prayers go unanswered because you do not realize that God is that part of you that revealed the problem in the first place and encouraged you to get to work. If God is not your cup of tea, you might visit a therapist. It is not clear what a therapist is going to say that you do not already know. Perhaps he or she will sidetrack you, give the ego clever justifications for its resistance: your mother did this, your father did that. Poor me! Maybe you are inclined to visit a psychic or have a Tarot reading, in which case you will learn that you are being tested. But wait! The Ace of Cups says you will come out of it a stronger, better person. Spiritual as it seems, magical thinking is delusional. You are not special and the universe is not eagerly sitting around waiting to deliver a much needed miracle. If you are looking for outside help or a sign from the cosmos, know that your mind is firmly in the grip of delusion. Resistance to change is tamasic. There are few things worse than the feeling of helplessness and low self esteem that comes from not doing what you know is right for your liberation.

Assuming that you have overcome your resistance and are actually ready to begin transforming your mind, how should you proceed? On the surface it seems as if you have no control over the three energies. One minute you feel good, but some little thing does not go your way and suddenly you feel angry. "Gotcha!" says rajas. Or you are having a very bland day, definitely nothing to write home about, and suddenly you feel very happy for no apparent reason. Sattva snuck up on you when you were not looking. Perhaps you were feeling fine when someone said that your candidate for president was three points behind in the polls. Instantly you become depressed—tamas hard at work. You cannot predict your next thought. You set out to get something in the kitchen, but by the time you reach the kitchen door you have forgotten what you wanted, because a more important thought has entered your mind. Our subjective life is controlled by the causal body, the unconscious, which dictates our moods. Our moods motivate our behavior.

It does not have to be like this. Rajas and tamas are unconscious energies, viruses that thrive in the dark. They survive because they fly beneath the radar of attention and replicate themselves secretly as we act. To expose them, we need to connect our actions and their results. This seems obvious, but it is not as easy as you might imagine. For example, you go out for a night on the town. You have a big meal with your significant other and hit the dance floor. The music tickles your fancy. You and your partner are very much in tune, so you dance till the wee hours, knocking back stiff drinks between the numbers. Rajas feels fantastic; you are excited. Whee! Great party. You are effusive, romantic and silly. The milk of human kindness flows generously in your veins. You overtip and hug the waiter, as if he were a long lost relative. When the taxi drops you off at home, you strip off your clothes as you make a beeline for the bedroom. Your wife's aunt in the guest room downstairs cannot sleep because of the all the commotion going on overhead. It is going to be a bit tense in the morning at the breakfast table. Finally, you run out of steam. The last thought before you drift off is, "Wow! This is great!! If this is life, give me more."

And the truth? It is great—until it isn't. The following morning you wake up late. It is a new day. The sun is shining and you have the day off. You will take care of some projects: mow the lawn, fix the sink in the guest bathroom, haul some rubbish to the dump, take your kids to the zoo and get to bed early. A typical happy Saturday in suburbia.

But tamas has arrived. Your head aches. Every muscle in your body is sore. Your mouth tastes like a cesspool. The light filtering into the room through the drapes sears your eyes. Your mind is so dull you can barely think. You stumble into the bathroom to brush your teeth and get into a fight with your wife because she used the last bit of toothpaste. Your kids come running up, excited about their outing. "Daddy, Daddy, let's go to the zoo!" they say, pulling at your pajamas. You know better, but you hate these selfish little bastards, your own flesh and blood. Why can't they leave you alone? Don't they see how you're suffering? They don't care. You promised, and you will have to deliver or they will hate you as much as you hate them. You shuffle to the kitchen, down a liter of coffee and a handful of antacids. You stuff your stomach with fried potatoes cooked in bacon fat and scarf down several cholesterol laden eggs, wiping up the yolky sludge with a couple slabs of white bread. Sloth is the best friend of cholesterol; it loves fat and carbs but, hey, anything to dull the pain.

All is not lost, however. The hangover makes you smart: it is not that much of a stretch to connect last night's behavior with your present misery. A swell of resolution, born of true knowledge, floods over you. You will become a better person. For the $n$th (and final, final) time you resolve to quit drinking. This time is for real!

But as the day progresses and the hangover slowly wears off, a few fond memories of last night's bender float by. You remember the liquor-induced bonhomie and the unconscious but great sex and you think, "Well, maybe my vow was a bit hasty but I'll definitely cut back." And just as this thought ends, fate seems to agree because good old boy Bob from down the block shows up to watch football with a six pack—its only beer, mind you, no harm done—and you settle into your Lazy Boy to watch the Vikings throttle the Rams. At halftime, Bob pops over to the corner store for another six pack.

Life's hangovers make you smart, all right, but not that smart. It takes more than a resolution to change. Inquiry is necessary. In this case, inquiry lies in understanding the big picture. Yes, chasing pleasure is certainly—well, pleasurable. It is a god given right and sanctioned by the Constitution, "the pursuit of happiness" it says in black and white. And what does it accomplish? It makes me feel good. And why do I want to feel good? Because I do not feel good as I am. Something is missing. I feel dull, bored and unfulfilled. I work like a dog, bring home the bacon, keep my family in iPods and Nikes and by the end of the week I am worn out. I need some fun. I get stoned or drunk and my problems go away. But next morning I have the same problems, and the solution to my problem is now a problem sitting on top of the original problem. So is feeling good a solution? I had better have a look at why I feel bad.

To make a meaningful change, one needs to realize that life is a zero sum game. This is not what we have been told. This is not what we want to hear. If God set up this unbeatable system, he or she is certainly a pervert. You cannot get ahead, no matter how hard you try. Every upside has its downside, every cloud its silver lining. If life is a zero sum game, why should I do anything? In the best of all possible worlds you would do nothing, but life is not the best of all possible worlds. You have no choice with reference to action. If you are here, you are a doer. Consciousness shines on your causal body and you move till the day you die. You have some discretion over the type of actions you perform and the attitudes that cause them, but you are compelled by your karma to act.

Self inquiry is the way out. It is the power to recognize rajasic and tamasic thoughts and neutralize them, with the understanding that they prevent radiant happiness and the assimilation of experience. In the dramatic and gross example above, our regular Joe has not inquired into the source of his suffering. He feels incomplete, but he does not know why. Therefore, he assumes incorrectly that there is an experiential solution. The solution he devises does not work, because he refuses to believe that life is a zero sum game. Although he intellectually knows that his solution does not work, he cannot break his habits, because his coping mechanism is built in. The alcohol tendencies are dynamic; they compel him to drink when he feels anxious, angry, bored or depressed. When he is agitated, he relies on alcohol to relax him. It does not really make him relaxed. It makes him dull. Dullness, however, seems like peace compared to anxiety. When he is dull, he relies on alcohol to lift his spirits. It does not really lift his spirits. It just stimulates his nerves for a short time. This, however, feels a lot better than depression.

When you are caught in the rajas-tamas cycle, you are not happy and cannot assimilate the knowledge you gain from experience. Thanks to the samskaras your bad habits keep replicating themselves, your will power deserts you and you stop growing. Therefore, cultivate sattva.

Do not think that because your life is more refined than the life of our mythical hard living materialist, you are free of rajas and tamas. They function at every level of evolution. Golden chains bind just as tightly as iron and silver chains.

## The Value of Values

The assimilation of experience depends on the interpretation of experience, and the interpretation of experience depends on the individual's values. Because the apparent reality is a duality and we have lived in it for a long time, we have inevitably picked up good and bad values. One part of the mind lives in daylight and another in darkness. Such is the nature of duality. Consequently, it often seems as if we are two very different people. Certain sattvic values facilitate inquiry and growth, while others inhibit it. So it is incumbent on anyone seeking happiness in this world—or freedom from this world—to take a fearless moral inventory. Before we enumerate some positive and negative values and how they impact on inquiry, it is important to value the absence of judgment with reference to yourself and others. Absence of judgment means that you do not put yourself up on the basis of your positive qualities, nor do you get down on yourself on account of your negative qualities. By and large, values are unconsciously assimilated and are woven into the very fabric of our being. So it is unrealistic to expect the negative values to disappear overnight, even when we vow to be done with them. Renunciation of negative tendencies, a companion value of absence of judgment and one of inquiry's core values, comes through understanding. When you discover how a particular value stacks up against your spiritual goal, you will be in a good position to cultivate it—if it is in harmony with your goal—or renounce it if it is not.

If enlightenment is freedom from dependence on objects and freedom is gained by self knowledge, it stands to reason that love of knowledge should be a core value. If you find yourself indifferent to knowledge and enamored by feelings, know that your values are distorted. If you have the right values, you will always feel good. If you focus on how you feel without an inquiry into your value structure, you will never feel consistently good. When you feel bad, it should be taken as an opportunity to inquire into your true nature.

If you value self knowledge, you cannot but value peace of mind, because inquiry cannot take place in an emotionally disturbed mind. In general, the mind suffers agitation or dullness when a negative value is in play. When the mind is agitated or dull, it is impossible to appreciate and enjoy the self. This is not to say that inquiry should not be practiced when you are feeling bad. On the contrary, the presence of dullness or irritation is an invitation to pinpoint and renounce the value that is causing the disturbance. When this is done, there is a qualitative shift in your experience. When clarity returns, the light of awareness reflects on the still lake of the mind and you feel good. Eventually, as you consistently examine and renounce the negative values, the mind becomes extremely subtle, the light of awareness shines in it more or less constantly, and self realization is inevitable.

Truth, another core value, is not an abstract principle. It stares you in the face every minute of the day. It is the appreciation of things as they are. Its negative counterpart is a value for getting what you want from the world. When the value for having it the way you want it overrides the value for truth, the mind is disturbed. Wanting what you want, when you want it, at the expense of what reality is presenting to you at the moment is vanity, a core negative value. It is vanity because you believe that life was created for your enjoyment, when the truth is more nuanced: yes, you are here to enjoy but you cannot enjoy properly unless you make your contribution to life. It gave you everything and you have the responsibility to pay your debt. If you do not pay your debt, you are a thief. You are a thief because you are robbing yourself of the opportunity for peace. If you do not value peace, how will you grow spiritually?

Straightforwardness is an alignment of thought, word and deed. It is know-ing what you think and acting accordingly. It is the opposite of crookedness, always trying to work the angles. Crookedness, like all negative values, is fear based. You are afraid that you cannot get what you want by straightforward means, so you scheme, manipulate and cut corners to get what you want. Un-derstanding straightforwardness is not straightforward because it is possible to injure others with your straightforward, unsolicited opinions and actions. So it is important to understand this value in the hierarchy of values, in so far as it is trumped by charity and compassion. If you are in love with yourself because you are an honest, straightforward, righteous person, it is wise to cul-tivate another important value, judicious restraint. Think about the effect of your views on others before you "share" your feelings. Unless the world sends a written request for your opinion, it is better to keep it to yourself.

Being honest with yourself is an important core value. How can you purify your mind if you do not want to look at your impurities? When there is a pre-ponderance of tamas in the mind, it is very difficult to be honest with yourself. Tamas is responsible for denial, refusal to see what is. If you are honest with yourself, you will be honest with others. If you find yourself cheating or telling lies, it is a sign that you need to investigate your relationship with yourself.

Sad to say, the mind has become so lost in ignorance it has come to think that fear is smart. This is not to say that prudence and caution are other than positive values, only that pandering to society's myriad gratuitous fears is com-pletely unhelpful. Fearlessness, another core value, should be cultivated be-cause it acknowledges the benign, non-dual nature of reality. The world is not out to get you. Rapists and robbers do not lurk behind every bush. You are not condemning yourself to a life of suffering if you do not eat organic vegetables. Nor are you setting yourself up for identity theft if the security code for your computer does not have twenty seven digits including randomly spaced upper and lower case letters interspersed with numbers and assorted arcane symbols.

It is wise to be reasonably critical, but unbridled criticism is a negative value and should be counteracted by cultivating compassion, a core value. Compas-sion is the understanding that nobody, including you, would be who they are if they could help it. Ignorance is not something you do. It is something that happens when you are not aware of who you really are. You should not make yourself feel bad because you are not a saint. Yes, it is natural to feel bad when you violate life's core values, but you should not wallow in the feeling. Neutralize it with compassion for yourself. Feeling bad is self injury. It means you do not love yourself properly.

Charity, a higher value than compassion, is the appreciation of your fullness. It should be cultivated to counteract miserliness. Like kindness, it is a higher value, because it is more than just the appreciation of your suffering and the suffering of others. It involves actually giving something to yourself and the world. A miser is someone who is so fear oriented that he or she cannot let go of things, especially his or her insecurities, monetary and otherwise. Charity means giving yourself the things you deny yourself out of irrational fears—time off from work, for example. Or giving to others things that are valuable to you but that do not contribute to a pure mind.

Renunciation is an important core value. It is a contrarian value because the samsaric view, which is built into everyone, is that less is never more. A pure mind is a simple, uncluttered, quiet mind. The more activities, relationships and objects you are involved in, the more agitated your mind will be. It should be practiced aggressively, because it is a sure way to break attachment. The one who appreciates this value lives a simple, austere life. Far from feeling deprived, he or she feels rich in peace and leisure. Renunciation, like dispassion, is a companion value of discrimination. When you understand the difference between what is real and what it apparently real, you can easily drop your attachment to the apparently real.

Another core value is non-injury. Non-injury is based on the fact that there is a universal and mutual expectation for non-injury. To cultivate non-injury is to counteract cruelty. Cruelty is so obviously unspiritual it hardly bears mention, but it is much more common than we like to admit. Cruelty, an intense fear inspired by dislike of oneself, motivates us to punish ourselves and others in many subtle ways: the father that beats his children, the wife that incessantly nags the husband, the scammer who robs, the child who puts the cat in the microwave and pulls the wings off a butterfly. To counteract it, develop empathy.

Self confidence, another important value, comes from accomplishing what you intend to accomplish. For a spiritual person, it comes from living up to the teachings, taking a stand in awareness and resolving doubts about who you are on a daily basis. Self confidence is difficult to cultivate in timid individuals, because they often confuse it with arrogance, a lack of humility. It is not arrogant to see yourself as non-separate from everything and to assert your divinity to yourself. Feelings of unworthiness, continuously second guessing yourself, and dithering excessively indicate a lack of self confidence.

If you are conditioned to unspiritual values, your ego will resist your attempt to live the higher values. If you discover resistance, it is important to identify the problematic values and understand why they are not serving you. The most difficult negative value to confront is desire for objects. Why is it a negative value? Because it is an emphatic statement by ignorance that you are incomplete and limited. If it seems impossible to live without craving for objects, know that your relationship to your desires needs to be investigated. Before we set out to do something about it, we need to know that only binding desires need to be eliminated, because they stand in the way of self inquiry. If they are sublimated into the desire for self inquiry, so much the better.

Although we have covered this point before, it bears repeating, because it is important to have a practical understanding of the problems associated with binding desires. When you value your desires unnecessarily, you are asking for anger. Oddly, many worldly people value anger, particularly those who count themselves among the virtuous, because they are filled with pride, another negative value. Jesus whipped the moneychangers in the temple because it was good for them and I am attacking you because you are a godless pagan. But anger is just frustrated desire. A person with desire for objects will always have anger, because the world does not care what you want. It apportions desired objects according to the needs of the total. Obviously, an angry mind is not suited to self inquiry. When desire is valued excessively and the mind is prone to anger, it becomes dull and when it is dull, it becomes deluded and is no longer able to discriminate properly. When discrimination goes, you are finished. When you value desire excessively, you end up living on hope. Hope is an unsuitable basis for a life. It is a statement that you are unable to accommodate yourself to reality.

Although there are many more, here are a few negative values to watch out for: greed, lust, pride, deceit, hypocrisy, willfulness, self glorification and arrogance.

# CHAPTER ELEVEN

# Lifestyle

## People, Food, Sex and Money

Once we are committed to the purification of the mind and we understand the importance of adjusting the relative proportions of the three energies, it is time to apply the knowledge. Just as we are what we eat on the physical level, we are our associations on the psychological level. Most of us think that we consciously choose our friends, but actually the samskaras do the choosing.

If you have difficulty understanding yourself, look at your associations. Just as all the people appearing in a dream are symbols of various parts of the dreamer's psyche, including the dream ego, in waking life each person represents some aspect of our conditioning. Rarely are our associations sinister, but many contribute little or nothing to our growth. They also tend to continue for less than noble reasons, often loneliness and habit. Even our significant others may feel threatened by our interest in enlightenment and make our way forward difficult, because they would like us to fit into the box they devised for us a long time ago. Once we have determined which associations are helpful and which are not, it is important to make the necessary adjustments. If your desire for freedom is weak or middling, attachment will prevent you from moving on when you see that your relationships are reinforcing unhealthy tendencies. If the desire for freedom is strong, you will have the confidence to let go of those that do not facilitate your quest and move into those that do.

It is wise to avoid people who do not share your passion for the truth, no matter how drawn you are to them. Here is a partial list of types who are not beneficial influences: workaholics, party people, glad-handers, small talkers, poseurs, romantics, cynics, the excessively ambitious, self-promoters, substance abusers, hangers on and hangers out, scammers, speculators, swingers, slackers, debtors, neurotics, whiners, back-biters, hypocrites, obsessives, compulsives, manics, depressives, the morbidly obese, anorexics, perverts, religious fanatics, cause-obsessed people with an excessively refined sense of injustice, conspiracy theorists, world savers, doomsday predictors, dandies, ne'er-do-wells, gamblers, loan sharks, addicts and criminals.

Many in this group are not bad people, but they should be avoided anyway, because their negative tendencies set up resonances with similar tendencies in your mind, bringing those tendencies into play and reinforcing them. As society continues to deteriorate under the pressure of materialism, it is easy to fritter away one's life on non-essentials. Encounters with dysfunctional people are also increasingly the norm. One should engage them politely, offer short term assistance if requested, but refuse to bond.

Associate primarily with truth seekers and finders. Associations with good people with worldly vasanas should be kept to a minimum. Association with the inner self in solitude and contemplation is best.

## Money

Because money is a means to satisfy desire, and desire is always present, I am always under pressure to spend. But if I have invested money with the power to make me feel secure, I become insecure when I spend. So there is a constant struggle between the long term desire for security and the short term desire for pleasure. When desire runs to security and pleasure, I have a readymade vasana generator. If my goal is peace of mind, which it should be if I want freedom, I need to sublimate the desire for money into the desire for freedom. I need to find the unchanging source of security and pleasure in myself.

Prudent spending is sattvic. Miserliness is tamasic. Extravagance is rajasic. Money obtained from hard work and ingenuity is sattvic. Easy money and other people's money is tamasic and tends to corrupt. Debt creates anxiety for both the borrower and the lender. Anxiety prevents the mind from remaining present and hinders inquiry. It destroys discrimination and faith. Yes, tether your camel, but trust the Lord too. Trust is a sign that you understand the benign nature of reality and that you are confident your inner strength will see you through the hard times.

Financial security can be very helpful on any path. To obtain it, live beneath your means. Nobody really cares how well you live, except you. Studies have shown that seventy percent of millionaires became millionaires by living beneath their means. Greed is theft, a violation of dharma, because it encourages you to take more than you need, thus depriving others of their fair share. Counteract greedy tendencies through charitable giving. Give until it hurts.

## Sex

Security, symbolized by money, is a dominant human fixation. But once we feel financially secure, the ever restless mind turns to luxury and pleasure. Security is a negative value, a perceived freedom from the vagaries of existence, but sex is a positive value because it produces ecstatic feelings. The more pleasure is derived from an experience, the more powerful the tendencies it creates. Powerful tendencies produce binding attachments and binding attachments compromise discrimination. Poor discrimination leads to accidents, losses and unappreciated opportunities. Sexaholics suffer low self esteem, brought on by a sense of helplessness in the face of overpowering cravings. An inquiry into sex is warranted, because an activity that causes extreme attachment and aversion is always accompanied by irrational beliefs, fantasies, judgments, opinions and prejudices.

The causal body organizes the vasanas in various patterns or archetypes. Sex and love belong to the same archetype. Therefore, it is difficult to discuss sex and spirituality without discussing love. Love has been around forever, because it is the nature of reality. It is just willing attention, consciousness engaging itself in sexual and non-sexual activities. Maybe in the beginning of human history there was no separation between love and sex. Perhaps sex was nothing special, just one of many expressions of consciousness loving itself. In any case, at some point in evolution it seems that love became an abstraction and sex was no longer non-separate from it.

How does my idea of sex and love hinder or enhance my pursuit of self realization? On the one hand, separating love and sex may be to my advantage. A commitment to another, with its concomitant emotional baggage, may be too high a spiritual price to pay to work out such a powerful tendency. On the other hand, a committed loving relationship with a supportive someone with similar values, in which sex played a minor role, might provide a stable emotional foundation for inquiry and sex, assuming the karma yoga view is operative.

On traditional spiritual paths, the sexual impulse is meant to be sublimated into practices that produce sattvic tendencies. Over time, the bliss that comes from the practice dwarfs the bliss of sex—and other non-essential blisses—and sex looses its luster, so to speak. Non-traditional approaches sometimes promote sex as a spiritual path. While it is possible for a mature individual to enjoy sex and pursue enlightenment, attachment is a clear and present danger. It is unlikely that a mature person would choose this path, because maturity implies discrimination and dispassion, qualities not in evidence in people fascinated by sex. Nonetheless, immature people are also attracted to spirituality and often feel that they would rather spiritualize sex than leave it behind—think Tantra. But it is impossible to spiritualize sex, because there is nothing spiritual or unspiritual about it in the first place, although lust is always a problem. If you can enjoy sex without attachment, it is no more unspiritual than eating a salad.

As we know, it so happens that every attempt to get happiness through an object is actually a clumsy and uninformed attempt to gain freedom from desiring the object in question. Sex is no exception because the goal of sex is orgasm, an intense experience of peace, ecstasy and freedom. There is nothing unspiritual about experiential liberation, but it suffers the defect of contact with all objects.

An individual with no spiritual core finds it virtually impossible to transcend sex, because it is an integral part of his or her identity. Self realization, uncaused freedom, can be realized only when all objects, including sex, have been observed, investigated, negated and transcended. Negation and transcendence comes about through a keen appreciation of the impermanence of experience. As long as romantic views of sex survive, growth is virtually impossible. To grow beyond sex does not mean that sexual activity necessarily terminates, although it may, but that its limitations are fully appreciated.

Attachment to sexual pleasure reorients one's priorities and pushes what should be at the center of life—inquiry—to the periphery. When a frivolous value displaces an important value, suffering is quick to follow. Because the joy of sex is so intense, it can also result in violations of dharma. When you want something badly that depends on the good graces of someone else, you are tempted to lie or make yourself susceptible to lies. People lie routinely about sex. They lie about their sexual histories, their circumstances and their feelings for each other for fear that they will not get what they want. They make promises they have no intention of keeping. When desire is frustrated by the object, violent feelings are often forthcoming.

Identification with sex poses a problem for a seeker and a sexual identity compounds it. Sex itself is exciting and dulling, with tiny dollops of peace thrown in for good measure. As such, it does not qualify as a spiritual path. It involves intense use of all sense organs, the emotions and the intellect. Its strategy is threefold: get rid of desire, pick up a bit of pleasure along the way, and hit the jackpot at the end. We know this because when orgasm is achieved, desire vanishes. The absence of desire is sattvic, non-duality in action. When the mind switches off, even the bedrock gender identity is suspended and you actually feel non-different from everything. Sometimes in the tangle of bodies, you cannot figure out where yours ends and your partner's begins.

But the price is high: the organs and emotions suffer fatigue after the initial high, the mind becomes dull, and you collect a big fat sex vasana. It is not an accident that most sexual activity takes place at the end of the day, in the bedroom with the lights off. Next stop: sleep. Even if you are energized and awake half the night, you pay dearly in the morning when the alarm rings and your mind is as dull as a loaf of bread. If you practice non-orgasmic sex, you avoid the downside of orgasm, but the good feelings are also accompanied by a karmic drag.

There is nothing wrong with sex from a spiritual point of view, assuming you go into it with your eyes open and do not expect it to solve the riddle of your identity or other important problems. But there is nothing particularly right about it either, in so far as it is just another vasana-driven dualistic activity. And if an identity is added—gay or straight or otherwise—it becomes a spiritual problem, assuming you are seeking freedom. Since everyone is seeking freedom, whether they know it or not, and freedom comes through self knowledge and self knowledge comes through self inquiry, any assumed identity not in harmony with your true identity is an obstacle.

What is sex, anyway? Does it refer to an actual object with certain qualities, something whose nature can be agreed upon by reasonable people whose senses and minds are functioning normally? Or is it only what you think it is? Normal people agree that there is a sun in the sky and that it produces heat and light. If it is only in the mind, you can lie under it all day and not get sunburned. But if it is real, you will turn red like a lobster. Even if it is only in the mind, it may have a profound effect on you. Therefore, it is important to find out what sex means to you. When you look into sex, it could be anything you want it to be. It is only an idea in consciousness that has no objective reality. Inquire more deeply to see why this idea is attractive. Ask yourself who you would be without it. See if there is a good reason, related to your ultimate goal, that you should act out this vasana.

Rules for healthy sex: Tell the truth. Be sure your partner understands what it means to you. Is it a one night stand? Are you in love? Let your partner know what you want and what you do not want. Be considerate and open to suggestions. See to it that you are as interested in your partner's pleasure as you are in your own. Think outside the box. Do not fall into boring patterns. Take chances. Avoid expectations. The fruits of the action are not up to you. No matter how it turns out, see it as a learning experience. Do it with love, whether or not you are in love. Do not be manipulative or coercive. Do not make a big story out of it. Keep it intimate. Do not discuss it with others. Open relationships are adharmic, motivated by greed. Greed is a sign of spiritual poverty. Once the sex vasana gets control of you, you are finished.

Clean up every last bit of karma from the preceding relationship and wait a long time before even considering another. Do not date anyone who is dating someone else. Adultery is a violation of a universal value: non-injury.

## Diet and Lifestyle

Because the materials in food affect the mind and the mind is the instrument of inquiry, a comprehensive science of diet that compliments self inquiry evolved thousands of years ago. The diet is scientific in the sense that optimum health and a clear, energetic meditative mind can be cultivated by experimentally adjusting the relative proportions of the three gunas in food. If the mind is pure, the body will remain essentially disease free.

If the goal is a clear pure mind, a tamasic diet is counterproductive because it creates sleepy, dull thoughts and depressing feelings. Although they are an important component in a balanced diet, foods in which the earth element predominates tend to be tamasic as they require more energy to digest, assimilate and excrete. A heavily marbled fried steak is an excellent example of a purely tamasic food. Only someone with an extremely active lifestyle, like a high performance athlete, can eat such food with impunity. It is dangerous for individuals with sedentary lifestyles. If the digestive fire is highly refined or weak, this kind of food will cause indigestion. The obesity epidemic sweeping the "developed" world is the result of a tamasic diet.

Compared to fruits, vegetables and grains, flesh is tamasic, although some flesh is relatively sattvic, fish and chicken for example. Because it is flesh, fish is tamasic, but it is an excellent food unless the digestive fire is exceptionally sattvic, in which case it may not digest properly. Because it is difficult to purify, pork is tamasic, although certain cuts of organic pork are less so.

Dairy foods are tamasic. For example, cheese is tamasic because it produces sticky mucous, which stresses the physiological system, and absorbs environmental toxins and the waste of putrefactive bacteria. Bacteria love warm, sweet, mucous-laden environments. Vegans and raw fooders rarely get sick, because they deny unwanted bacteria conducive environments. In any case, in the warm intestinal environment, a thin layer of sludgy, toxic mucous bakes on the colon wall, slowing absorption and excretion. The colon is the most important organ of elimination next to the skin and should be kept sparkling clean. When absorption, assimilation and circulation are compromised, the brain eventually becomes sluggish. The mind becomes cloudy, making creative thought and discrimination difficult. When the physiological processes become tamasic, disease is sure to follow. The diet of choice in Western societies is tamasic.

Rajas and tamas should be regulated by knowledge of the gunas. Unthinking people try to manage rajas with tamas. A pepperoni pizza is the king of tamasic foods. Eat it and die. If pizza is king, an egg is queen. It would be hard for nature to devise a more plugging, clogging food. The animal protein myth that has kept the public hypnotized for a hundred years was concocted by the advertising industry, to keep the barons of the meat and dairy industry happily ensconced in their mansions. There are hundreds of millions of strong, limber, healthy individuals in India who have never eaten meat or meat products.

Is it a wonder that the price of health care is astronomical and that pharmaceutical companies are some of the richest institutions in society? Cholesterol is tamasic and cholesterol-reducing drugs are rajasic in the short run because they break down fat or block fat absorption. In the long run they are tamasic because they leave residues in the cells that compromise their functions. On the other hand, yogurt in reasonable quantities is a relatively benign tamasic food because it contains enough water to pass through the system easily. It also consists of beneficial lactobacteria, vitamins and minerals, so it is sattvic when ingested in reasonable quantities.

The Department of Health is not your friend. Its recommendation of animal products as essential components in a healthy diet is irresponsible. You can eat meat and dairy and be healthy, assuming you use discrimination and have a very active lifestyle, but these foods are not necessary for health. No food is actually bad, if its effects are understood by experiment and analysis.

However, one should eat from knowledge, not from emotion, taste, habit or the recommendations of experts. There is a raft of experts on every side of every issue. Their recommendations should be viewed with skepticism.

Methods of preparation impact on the quality of the food. A potato, for instance, in its natural state is a nice blend of sattva and tamas. Root crops are tamasic, but beneficial. Fry a potato in fat, cover it with butter and sour cream and eat it in large quantities and it becomes decidedly tamasic. A broiled or grilled steak is less tamasic because some of the fat drips out. Boiled food is less tamasic than fried food, but it is more tamasic than steamed food because boiling removes more nutrients than light steaming. Raw food is sattvic in general, but it can become rajasic after prolonged use as it purifies tamas. In addition to frequent trips to the toilet, raw fooders tend to have busy minds and suffer insomnia because too much helpful tamas has been purified from the body. Because raw food is generally superior to cooked food in terms of health and energy, raw fooders often suffer one of sattva's unbecoming side effects—vanity.

Eat life. Food should be eaten fresh. An apple plucked from a tree on a cool fall day and eaten immediately is obviously more purifying and energizing than one shipped from South America, stored in a refrigerator for months and eaten after a week's stay in a supermarket. A side of beef sitting in a freezer for a year is completely tamasic because all the energy has dissipated. Refrigerating food for a short time is sensible, because it preserves its energy, but the longer it sits in the fridge, the more tamasic it becomes. Frozen food is caused by a hoarding mentality and a convenience-driven lifestyle. Freezing began in earnest in the late 1940's as a response to the food anxieties spawned by the Great Depression (buy huge quantities and save!), gained ground during the prosperous fifties, and continues unabated today. It also promotes waste.

The more a food is heated and mixed with other foods, the less sattvic it becomes. Food cooked in complex sauces and mixtures of spices places undue stress on the digestive fires, increasing rajas in the short run and tamas overall. Raw fibrous foods—think salads—are exceedingly sattvic, because they supply clean nutritious energy and absorb toxins on their way through the digestive tract. The less work you give the body to do, the longer it lasts and the better it feels.

Because tamas makes flesh, it should be carefully balanced with rajas and sattva to create the desired body. A sumo wrestler obviously prizes tamas but a ballerina eschews it, opting instead for a predominance of rajas and sattva. A meditation lifestyle and other creative lifestyles demand a large percentage of sattva and smaller proportions of rajas and tamas.

Rajas, the activity principle, is also found in food. Although many bitter and astringent foods are rajasic, the most common and popular rajasic food is coffee, prized for its ability to prod the mind into action. Caffeine and other stimulants are not recommended for a meditation lifestyle. They artificially activate the mind and produce tamas, which induces increased coffee consumption and masks the body's need for rest. If the lifestyle is sattvic, the idea of what has to be done will supply the energy directly from consciousness. Remember, you are consciousness with a body, not a body with consciousness. Sugar, which provides bursts of rajasic energy in the short run, becomes tamasic as it passes through the system. The letdown following the consumption of processed sugar indicates a tamasic condition of mind. The depressions suffered by alcoholics are sugar induced.

Stimulants like drugs, alcohol and coffee provide virtually no health benefits, although the coffee industry now informs us that it is loaded with beneficial antioxidants. Before long, the advertisers will find a way to convince us that alcohol is a cure for cancer. These industries thrive because the public has little common sense and is woefully ignorant of the post digestive effects of foods. If the lifestyle is sensible, there is no need to artificially boost energy.

All substances suffer a loss of effectiveness over time. When this happens, individuals often resort to will power to accomplish what needs to be accomplished, ignoring the signals that indicate a breakdown of a particular physiological system. For example, a person with a very active lifestyle will often feel tired during the day. Instead of taking the feeling as a sign from the self to slow down, take a nap, or budget more time for sleep at night, he or she ignores the feeling and overcomes the sleep vasana with will power. This is not wise, because the body-mind organism is controlled by consciousness through a complex set of natural laws. If the laws are not respected, suffering comes. If the mind is suffering, how can it inquire dispassionately into its own nature?

## The Rajas-Tamas Complex

Rajas and tamas are incestuous bedfellows. On the psychological level, desire and fear, abuse and neglect, projection and denial, attraction and aversion—the dualities—operate non-stop and are at work in every sphere of life. When you awake in the morning feeling tired, you immediately down a couple cups of coffee to stimulate the nervous system and activate the mind, so you can deal with the world. Everyone knows that facing life with a dull mind is a recipe for disaster. People in the business world, for example, tend to be rajasic, although rajas more or less permeates every aspect of modern life. Even without coffee, rajasic people have excessive desires and an abiding interest in satisfying them. When you show up at the office with your triple espresso from the drive-up kiosk on the corner, you enter a highly charged atmosphere, which further stimulates you. You are now ready to work. The rajasic mind believes that the more results it can produce in a short time the better—got to get that promotion, kids are nearly ready for college!—so off you go. When your energy level flags, you take a big swig of espresso and you are back in the ballgame.

Highly competitive rajasic environments produce conflict. Like children, everyone wants something every minute—not necessarily what you want—and they want it now, so there is always an undercurrent of anger and aggression. Modern life is a little like war. You never know when you are going to step on a mine—think road rage. And when a conflict breaks out, the emotions reverberate in your mind and produce an incessant string of unhappy thoughts that only serve to irritate you more. When tamas rears its ugly head and you start to nod off, you swat it down with another cup of java. By quitting time you are completely wired—and tired. If you had control of your mind when the day began, you have lost it completely by now. It is like a big freight train without an engineer, going down the tracks at full throttle.

You deal with it the only way you know. You stop off at the sports bar down the road and quaff a few—well, quite a few—brews. The vibrations in your head begin to settle down, but do not go away completely. Good old Tom from the office shows up—he has had a rough day too—and offers you a smoke. It does not occur to you that not one of the untold species of creatures endowed with mouths and lungs, except man, is foolish enough to consciously inhale hot smoke from burning vegetable matter, but you are not that conscious, so you puff away.

Alcohol makes you dull, no doubt, but tobacco is king of tamas. It plugs the alveoli in the lungs with nasty tars—think asphalt—which inhibit the natural flow of oxygen from the lungs to the bloodstream, depriving the brain and other assorted cells of oxygen, which sends rajas reeling. By this time you are feeling no pain. But wait, rajas is down but not out! It has retreated to your stomach and you are now ravenously hungry. There just happens to be a pizza joint next door, so you and Tom order—guess what?—a large pepperoni pizza! You are feeling no pain when you get home, but somehow you forgot that your drinking/smoking/sports watching/dinner missing/kid ignoring complex does not have the same calming effect on your wife as it does on you. Her rajas goes ballistic and your tamasic fog is not strong enough to mute her shrill ultimatums. You get a nasty headache, which you treat with a stiff nightcap. The first thing you do in the morning is to switch on the coffee pot.

The rajas-tamas cycle acts itself out in one way or another on many levels, billions of time a day, throughout the world. And the moral of the story? Managing tamas with rajas and rajas with tamas is not the way to go.

The solution is a conscious sattvic lifestyle. If you rob a bank and cannot sleep for days, even an intellectually challenged person may draw the conclusion that the lack of sleep is somehow connected to the robbery. If you insult a stranger and get punched in the nose, it does not take a lot of smarts to connect the two events. But if you wash down a piece of chocolate cake with a big latte every day for years, it is a little more difficult to determine the long term effect on your health and state of mind.

To spiritualize your diet, you first need to figure out whether a food is sattvic, rajasic or tamasic for you, by observing its post digestive effect and then looking into its connection with your emotions. There is no magic one-size-fits-all formula that makes it easy and convenient. A food that is sattvic for you at the early stages of your diet may become tamasic when the body has achieved a high degree of purity. A food that is rajasic for one person may be sattvic for another. Each individual has a different body and different energy requirements, so you must experiment.

Our relationship to food is almost exclusively related to taste, and our tastes were conditioned before we had enough intelligence to understand what was going on. Parents worldwide use food to manage the feelings of their children. When baby is emotional, they do what works. What worked on your grandparents, your parents and you was fat and sugar. Vegetables never work. They are too healthy. Dissatisfaction is rajasic and fat and sugar are tamasic. Tamas temporarily neutralizes rajas. So baby gets a sweet. Sweets work. The bad news: a vasana for sugar has been created. Now, every time junior is unhappy, he wants a dish of ice cream, a Baby Ruth or a Coke. And before he is ten, he has diabetes. It makes you wonder if doing what you have been conditioned to do for your children is actually love.

When you drive to the mall, you pass a MacDonald's on the corner. If you are not too busy thinking about a parking place in front of Office Depot, you will notice a nice colorful little playground with a plastic swing, teeter totter and a slide. It warms the cockles of your heart to think of the depth of Ronald MacDonald's love for kids. "How lovely," you think. "They don't have to do that." It is true. They do not have to do it. They want to do it. Get those Big Mac vasanas going early and they will stick with you for life. "Let's see, that's seventy-five years—assuming they do not die early, which they tend to do if they eat too many—times 200 Big Macs a year plus fries—lots of good yummy fat there too—at let's say $5 a visit—what does that come to?—um, seventy-five thousand dollars. Not bad!"

Do not shed tears for MacDonald's. They're in on the secret: fat works. You start to feel better after the first bite, because those nutritionless greasy molecules jam the pores in your stomach lining, taking away the hunger. Now every time junior needs to calm down, you toss him in the SUV and streak to the Golden Arches. Problem solved. Well, sort of. By the time he is nine, he weighs a hundred and fifty pounds and cannot climb the stairs to his bedroom.

The doctor has him on some very expensive special medicine and you just cannot figure out what went wrong.

Every action has both an immediate noticeable result and an unseen result. In the case of our examples, the immediate result of sweets and fats was emotional satisfaction: the brats stopped whining. Sweets and fats do not taste good because there is something inherently tasty in them; some people even hate them. They taste good because they solve a problem. Tamas temporarily neutralizes rajas. This is not to say that sweets and fats have no place in a healthy diet, only that the food you eat should be eaten for its health benefits, not to make you feel good emotionally. You need a diet of healthy emotions to solve emotional problems. You need a healthy diet of the right foods to solve the energy and disease problem.

So the first step is to separate your emotions from your diet. Eating for taste is a sign that emotional motivations are in play. There is nothing objective about taste. It is completely vasana driven. Once you get into a pure sattvic diet, even the smell of the food that you once found so tasty makes you sick. The broccoli you hated in your steak and potato days now tastes as good the steaks once did. Sattvic food tastes good, assuming you have cleared your attachment to rajasic and tamasic foods, because it is good. It is healthy, nutritious, cleansing and energizing. It is the kind of food that the body actually needs to be healthy. It keeps the mind focused and alert.

The body is consciousness, in the form of an amazingly complex and subtle instrument. None of its components are actually conscious but they function because consciousness enlivens them. Food is a fuel like gasoline and the body is a machine that burns it and distributes the energy to its various systems. It is made of the four elements: air, fire, water and earth. The earth element gives it substance. You need tamasic food to maintain the muscles, bones, nerves, arteries and organs. The fire and water elements burn and digest the food. Fire heats the food to a certain temperature and the digestive juices, the water element carrying certain rajasic chemicals, digests it. The circulatory system, the water element, distributes it to the cells, picks up waste and so forth. The air element carries carbon dioxide to the lungs, where it is converted to oxygen, and carries carbon dioxide away.

Although certain crude combustion engines run on vegetable oil, a jet cannot do so. It requires a highly refined type of gasoline, one almost completely free of impurities. If you filled a jet with vegetable oil and it got off the ground, you would see a vile black cloud of pollutants issuing from it. It would undoubtedly crash after a couple of hours because the engine would be so gunked up, it could no longer function. Sattvic food is like airplane fuel. It is relatively free of rajas and tamas. If you put it in your body, you will fly high and long.

Garbage in garbage out: if you fill your body with tamasic foods, all your systems, from your brain on down to your feet, will be compromised. Everything will slow down until you come to a complete halt. One day they may have to call emergency rescue to cut away the ceiling of your bedroom and lift you out with a crane. You will end up a stupid, dull person, prone to depression and disease. Granted, you have to be stupid and dull to eat predominately tamasic foods in the first place, but this only goes to show that the desire/action cycle works both ways. Because you are dull, you eat dull foods and dull foods keep you dull.

To get a sattvic body-mind, you need to distinguish the short term effect of the food from its post digestive effect. This is often difficult, because you tend to eat several foods at one time. Just to make a point, here is another exaggerated example.

Beer is a popular beverage. It is essentially water, but it contains some helpful nutrients. Before you go ahead with this little experiment, wait until your mind is clear, still and alert and you do not have a reason to drink beer. Drink a whole beer quickly. Normally, you would sip it carefully during a nice conversation with a friend, perhaps with a meal. You do not want to do this, because it will be difficult to isolate the effect. Carefully observe the quality of your mind. If there is no change after twenty minutes, one beer is sattvic for you. If you start to feel dull and sleepy, beer is tamasic for you. If you keep drinking, note the point at which you crave another beer or become dull and sleepy. This is the quantity at which beer activates either rajas or tamas. If you are using beer to relax, beer is tamasic for you and you can keep drinking until you are as relaxed as you want to be. At some point, of course, you may get so relaxed you are no longer conscious. When you do become aware again, try to remember how many beers you had and how much time passed before you passed out. Presuming it was your intention to pass out, beer is working for you. Continue observing the quality of your mind. If it is clear and still and you feel excellent and do not have cravings for more, you can use beer as your spiritual path. It will take you straight to enlightenment. If you are sluggish and lazy, beer at that quantity is tamasic for you.

If at some point after your first beer you feel good and want another beer, one beer is rajasic for you. You can now choose if you want to feel even better. Yes, definitely, two is better than one. Keep watching your mind. Is it clear and happy? Does the milk of human kindness flow generously through your veins? If so, X number of beers makes you sattvic. So far, so good. Keep observing. Are you starting to get hungry? If you are, rajas is now in charge. Go to the fridge. Open it. What kind of food appeals to you? There is a nice nutritious crispy carrot and a fresh bell pepper just bursting with wholesome sattvic energy, sitting next to a couple of slices of two day old cheese and ham pizza, left over from your son's birthday party last week. What do you choose? If you mix the carrot and the peppers with some lettuce and make a nice salad, the post digestive effect of X number of beers is sattvic. You're a huge spiritual winner: you had a nice drunk, suffered no hangover and you went right into sattva with nary a hitch. If you choose to microwave the pizza, keep observing. You have just chosen a very tamasic food. If your hunger goes away and you feel light and high and you head for the meditation room to sit for a couple of hours, you are a transcendental yogi and no rules apply; you can eat nails if you like. However, if you are a normal person, the tamas produced by the pizza will combine with the tamas created by the alcohol, which was secretly parked behind the hunger vasana, and you will probably fall asleep on the floor on the way to your bedroom. You are also likely to awaken in the morning feeling rotten. If this is true, you now understand what tamasic foods do to your energy level.

To purify the body of excess rajas and tamas, it is helpful to understand the actions of the elements. Fire is an activating and purifying element. If you go out for Mexican food and order a burrito, you are looking at a healthy but tamasic meal rife with fiber. Unless you are a hermit living in a mountain cave without access to the media, it has probably not escaped your attention that fiber is good for you. The beans and rice make a complete protein, forestalling the need to add chicken or pork and make it more tamasic. You told them to put a lot of lettuce and tomatoes to add some sattva. Now go to the salsa counter and slather on some hot sauce. If you really want to rock with rajas, you can ask for habanera peppers. Jalapenos are hot, but the number of BTUs in a habanero is astronomical. If you are dying of hypothermia in Alaska, a handful of habaneros could conceivably save your life while you wait for an Eskimo to happen by with an extra parka and some nice tamasic whale blubber. Deep tamas works fine in Alaska because the body generates rajas to compensate for the cold, raising metabolism to a level where it can burn nearly anything.

You unwrap the foil and sink your teeth in. Aaah...lovely! The wheat, beans and rice are a tad heavy—earth elements are that way—but the pepper adds a bit of fire which heats the goop and draws water from the cells. The water breaks apart the stodgy carb molecules and gets them moving through the system. Want a really nice touch to complete your meal? Sin intelligently and have a Coke. Yes, the sugar and the carcinogens are not all that helpful, but the water replaces the water the peppers leached from your cells and the bicarbonate of soda insures against indigestion.

Before the Industrial Revolution, most cultures had simple honest diets that provided a reasonable balance of sattva, rajas and tamas because they were evolved by hard working common sense people. It is only in the last one hundred and fifty years in wealthy industrial nations that the balance has become distorted, and fiber, which is sattvic and essential for health, removed or greatly reduced in modern diets.

Wealth makes luxury possible and luxury is the enemy of common sense. When elites, ever on the lookout for more pleasure and stimulation, develop diets, they tend to eschew simple foods. Snobby, rich foodies, for example, often make a big fuss over French cuisine for its meats and exotic sauces. "Ah, oui, extraordinaire!" Sauces are basically dishonest. Relics of the pre-Industrial age when refrigeration was virtually non-existent, they were used to disguise rotting meats. If a steak is so wonderful, why hide it behind a complex sauce? Indian cuisine—particularly North Indian—suffers the sauce disease.

Masalas and gravies add very little to the actual content of the food. They are used to kill bacteria. Ninety percent of the population does not have access to refrigeration in India. As food is expensive in India, a poor country, they make bland food tasty so as to suppress appetite. Sauces can be healthy, like salsas, but by and large they only serve to distract bored palates. In any case, our tamasic burrito has suddenly become much less tamasic with the addition of the fire and water elements and we leave the taqueria without any karmic drag. Well, all that sugar and chemicals from the Coke cannot be doing a lot of good, but what the hell, you're only young once, right?

Citric acid, found in fruits, is water and fire and is an effective purifier. The water flushes the system and the fire purifies. If you pour oil, which is tamasic, in a saucer and squeeze lemon juice on it, the terrified fat molecules break apart and run away. At one time, the latest most incredible fat burning diet in the US was the grapefruit diet. Extract of the seeds of grapefruits can prevent colds in their early stages, because rajas destroys the tamasic mucous laden environment that bacteria and viruses favor.

Knowledge of the air element is useful too. It can be used to control the fire element. For example, if the mind is too active, regulating the breath can bring it to clarity. If the water element is excessive, the mind may become emotional. Through conscious breathing, the air element can dry or evaporate the water element and produce a sattvic mind. If the body is heavy and uncomfortable, cardiovascular exercise increases the air element in the blood, which activates the metabolism—fire cannot burn without oxygen—which consumes fat. Exercise, not rajasic food, is the best way to attack tamas.

Water is all the rage these days, as if it was a recent invention. The water craze is good in spite of the fact that it was cooked up by greedy geniuses on Madison Avenue. They will get us to buy air next. It may not be common knowledge any more, but you can still get water from the tap and save. It is a sign of the sorry state of western civilization when the public needs to be informed that a thirsty body only wants water. It might be helpful to note that the human race did quite well for a few million years without Coke and manufactured water soluble vitamins. The addition of caffeine, sugar and other tastes panders to psychological needs and does not contribute to health.

Sugars, for example, are useless empty calories in their refined state. Taken in the form of fresh fruit, however, they provide clean-burning, efficient fuel. Pure water, uncontaminated by sugars and stimulants, collects rather than deposits contaminants as it passes through the body.

To further refine our model, we need to look more closely at the relationship of the three strands of the guna rope. So far it seems that rajas is rajas, sattva is sattva, and tamas is tamas. But when we put the eye of inquiry on each of these energies, a more complex picture emerges. We see that each guna has elements of the other two. Sattva has a bit of rajas and tamas. Rajas has a bit of sattva and tamas and tamas has a bit of sattva and rajas. No guna is completely pure. If we take edible oils, for example, which are tamasic, we see a range from tamasic tamasic to tamasic sattvic. When you first press an olive, for example, it has a lot of earthy substance to it; you can even spread it on a piece of bread like thick butter, but as you filter out more and more of the earth element, it becomes more and more watery until the oil becomes extremely sattvic or "lite." Butter is fat from milk and is very tamasic. It is bad or good depending on the quantity and the quality. It is very tamasic, no doubt, but it is sattvic compared to the thick white fat surrounding a cut of beef, for example. Cholesterol is bad, assuming heart attacks are bad, because it clogs. You cannot break apart the fat molecules with the water element; you need rajas, the fire element. Because aspirin is rajasic, it can break up clusters of fats in the arteries. Feelings of sluggishness and laziness are caused by too much tamas in the body.

In the example above of the man caught in the stressful rajas-tamas food cycle, sattva played almost no role. Yes, for a few moments he experienced clarity, but fundamentally he went from stimulation to sloth to stimulation, using one guna to manage the other. If we check in on him in his forties, we will see him suffering from a raft of medical issues and he will be a prime candidate for an early heart attack. For his life to work, he would have to break his addiction to coffee, cigarettes and tamasic foods, so that he has the clarity to see what he is actually doing to himself. Spiritual types, unlike worldly types, tend to be sattvic and are not as caught up on the gross material level as worldly types, but they have bodies and minds nonetheless. The struggle to find the right guna balance continues at all levels of evolution. There is no universally right body-mind. The body-mind instrument is only a tool the soul uses to achieve its goals.

According to the soul's desire, the vasanas determine the type of body. They select the appropriate materials and carefully craft the body. If I want to be a sumo wrestler, for example, I will need a preponderance of tamas for the body. But a big tamasic body is only useful if it can move efficiently; so to excel in my sport, my vital air sheath, the next level inward, must be very rajasic. The vital airs are the physiological systems: digestion, excretion, respiration, absorption, circulation and assimilation. They are rajasic by nature, but if the body becomes too tamasic they slow down and become inefficient, compromising the body's ability to move. The body cannot change itself, because it is not conscious. It will only change at the behest of consciousness. I am consciousness. So, if I find that my vital air sheath is sluggish, I must restrict the intake of tamasic foods, increase rajasic and sattvic foods and force the body to move.

Motion takes will. Will is located in the subtle body. If my subtle body is also predominately tamasic, my will power will be weak. Pleasure vasanas, like gluttony, sap the will. The food industry knows this and pitches diets that are meant to provide a nice light body without having to give up the foods you like! If will is strong, you will exercise. Desire is like fire and consumes excess tamas in the vital air sheath—raises metabolism to keep it simple— and makes movement easy. I now have my big tamasic body and lots of vital energy, but to move the body in tricky ways to confuse my opponent, I need the ability to think creatively. The thinking faculty is located at an even deeper level of the subtle body than the will. If it is tamasic, I am certainly at the mercy of an opponent whose intellect is sattvic, assuming similar energy levels and body weights.

Consciousness shines brightly in a sattvic intellect. The less rajas and tamas in the intellect, the more intelligent it is. Intelligence is consciousness reflected on the intellect. It is not a property of the ego. But pure sattva is not enough. You can be very intelligent and very unsuccessful at the same time. Sattva is the aspect of consciousness that sees, but does not act. It gathers information. If it is disturbed by too much rajas or distorted by too much tamas, the information will be faulty. To act—thinking is an action—rajas is required. So to outsmart my opponent, I need a clear active mind and the power to think creatively. Creative thought is the ability to see the variables in the field, their relationship to each other and how they relate to what I am trying to accomplish. You may have a big sluggish body, but if your intellect is predominately sattvic, with a generous dollop of rajas, you will be creative.

If tamas has penetrated so deeply into my being that my intellect is dull, I will not be successful. Success requires adaption because life is constantly changing. Life continually makes suggestions to help me grow. If I resist everything, I am as good as dead. Changing diet is difficult, upping the energy level is difficult, keeping a high level of desire is difficult but changing the nature of one's thoughts is exceptionally difficult.

Tamasic thinking is conditioned thinking. Partisan thinking and religious thinking are good examples. We have been conditioned to a set of beliefs and opinions by our environments. We take them to be the truth and cling to them tooth and nail. We are convinced they are right and that having them makes us right. Even if they conflict with reality and make us miserable, we tend to cling to them. Ex-Vice President Cheney still thinks that going to war in Iraq was the right thing. Let us say you are a fundamentalist Christian and believe the world was created in seven days, five thousand years ago. When they find a two-million-year-old dinosaur skeleton on your Montana ranch and offer you a million dollars, you have a problem because the scientific view does not fit your view of reality. If you sell, you are selling out, admitting that the evolutionists are right. Better forgo the million and stick to your irrational belief. Your church, meaning other dull people who think like you, will honor you for sticking to the truth. Unless, of course, you offer to donate the million to Jesus.

If our sumo wrestler cannot think quickly and creatively, he will not become a champion. There is virtually no progress in the world, because most people, no matter how active, have dull intellects. Fear causes dullness. Fear is ignorance and ignorance is a cloud that veils the truth. There are simple ways to solve the Israeli-Palestinian problem, but neither side will let go of its fears, so the same tired arguments surface over and over *ad nauseum*. Whether your goals are worldly or spiritual, they will not be realized if your thinking is tamasic.

If you want to change your thinking, you need to expose your mind to the truth. Not the religious truth, the political truth, the scientific truth or the artistic truth, but the truth truth. What is the truth? Reality is non-dual, all appearances to the contrary notwithstanding, and I am non-separate from it. All self-defeating and conflict-inducing thoughts flow from the non-appreciation of this fact. If you want to realize it, you need to expose your mind to it in a disciplined way.

When the emotional sheath is sattvic, the individual loves without attachment. If it is rajasic, love will be passionate, obsessive and possessive. When love turns to hate, it is under the influence of tamas. If our wrestler's girlfriend runs off with his best friend and his emotional body is tamasic, he will become despondent and perhaps lose interest in food. If the tamas persists, he will lose weight and become non-competitive. If his emotional sheath is sattvic, he will momentarily be angry but will soon accept her decision and be happy for both of them.

At the level of the thought sheath, if the diet is too rajasic, the mind will be scattered and unable to concentrate. If it is tamasic, clear thinking will be difficult. Only knowledge and will, not food or emotional harmony, can change thinking patterns. Because the intellect is the subtlest sheath, it has a disproportionate impact on the emotions and the body. If you change the idea of who you are in line with the highest knowledge, emotional problems will resolve more or less effortlessly. When the emotional center is resolved, it is easy to effect diet and lifestyle changes.

Because reality is non-dual, nothing stands alone; everything impacts on everything else. The subtle sheaths are more powerful than the gross sheaths, but the gross sheaths impact on the subtle as well. Sadly, you cannot eat your way to happiness. The obsession with food in America shows that the group mind—which is always tamasic-rajasic in materialist societies—is under the grip of a delusion. Unable to determine the spiritual, moral and intellectual causes of its unhappiness, it predictably looks to the material aspect alone for a solution.

To make food work for you spiritually, you need to change the way you think about food, hence this discussion. This is difficult, because food thinking is related to your vision of your self and the world. Instead of blindly accepting how you have been conditioned to think about yourself and the world, inquiry is necessary. Inquiry should be guided by impersonal knowledge of the nature of reality, action and the dynamics of the psyche.

Our sumo wrestler prizes a tamasic body, but a ballerina eschews even an ounce of fat. She needs an extremely light and limber sattvic body. Self inquiry does not require a particular body type, although the body should be strong and healthy, because meditation and self inquiry are acts of mind. However, a meditation life style needs to be particularly sattvic, because the mind should be relatively free of agitation and dullness. A fight with strong extroverting and veiling energies is the last thing you want. In meditation, the mind should be clear and fixed on the self, so that self knowledge can take place.

The goal is peace of mind. Your sacred mantra should be: less is more. The more decisions I have to make, the more activities I do, the more possessions I am responsible for, the more relationships I maintain, the less peace of mind I enjoy. A pressurized, city dwelling, multitasking lifestyle does not work for inquiry. A sattvic lifestyle provides the opportunity to allocate time to cultivate higher values and to conserve the energy necessary for self inquiry.

Most health problems in Western materialist cultures are caused by psycho-spiritual factors, i.e., rajas and tamas. They can be reduced to a single cause: stress. Stress is anxiety over results. Debt-financed spending causes psychological anxiety. Overwork is debt financed activity. You cannot keep it up without paying the price. The more unfulfilled I am spiritually, the more stress producing activities I will do, not realizing that non-doing is the solution. Thanks to the vasanas, stressful activity only produces more stress. When I override the need for rest and drive the body excessively for long periods, it gets sick. Here are three ways to relieve stress. Realize who you are. Unless you are particularly lucky, this is like exhorting you to win the lottery or inherit a fortune. Reduce the number of extroverting activities. This will be particularly difficult without option three, karma yoga. If you take this attitude toward action and its results, it will reduce stress. The purpose of a simple lifestyle is to accumulate energy for the purpose of self inquiry.

The fatigued conservative part of the mind will resist a move to a simpler life, because it resists all changes, good and bad. It would prefer to have you sit still and make excuses. The dramatic rajasic part will try to convince you that the project involves great expense and commitment, one that you are not quite ready to undertake, considering all the other important things that require your attention. But if a sudden awakening inspires you to leave your hectic life and head for a cave in India to fast, meditate and pray, do not sell the farm. You will be back in the center of your busy life before you know it. There are no quick fixes.

To gain the freedom to live a pure life, you need to start small. Look at your schedule and drop one small item. Work through the resistance to letting go. Once you are comfortable without your superfluous X, let go of one more activity. Do not return the calls of an energy sucking friend who just wants you to hold his or her hand and say, "There, there, you poor dear." Buy the house with the one-car garage, not the three-car garage. Instead of renting storage space, sell, throw out or donate to charity all the stuff that forced you to park outside your three-car garage. Tell your spoiled, lazy brats to get a job when they ask for the latest iPhone. Drink one less cup of coffee a day. Go out for Thai food instead of pizza. Go tent camping close to home instead of renting a thirty foot Winnebago with satellite TV, microwaves and a Jacuzzi and heading for the Grand Canyon. Once you get the hang of it, you will notice that you have more energy and feel better overall. Your bank account will grow. Keep at it day after day, year after year. If you are meant to live in a cave, the cave will appear one fine day and you will enjoy the experience.

Eat to live, do not live to eat. Enjoy a diet of easily digestible and effortlessly excreteable, high energy, fresh foods that keep the physiological systems humming. Develop sensible work and sleep patterns. See to it that your environment is clean and the objects are placed consciously with reference to each other. Listen to uplifting music and chose art that reminds you of who you are. Do sex with love. Manage relationships with the karma yoga attitude. Pay attention to every detail. No object or activity is more or less important than any other. No matter how relatively quiet your mind becomes, relentlessly burnish it until the radiant, charismatic, unalloyed self shines in all its glory.

# CHAPTER TWELVE

# Knowledge Yoga

Devotional yoga transforms emotion into devotion, action yoga exhausts subconscious tendencies, the yoga of the three gunas transforms anything on any level, and knowledge yoga utilizes the intellect's power of discrimination, analysis and inquiry—guided by scripture's proven teachings—to separate awareness and the objects appearing in awareness. As long as confusion between the self and objects obtains, the individual remains bound to objects. Freedom is freedom from dependence on objects.

As we know, knowledge—not experience—destroys ignorance. Experience of the self in the form of its reflection in an arrested mind will result in enlightenment, assuming the knowledge "I am whole and complete, actionless awareness" arises and is completely assimilated. Unless you understand that enlightenment is self knowledge however, you will probably not take the self as your primary identity. The spiritual world is little more than hundreds of thousands of individuals whose sense of limitation has survived epiphanies too numerous to mention. Knowledge born of inquiry is not a one-off. It requires constant practice, until the last vestiges of duality are removed.

Because the intellect is the self's subtlest function, it is the most influential. Emotion and action proceed from thought, because the mind and the body are down line from the intellect. Even impulsive, emotionally inclined individuals, who seem to react irrationally at every opportunity, are motivated by ideas. They do not realize it, however, because their attention is extroverted, making them incapable of introspection. Self ignorance manifests first as confused and unrealistic thinking. It subsequently trickles down to disturb and delude the emotions and eventually contaminate the individual's contact with the world. Because it eliminates incorrect, ignorance born thinking, self knowledge produces a harmonious, clear and luminous subtle body.

Knowledge yoga is self inquiry. Knowledge has always been a hard sell, no more so than in today's materialistic world, where people are so stupefied by their senses, they are too confused and lazy to think. That it is "only intellectual" is the most frequent argument used against self knowledge. This view is understandable, because individuals often claim to know things of which they have no direct knowledge. A person who has never been in love, for example, cannot claim to know what love is, except as a concept. However, knowledge does not need to be backed by personal experience to work. One need not personally split an atom to get the knowledge of how to split an atom; application of pre-existing knowledge will split it.

The indictment that self knowledge is only intellectual is based on ignorance of how knowledge works. To bolster the charge that knowledge is only intellectual, it is believed that self knowledge is a special kind of "experiential" knowledge. Self knowledge is not experiential, not that such a category of knowledge actually exists, because the self is always experienced—whether or not it is known. It is apparently not experienced because ignorance stands in the way, so inquiry removes ignorance. Self knowledge is like the knowledge of anything else, with an important difference: once the self is known it cannot be forgotten, because it is always present, unlike all other known objects.

However, it is possible for an individual to lack confidence in the knowledge for various reasons, in which case it might be said that his or her knowledge was only intellectual. But the fact remains that all knowledge is intellectual, in so far as the intellect is the only instrument of knowledge we have. Even those who claim that knowledge is only intellectual are guilty of the sin of intellectual knowledge, because the idea that there is another kind of knowledge is also an intellectual belief.

The argument that self knowledge is intellectual can only stand when you are ignorant of the amazing power of knowledge to transform your life. Those who argue against it are forced to sit around waiting for the next epiphany to set them straight. Or they are forced to use false knowledge—that knowledge is only intellectual, for instance—to deny the reality of their experience. But when you realize how knowledge works, you will become a convert.

When you first hear the idea that you are whole, complete, ordinary, actionless awareness, they are only words. But when you reflect on them, you discover a depth of meaning that takes you beyond whatever suffering you happen to be experiencing at the moment. The meaning does not reside in the words, but in the change in your relationship to your suffering. You can no longer own it. You discover that you are free of it. The knowledge does not cause the transformation, although it seems to. It simply removes the ignorance that produced the suffering in the first place, and the reality of who you are is obvious.

When the knowledge that friction is caused by an improper understanding of the nature of reality and is a symptom of self ignorance becomes established in the mind, our daily sufferings become an instruction to turn our attention to the self. Any point of conflict is an opportunity to practice knowledge. When you really understand that self ignorance is the cause of suffering, you become powerless to act, think and feel in any way that is contrary to the truth of who you are. If self knowledge is merely intellectual, it is certainly superior to any other kind of knowledge.

Self knowledge is not "intuitive" knowledge either. Self knowledge cannot be negated because the object of knowledge is always present and eternal. But intuition, which is a subtle perception, is unreliable because it is subject to error. It may tell you one thing about an object one moment and something else later. Although the notion of predetermination is as old as the hills, recent studies have shown that your mind is made up before you make it up. In some way you know what is going to happen—or the nature of a particular object—before you think you know. When the mind is particularly still, it may present this unconscious determination to the conscious mind as a flash of insight or as a very subtle attraction or aversion. The value that an individual places on intuition is often connected to anxiety about what is happening or about to happen. If the karma yoga attitude is in place, any outcome is acceptable, because the goal is not to obtain a particular result, but to neutralize likes and dislikes, in this case the anxiety about what will be. Knowledge of reality is required to make sense of our intuitions. Finally, the karma yoga attitude is based on incontrovertible hard and fast knowledge of reality: the doer is not the giver of results.

To gain the vision of non-duality, words are extremely helpful. The argument that enlightenment only happens in silence is untrue, because silence is not opposed to ignorance. If inquiry takes place in silence, it may result in enlightenment. But words are much more likely to result in enlightenment, because they can function as vehicles for knowledge. Only knowledge cancels ignorance.

Self inquiry uses many negative words to reveal the self, because awareness is not an object of a given word. It is the awareness in which words arise. It is simultaneously everything and free of everything, so what word can describe it? To say that it is beyond everything is not correct, because awareness is everything. It has no qualities or attributes, so what can be said except that it has no qualities or attributes? We cannot use words to directly describe awareness, because it is not the ostensible meaning of any word.

Even though words need objects and the self cannot be objectified, words can be used in such a way that their implied meaning reveals the self. Because the perceiver cannot see the self, words are required to reveal it. The words of scripture come from awareness. Awareness knows itself and knows that some part of it does not know. Because it is limitless, it has the power to seemingly not know itself and to evolve the teachings that can remove its seeming ignorance. In any case, certain experiential things cannot be described in words, like love. The only way it can be known is through experience. But experiential knowledge does not apply to awareness, because it is the essence of every experience and as such, cannot be turned into an object.

Therefore, how are you going to see awareness? You cannot see awareness just as you cannot see your eyes, because whatever self is seeing now is awareness. The fact that you see means that you have eyes. All that can happen is that awareness recognizes itself. The right words can bring about recognition. So when we say that awareness cannot be described, it can only be the implied meaning of a word, not the direct meaning. For instance, as you read the words on this paper, it seems that you are only experiencing the words, but if you investigate the situation you will see the existence of words implies the existence of paper. The paper provides the context for the experience of the words. They are separate from the paper, but they are also not separate from the paper either, because they cannot exist without the paper. It is important to understand this point, because if awareness is not available through words, what is the point of the scriptures that make up the science of self inquiry?

Perhaps you would like to argue that the implied meaning of words cannot give direct knowledge. If a black dog is chasing its tail next to a black chair, and you say "the black is chasing its tail," I understand by the context that the black dog, not the black chair, is chasing its tail. In this case, direct knowledge is delivered by implication, even though the word *black* refers to a color, not a dog. Scripture says that the self is neither near, nor far; that it is neither inward turned consciousness, nor outward turned consciousness, nor a mass of consciousness. This does not describe it directly but by contemplating the words, the implied meaning becomes clear.

Words convert experience into a language that can be helpful for negotiating the body and mind through life. Ideally, we would understand the abstraction involved and not take the words to be accurate descriptions of what is experienced. But we often imagine that the way the mind describes experience is true to experience. When consciousness, under the spell of ignorance, perceives an object, it creates a word, an "I," that is apparently separate from the object. The statement "I see you" is not the experience of seeing you. The experience of seeing you is the experience of the self seeing the self in the form of an object. It is therefore assumed that the mind is the problem, as far as the realization of the self is concerned. And since the currency of the mind is words, it is assumed that both the mind and its words are the problem. But they are not the problem. The concepts that it has abstracted from its experience are in conflict with what is actually experienced. Experience will not rid the mind of erroneous notions. Only knowledge will. And knowledge comes in the form of words. So we need words that destroy ignorance. We need a word mirror that destroys belief or converts beliefs to knowledge and reveals reality as it is.

## The Methodology of Inquiry

In reality there is no knowledge and no ignorance, no bondage and no liberation; I certainly exist but I do not exist as a unique individual. If I feel incomplete, separate and inadequate, denying my individuality is not helpful. This is why Neo-Advaita, the latest iteration of the instant enlightenment idea, is an inadequate means of enlightenment. It takes more than a few negative affirmations—no path, no teaching, no teacher, etc.—to solve my problem. I need a way to work myself out of my ignorance, step by step.

Vedanta's proven methodology is called superimposition and negation. It posits the existence of duality, which coincides with the experience of everyone, even though it is not true, and then proceeds to systematically destroy duality by inquiry. The negations arrived at by understanding the teachings of self inquiry are effective, unlike the mindless denials of Neo-Advaita, because they are backed by logic and experience. By far the most common method is the discrimination between the self and its many forms.[34] Although belief is an aid to inquiry, how is the belief "I am awareness" different from believing in the existence of God? I need to know why I am not separate to give my belief in non-duality teeth.

In the twilight a thirsty traveler approached a village well. Reaching down, he recoiled in fear when he saw a big snake coiled next to the bucket. Unable to move for fear of being bitten, he imagined terrible things, including his own death. An old man that was coming to the well noticed him standing petrified with fear.

---

34. This teaching is called *sat-asat viveka*, the discrimination between the real, i.e., the self and objects.

"What's the problem?" he asked kindly.

"Snake! Snake! Get a stick before it strikes!" he whispered frantically.

The old man burst out laughing.

"Hey!" he said, "Take it easy. That's no snake. It's the well rope. It just looks like a snake in the darkness."

Though the traveler was never in danger, the misperceived rope produced intense fear. Our existential fears come from confusing the self and the world of duality. The fear of the snake arose simultaneously with the misperception of the rope, and it vanished when the rope was known.

Superimposition can be conditional or unconditional. The snake and the rope is an example of unconditional superimposition. It means that once the rope is perceived, it is impossible to take it to be a snake, because the snake has vanished. You may understand how the mistake was made when you consider the conditions obtaining when it occurred, but you cannot actually perceive a snake as long as you are looking at the rope. This means that as long as you know that the self is whole and complete and non-separate from you, you will not take yourself to be separate, inadequate and incomplete.

Even if you are dying of thirst and see a lake on the desert, you will not try to drink the water, because you know it is unreal. This is called conditioned superimposition. The self is known but the world remains, apparently, but not actually, conditioning it. In other words, you can go about your life as usual when you know that you are awareness, minus the suffering that was brought on by the confusion between the self and objects.

## The Practice of Knowledge

The practice of knowledge is discrimination. Discrimination negates superimposition. Because the self is not known, the gross, subtle and causal bodies are assumed to be real. To take them to be the self causes suffering, because they are only apparently real. Reality, awareness, is always present and never changes. The three bodies are "not-self." They are to be negated, until identification with them and attachment to them is dissolved. Identification and attachment to the apparently real prohibits identification with the real. Non-attachment

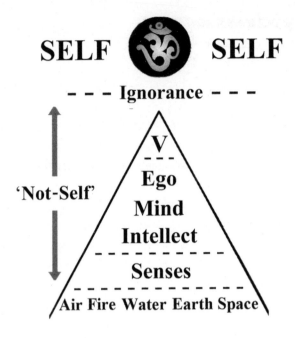

is not merely the intellectual conviction that the states, bodies, and objects are unreal, but it is the experience of freedom arising from the destruction of one's connection to them. Of course they are not "not-self," because reality is non-dual, but some part of you does not appreciate this fact, so you have to go through this process until you do, assuming you want to be free.

The three bodies are often referred to as sheaths, in the sense that they hide or cover the self. In fact, the self is self evident and cannot be covered by anything, but attachment to thoughts, feelings and bodily sensations keeps attention on them and not on the self. To reuse an example, although I cannot actually read the words on this page without experiencing the page, my focus on the words keeps me from appreciating the presence of the page. To know the background of my experience, my perceptions, sensations, thoughts and feelings need to be separated from it. Discrimination is not an experiential separation of the subject from the objects, astral travel or an out of body experience. The self cannot be taken out of the bodies because it was never in them in the first place, although often when the self is realized, it seems like an experiential shift, because we are so deeply accustomed to take the physical body as our point of reference. The shift is purely in terms of understanding although inquiry is also experiential, in so far as effort is involved and there is a positive result every time the not-self is dismissed. In fact, the bodies are "in" the self, in the sense that they are within the scope of awareness, not outside it, even though they appear as objects.

Discrimination is not intellectual; it is experiential. But ironically, it works only if experience is negated. To negate experience, you have to have had enough experience to have become disillusioned by experience. If you still entertain doubts about the futility of the pursuit of fulfillment in samsara, discrimination will not work. But if you are doubt free on this issue, discrimination works. The criticism that discrimination is "only intellectual" is based on the assumption that there are no qualifications for enlightenment. But, as we have shown, there are many qualifications, all of which can be reduced to the hard and fast, experience-based conviction that the world is not real and the self is real. The negation implied by discrimination is not intellectual either. To simply assert that something is not real is only a preliminary step. You have to actually refuse to indulge the vasanas pushing you into experiences, until they are rendered non-binding. You may very well know who you are and who you are not, but your vasanas do not. And even if they did, it is unlikely they would eliminate themselves. You have to do it. There is nothing intellectual about it. Discrimination is a practical, experiential method that has quantifiable experiential results. Every time you negate the not-self, peace and happiness ensue.

To practice discrimination, you need to keep up with the incessant stream of subjective events, dispassionately observing the quality, texture and volume of thought and feeling, not to change it but to simply understand how ignorance works. As the *whys* become apparent, unhealthy thought and feeling patterns drop off naturally. Consistent observation of the subtle body will eventually expose the true observer, awareness. In reality, observation is not something to be done. It is what one is.

Awareness of the observer indicates that the mind is becoming subtle and raises a new question—who is the observer? Is it the ego? The mind? The intellect? The self? All or none of the above? Is the ego to be discriminated out of the picture? If so, who will do it? If the self is the discriminator, what will it discriminate, since from its position nothing other than it exists? These and other equally weighty questions need to be resolved for inquiry to bear fruit.

## Cause and Effect

This discrimination shows that the self is limitless and that the world is not separate from it. It presents awareness as the cause of the universe and the universe as an effect enjoying a different order of reality.

An effect depends on its cause. The individual's body and mind are within the creation and are dependent on it. The body and mind are inert and cannot create anything; to create, a conscious factor is required. Therefore they depend on awareness. Although awareness is not an individual, the individual is awareness and the reality of everything. If an effect is just its cause in a particular form, then the cause and the effect are non-separate. For example, although there are many different ornaments made of gold, from the standpoint of the gold, they are all the same. If everything in the universe is fashioned by a single cause, limitless awareness, then everything in the universe is limitless awareness. Therefore to know the essence of one thing is to know the essence of everything. To know salt water I need not drink the seven seas; I need only to take a sip from one. The realization that I am limitless awareness and that the whole universe is not separate from me is the result of this teaching.

The nature of fire is heat. If you take away the nature of something, it ceases to be what it is. Awareness is the nature of the self. It is not a quality that belongs to the self. The self is awareness and only awareness. Awareness supplies existence to the creation and all the things in it. What we call existence is limited to things that change. But awareness exists out of time. It has no limits and no divisions in it. You cannot find a beginning or an end to it. Because it has no beginning, it is unborn and non-dual. It is not created. None of these words say that awareness has a particular quality. In fact they negate all qualities. We call awareness the "cause" or the "higher" nature, for the purpose of discrimination, even though the notions of cause and effect, higher and lower do not obtain in reality.

To create, a cause is necessary. For example, to make a pot you need clay and a potter, someone with an idea and the energy to turn the clay into a pot. When we speak of the whole of existence, we say that the cause is awareness. But our metaphor breaks down when we try to apply it to awareness and existence, because awareness is non-dual. In our example, the potter and the clay are two different things. One supplies the substance and the other the intelligence and the energy. But awareness cannot be split into two. So it has to create in another way.

It has to be the cause and the effect, the potter and the pot. Normally, when something is created, the substance undergoes a change. If we want to make glass, we start with sand, apply heat, and end up with glass. But awareness creates by assuming a form, without surrendering its nature. You cannot find the sand in the glass because it has become the glass, but you can always find the awareness in anything because ignorance is the creator of the world.

In other words, the creation only seems to be something other than awareness. For instance, when you dream you are awareness observing the dream world, which is concocted out of your awareness. You are the substance of the dream, you are the intelligence that creates the dream world, and you are the energy that makes the dream happen. You are the subject and the object, the cause and the effect. Because you are the cause, you are not affected by the effect. It depends on you, but you do not depend on it. A spider's web is the spider, but the spider is not the web. The clay is always free of the pot, but the pot is not free of the clay. Enlightenment is the realization of this fact.

The effect, the creation, is called the lower nature. It is made up of the vasanas, mind, intellect, ego, the five physiological systems, the ten senses and the gross elements. It is in a state of constant flux and if you find yourself caught up in it, you will definitely suffer. If you try to get out of it by doing something, you will not get out, because it is not really there. So you are not actually in it, although you believe you are. However, if you are caught up in a dream, you can wake yourself up by making an inquiry into the dream. If you allow the teachings of self inquiry to guide your investigation, you will resolve the problem into its cause and the cause into awareness. All problems are apparent problems, never real problems.

## The Real and the Apparent

An object that on analysis cannot stand alone, or that can be resolved into another object or the self, should be considered "not-self" and taken to be only apparently real. Nothing that an unenlightened ego identifies with is real. This teaching exposes ego's false identifications. Something that is merely apparent is unsuitable as the basis of an identity. Apparent does not mean that an object is not experienceable. It means that it is not substantial and enduring. If my sense of well-being depends on something insubstantial and non-eternal, I will not be happy when it changes or when I discover that it is not what I think it is. The self, awareness, stands alone. Hence, if I am the self I am free of objects. To make identification with the self possible, I need to free myself of unsuitable identifications. Since my goal is freedom, I need a standalone identity.

For example, although it seems to be real, the physical body can be resolved into awareness. It is made of four gross elements: air, fire, water, earth. If we remove any one of the four, the body will no longer exist. Do the elements stand alone or do they depend on something else? They depend on much smaller units; let us call them atoms. How real are atoms? If we analyze the atoms we find that they are space and electrons, protons and neutrons. We can now discard the atoms, because they do not stand alone. As we move even deeper, we come upon mesons, quarks and neutrinos and we see that the spaces between them are as vast as the spaces between galaxies. We can now dismiss the electron level. At this point, a new factor enters our analysis. The particles lose their shape and become waves of energy. Now we have waves of energy playing in space. How real is something if it is one thing one minute and something else the next? If we keep concentrating on energy we find that it seems to come out of space and disappear back into space. So space is the reality, the substrate, and energy is the apparent reality. When we discard energy, we are left with space and awareness. We cannot resolve awareness into space as it does not depend on space for its existence. Space, however, depends on awareness because without awareness space cannot be perceived. Therefore, we can resolve space into awareness. From the level of the gross body, all the way down to the level of infinite space, all existent objects are only names and forms. They have no existence apart from their substrate.

Now, try to negate awareness, the substrate. It is impossible, because awareness is non-dual and cannot be objectified. To turn awareness into an object there would have to be a second awareness somewhere that was subtler than the first awareness. But this is not possible, because awareness cannot be split up into layers, levels or parts. It is irreducible. The final stage of this discrimination is to determine whether or not awareness is the same as you or different from you. It obviously cannot be different. Therefore you are awareness and not the body.

This inquiry can be applied to any object, including the subtle and causal bodies. Do my thoughts and feelings stand alone? If they do, I can take them to be me. But analysis shows that the content of the subtle body is wholly dependent on the causal body, the seeds of my past actions. And does causal body, the source of my fears and desires, stand alone? The causal body is dependent on ignorance of who I am. Ignorance of my identity is not who I am either, because it depends on awareness. If I am not aware, how can I be ignorant?

All subtle body phenomena depend on each other. The mind is a rich tapestry of interwoven, interdependent psychic threads. So the self cannot be a thought or a feeling. Ego, the "I notion" depends on self ignorance. Ego is also unreal because it does not exist in deep sleep, where all differences are dissolved. Ignorance is destroyed by knowledge, because it ends when knowledge arises. Knowledge depends on awareness. You cannot know anything unless you are aware. Therefore I am not what I know. Thinking depends on the intellect, the thinker. The thinker depends on awareness. Thought depends on the conditioning and conditioning depends on experience, and experience depends on awareness. So I cannot be what I think or experience. Without me, awareness, nothing exists.

Identification with time is an obvious source of suffering and can be removed by analysis. As we increase the units from nanoseconds to milliseconds, to seconds and on up to years, centuries, ages and so on, the space between the units increases until time eventually disappears and only space, which on analysis turns out to be nothing more than a concept, remains. As noted, space is a concept that requires a witnessing consciousness. Concepts can be further reduced to mind and mind to awareness because the mind is just one of the functions of awareness. Awareness is not reducible, because before you know of the existence of an object, you have to be there as awareness.

Or if this analysis seems to be too abstract, consider the fact that time is different for every individual. One hour in a torture chamber is not equal to one hour at an exciting movie. Time, like space, is dependent on the desires and attachments of the one that experiences it. Attachments and desires are only transitory phenomena. In deep sleep they do not exist. So they cannot be me. How real, meaning enduring, can something that depends on something else be?

That everything on any level of existence is merely apparently real may be difficult to accept. These inquiries are not meant to become objects of faith, but they are intended to encourage us to think about reality in a radical way. When we discriminate the apparent from the real, the inner worlds defrost, and the rigid barriers that make life painful break up like ice in spring. If the intellect no longer makes uninformed judgments about an apparent reality, or fritters away time gathering objective knowledge, but instead turns attention on itself and discriminates dispassionately, our responses become natural and spontaneous. And ultimately, although discrimination means we must face continual disillusionment, in the end we are paradoxically led to the realization that everything on every level of existence is real, because it is the self.

## Essential and Non-Essential

The self is free of attributes. What is essential to an object should be present as long as the object exists. If it is not present, then it is an incidental attribute. Clear water in a green glass is perceived to be green. But when the glass is removed, it is no longer perceived to be green. The apparent waking state entity—me—is a perceiver of gross and subtle objects. This fact leads to the erroneous conclusion that the self is a perceiver and that perception is the essence of the self. But what happens to the perceiver and perception in the deep sleep state, where there are no objects to perceive? What happens to the notion that the self is a doer and an enjoyer in deep sleep? They do not exist. Therefore they are incidental, non-essential attributes and cannot be the self.

There is a notion in the spiritual world that there is no self. It probably arose from the belief that something without attributes cannot exist. But even though the self has no attributes, it is not non-existent. Non-existence is just a concept. It is a concept because we need a knower to know non-existence. If we inquire into the knower, we can only conclude that the knower is awareness because knowledge cannot happen without awareness. And since awareness is never non-existent, there is no such thing as non-existence.

Is there a world without someone to see it? Yes, if that someone is the perceiver-feeler-thinker entity, a non-essential attribute of the self, because this would mean that the world did not exist when the ego was non-existent, as it is in deep sleep. However, the existence of the empirical reality does not depend on the existence of any individual. It cannot be said to exist, if it is not known to exist. To say that it exists independently of awareness is meaningless. Because the self is awareness, it is limitless. The world that depends on the perceiver, the ego and its projections, is only an apparent reality, neither completely existent, nor completely non-existent. This is why it is inaccurate to say that the ego does not exist. It neither exists, nor does it not exist. It is an incidental attribute of the self.

## Change and Changelessness

If the discrimination between the real and the apparent is too difficult to understand, the discrimination between change and changelessness is a simple way to separate the self from the not-self. Experience takes place when the ego, motivated by the vasanas, uses the gross and subtle bodies to contact or avoid contact with objects in their respective fields. In spite of the unhappy fact that the bodies and their objects are in constant flux, the ego has somehow been led to believe that hooking the bodies up with objects will resolve its sense of limitation. But because all transactions, even the good, are perishable, this approach is bound to fail. If something changes—and what object does not?—it is only apparently real and can be dismissed as not-self.

## Subject-Object

Subject-object is a discrimination we set up in the first chapter and have employed throughout this text. Like the other teachings of self inquiry, it provisionally accepts duality with the intention of leading the inquirer through the process that destroys the belief in duality.

That physical objects are perceived is easy to grasp. For example, I see my hand. My hand is certainly me, but I am not my hand. I perceive my hand, but my hand does not perceive me. This means my hand is not conscious. But I am conscious. Therefore, I cannot be my hand. It should not be difficult to understand that emotions are also perceived objects, even though they are subtler than physical objects. It is only marginally more difficult to see that thoughts are perceived objects. It is more difficult, however, to see the thinker as a perceived object, because we think we are the thinker. For the same reason it is almost impossible to see the ego as an object. The more subtle an object—the ego is just an idea—the more difficult it is to objectify. This discrimination is based on a simple fact: I cannot be what I perceive.

If inquiry is going to bear fruit, it should continue during periods of happiness. If the one feeling fine today was not feeling fine yesterday, the inquiry has objectified the ego. When the ego is objectified, the expectation that happiness should last disappears, since the ego is nothing more than the self identifying with ever changing fears and desires. Happiness is an object and should be understood to be not-self. It is not-self, because it is not conscious. It is an experience that comes and goes. Discriminating the subject from the objects is difficult, because ignorance has conditioned us to believe security and pleasure reside in objects.

The ego, an incidental attribute of the self, need not be weaned from its attachment to happiness or to helpful objects. It will always be attached to something, because it is within the framework of existence. As long as the object is beneficial, like the practice of knowledge, prayer or meditation, attachment is temporarily useful. The purpose of discrimination is to see the ego as an object and to realize that the self is always separate from everything. A non-attached ego is not liberation. In fact, it is a contradiction in terms. Liberation is freedom from the ego. Once the self is owned, perceived objects are known to be non-separate from the self.

When we see objects, we presume that the body-mind-ego, the apparent "I," is the seer. But analysis of experience shows that this is not true. Is it not true that I experience my body, my mind and my ego? If your body is sick, you know it is sick. If you are emotional, you know that you are emotional. When someone inquires into your welfare, you can assess all the variables of your experience and issue a report. This means that there is another factor to which the body-mind-ego appears as an object, something that is there before they appear, something that knows them. For you to know something, you have to be conscious. So this factor is conscious. If you investigate your conscious-ness/awareness, you will discover that it is free of attributes and qualities. Ev-erything that has an attribute or a quality is limited. Heat is limited by cold, light by darkness, action by inaction, and love by hate. Every body-mind-intel-lect-ego has qualities. When you identify with them you limit yourself. To be limited is to suffer. But if you identify with the true subject—awareness—you are free of all qualities and not subject to suffering.

## The Three States

One of our most sophisticated discriminations involves an analysis of the three states of consciousness and their experiencing entities. The first entity is the waking state ego, the primary identity of everyone. When I say "me" in conversation, I am referring to the waking state entity. The belief that I am a waking state entity comes with the conviction that physical, emotional, and intellectual objects are real.

The waking state entity is consciousness turned outward, shining through the senses, mind and intellect, illumining their respective objects. The wak-ing state entity is a consumer of experience. Self Inquiry calls it "the one with thirteen mouths." The thirteen mouths refer to the ten senses, the mind, the

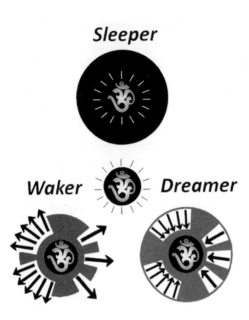

The three states

intellect and the ego. These instruments aggressively eat experience. The physical body consumes matter, the five elements in various combinations. The mind devours emotions; the intellect nibbles ideas; and the ego gobbles any experience it believes will make it feel whole, adequate, and happy.

The dreamer's consciousness is turned inward, awareness illumining a world similar in some respects to the waking state world and radically different in others. In the dream state, awareness illumines the vasanas playing out as images on the screen of awareness. In the waking state, the vasanas express as the waking state entity's thoughts and feelings. The waking world is not distorted like the dream world, because the senses structure it. Like the waking state entity, the dreamer believes his or her world is real. The dreamer is equipped with the same instruments for experience as the waking state entity: dream senses to consume dream objects, a dream mind to emote and feel, a dream intellect to think dream thoughts and a dream ego to go about the business of experiencing the dream life. In Sanskrit the dreamer is called *taijasa,* the shining one, to indicate that it is actually awareness. Dreams appear in light, even though the waking senses are inactive, because awareness shines through the dreamer, just as it shines through the waking state entity.

Sleep is defined as the state, saturated with happiness, where the self does not desire external objects, does not illumine internal objects and is self ignorant. The sleeper is called *prajna,* or mass of consciousness. In the other states, consciousness flows outward and inward but in sleep it is formless. The sleeper ego is extremely subtle, its presence indicated by the fact that we experience limitlessness and bliss. In the waking and dream states, bliss is sporadic because it is broken by many divisions of thought and feeling, but in sleep it is continuous. We know of the sleeper's experience because it reports a good sleep after transforming into a waking state entity. Were the waking state entity actually a different ego from the sleeper or the dreamer, it would not recall the experience of sleep or dream. In reality both are just consciousness.

The deep sleep state is free of both the waking and dream egos and their respective objects, because the vasanas projecting them have become dormant. Hence, it is referred to as the seed state. When the seeds sprout, the sleeper, who is actually the self, seemingly becomes a waking state entity or a dreamer and experiences the appropriate world.

Because the waking ego is transformed into a very subtle sleep ego, we do not think that we are conscious in deep sleep. This fact has erroneously lead metaphysicians to conclude that deep sleep is a void. But it is actually the womb of creation because the waking state entity, the dreamer, and their respective worlds emerge from it. When you wake up in the morning, your whole life is neatly laid out consistent with the day before, which indicates that the experiencer had simply entered a dormant state. The sleep state is called the causal body and contains the vasanas of every living being.

Because of its association with one of the three states of consciousness, non-dual awareness appears to be three distinct entities. Associated with the waking state, it "becomes" a waking state personality, suffering and enjoying the limitations of its world. The dreamer suffers the limitations of the dream world. And the sleeper suffers self-ignorance and limitless bliss.

These three states and egos are known to everyone and constitute the totality of experience. Once these facts have been established, the inquiry begins. If I am the waking ego, which I am convinced I am, what happens to me when I become a sleeper? I willingly surrender everything essential to my idea of myself (my body, mind, intellect, and all my physical possessions) and turn into a mass of limitless awareness. Yet in spite of the pleasure of sleep, I am not content, because I sacrifice my sleep identity to suffer and enjoy the worlds created by my vasanas in waking and dream states. My identity as a dreamer is obviously unsatisfactory, because I consistently leave it to become a sleeper or a waker. So my status as any ego or ego aspect is limited, and my true identity is open to question. Furthermore, if I identify with experiential happiness, I have a problem, because the happiness experienced in sleep disappears in the waking state. Dream happiness dissolves on waking, and waking happiness does not transfer to the sleep or dream states.

The answer to "Who am I?" is: I am not any of these ego entities. If I am real I have to exist all the time. I cannot suddenly be one thing one minute and something else the next. I experience life as a simple conscious being. In fact, the three ego entities are non-dual awareness, identified with the particular state they are experiencing. Awareness is the witness of the three states.

It is easiest to understand awareness by considering the dream state, because the physical senses are inactive. The dream is playing on the screen of awareness like a movie. Even though physical light is absent and the eyes are closed, the dream ego and the events in which it is participating are clearly illumined. The dream light is awareness functioning as the dreamer, "the shining one." However, ignorance operates in the dream as it does in the waking state. It causes the self to identify with the dream ego and its doings, preventing the realization of the dream light as me, the self.

The self is unknown in the waking state for the same reason. Preoccupied with the happenings in our worlds and minds, we are completely unaware that both the sense objects and our thoughts and feelings are bathed in the light of awareness.

In deep sleep the ego-intellect is dissolved into its source, the dormant seeds of its past actions. It is not aware of the self or anything external. Yet awareness is there, making the experience of bliss possible. And when we wake up we know that we slept, even though we were not there as the waking state entity, because awareness was there.

The three egos are called limiting adjuncts. A limiting adjunct apparently conceals the nature of something else. If I put clear water in a colored glass, the water, seen through the glass, appears colored. Similarly when I look at myself through my waking, dream and sleep personalities, I seem to be three distinct personalities. However, when I remove the adjunct I can see what I really am.

The removal or negation of the three experiencing entities is accomplished by simply knowing they are unreal. In the wake of this understanding, I am free to assume my true identity as awareness, because it is the only other option. Awareness cannot be denied or negated.

Over time, the waking state entity becomes fractured into many sub-identities, adjuncts within an adjunct, so that it is possible to be confronted with a confusing array of selves, none of which are real. Remember, real means enduring, unchanging and unlimited. Because something is experienced does not make it real, the blueness of the sky or a mirage on a desert, for example.

With reference to my son, I am a father. With reference to my father, a son. With reference to my wife, I am a husband. To my boss I am an employee. I am a devotee with reference to God and a taxpayer with reference to the government. With reference to myself I am a success, failure, victim, victimizer, sports fan, audiophile or any of the thousands of ready-made identities available today. The many often conflicting roles we play as waking egos are limited by each other, other selves playing similar or different roles, and our ideas about the meaning of these selves. Caught in this thicket of identities, is it any wonder I suffer? In the end, spiritual life, no matter what the path, always boils down to finding out who I am—minus all my roles and experiences.

Playing a role is fine, as long as you know you are playing a role. Society only functions efficiently when our roles are well-defined and we play them impeccably. But when we identify with our roles we suffer. The identification, not the role, is the problem. For example, although an actress identifies herself with the character she plays, she seamlessly returns to her original identity when the curtain falls. Even though the audience completely believes her illusion, she remembers her real self throughout.

After patient analysis, I can see that I am not any of my roles. What am I then? The limitless "I." And what is the limitless "I"? The limitless "I" is called the substrate. A substrate makes the error that I am limited possible. The rope in the example of the snake and the rope is a substrate, something whose nature makes it possible to mistake it for something else. The fact that I am formless awareness makes the playing of myriad roles possible. It is very easy to identify with conditioned roles because awareness cannot be perceived by the senses or the mind. It makes a perfect substrate, one that can support any identity.

When I inquire into the substrate, I find that I am whole and complete. I see that nothing is missing. Because nothing is missing, I am free of desire and because I am free of desire, I am peaceful. I see that I never change. When I look into my self, I see that it is free of all the forms appearing in it. The freedom of self realization is blissful like deep sleep, but I enjoy it consciously. When I inquire into bliss, I discover that I am pure love.

If I am awareness, why would I identify with anything else? Even when life asks me to play a role, I will never get caught up in the role if my self knowledge is firm. Freedom is not a mind-blowing mystical state. It is simply the condition of abiding in my true nature. To suppose that we need to transcend the three egos and enter the fourth state is incorrect, although it is a common belief. The enlightened sleep, dream and carry on a normal waking life, minus the feeling of limitation that bedevils the unenlightened. They are free of the expectation that experience should bring lasting happiness and they never deny the experience of duality, only its reality, because, like the snake in the rope, it is not actually there.

## The Five Sheaths

The five sheaths is a variation of the teaching of three bodies and the three states. It points out the universal errors in self understanding that occur at each of the five levels of experience. The non-apprehension of the self gives rise to five misconceptions about its nature. These misconceptions are called sheaths because they apparently hide the self. They need to be removed if the self is to be known as it is.

The most obvious self misunderstanding is "I am the body." The notions "I am mortal," "I am fat," "I am male or female," etc. indicate an association of the self with matter. Association of the "I" with the physiological systems causes one to say, "I am hungry," "I am thirsty," when in fact the "I," awareness, does not experience these sensations. The universal statements, "I am happy," "I am sad," etc. show that the "I" has been confused with the emotional body. When a person says "I did this," for example, it means the self has been confused with the ego. It is untrue, because the self is non-dual and cannot act. If someone says "I know this" it means that he or she has confused the self with the intellect. When you say "I feel good" you have confused the self with the causal body, the bliss sheath.

The application of this teaching follows a certain type of logic. First the self is introduced as the gross body, a common belief. Then it is shown that there is another subtler body, the feelings and emotions, which also are thought to be the self. When one's feelings are hurt, one will instinctively say "I was hurt by what she said." The second "self" negates the previous self because for a self to be a self it cannot be two, modern theories of multiple personalities notwithstanding. The word *self* means essence, that which is not made up of parts. Once the belief in oneself as the physical body is dropped and one accepts oneself as one's feelings, the teaching brings in the intellect self. It shows up as the concept "I am the doer/enjoyer" or "I am the knower," which is meant to remove the notion that the self is a feeler/thinker entity. When the limitation in the concept of the self as a doer or a thinker is grasped, the idea of the blissful self is introduced. The self is not blissful. Bliss is a condition that occurs when the self identifies with an incidental attribute, the causal body or bliss sheath. The bliss sheath is responsible for pleasure and its companion concept "I am an enjoyer." The doer and the thinker will give way to the enjoyer in every case, because doing and thinking are for the sake of enjoying, but enjoying is not for the sake of doing and thinking. Finally, the self is introduced as the source of bliss. I cannot enjoy anything unless I am there prior to the onset of the enjoyment. I know I am there prior to the enjoyment because I do not disappear when the enjoyment stops. Thus by tracing the "I" concept from the gross to the subtle, we are led to the self, the fundamental "I." The realization of the whole and complete "I" negates all the lesser selves and embraces the unlimited identity.

The teaching works when it becomes clear that the association of the "I" with these five basic but conflicting concepts is absurd, since we know experientially that we are only one being. The renunciation of limiting self concepts is tantamount to gaining or realizing the self. Although it shines on all concepts, the self is easy to recognize when the mind is free of attachment to concepts.

The idea that I need a technique to gain experiential access to the self because it is actually covered by the sheaths is a corruption of this teaching. Even if such techniques work, the transcender would enjoy only an experience of the self. Experience of anything is not liberation. If you think you went to a transcendental state, you are deluded because there is only one self and it cannot move. Finally, because both the experiencer and experience are impermanent, transcendence provides no lasting solution to the problem of limitation. It does not work because there is nothing to transcend, except ignorance.

## Why There Is Only You

Is the experiencer, the perceiver, the person you think you are, actually conscious? Let us assume you are conscious and you can see awareness. What do you see? Do you see any qualities or properties? How big is it? How far away is it? What color is it? If it is blue, how do you know if the blueness belongs to awareness or to you? After all, you look at the sky and it appears to be blue, but we know it is colorless. If the blueness belongs to the self, how can you see it if the self is beyond the scope of perception? To see it, it would have to be divided into a conscious subject and an object. But it cannot be divided, because it is non-dual. It can never become something else, because there is nothing other than it. It may seem to appear as an object, but ignorance can make the mind see many things that do not actually exist. Therefore, even if there is another self, it is impossible to know it. If you cannot know it, does it actually exist? Even if it did exist and it could not be known, what use would it be? The assumption that your means of knowledge, which you take to be you, is conscious is incorrect. The mind, intellect and senses are material instruments, no more conscious than a desk or a chair. They do not know anything. They reflect awareness and make the objects in their respective fields known, not to themselves but to you, awareness.

Let us assume for the sake of argument that duality exists. Is duality different or the same as awareness? If you say that it is different, it becomes a property of awareness, which is not possible, because awareness has no properties.

If you say that it is the same as awareness, we have the problem of establishing how you know that it is the same. You cannot know it is the same, because awareness cannot be divided into subject and object, so there is no way of knowing if it is the same. All you ever see-know-experience is you.

## The Location of Experience

Ignorance makes it seem as if what we experience at any moment is outside the physical body or in the subtle body. It also teaches us that the mind is in the body and the body is in the world. But this is not how it is. The body cannot be in the world, because the body and the world enjoy the same level of reality. The world is the five elements and the body is the five elements, nothing more or less. Upon investigation, it is clear that the body is just a cluster of ever changing sensations appearing in the subtle body, the instrument of experience. So the body cannot be in the world. If these sensations are removed, as they are in deep sleep, or simply understood to be sensations, the world and the body no longer exist for you, except as an idea.

The idea of the world appears to be in the mind, but is it? The idea of the world and the mind enjoy the same level of reality, so one cannot be in the other. What is called the mind is nothing more than the thought that is appearing at the moment. When we investigate the mind, we discover that it is nothing but consciousness in an inert form. Because the mind does not enjoy the same level of reality as pure consciousness but depends completely on it, any sensations or ideas appearing in it cannot be real, meaning enduring. Yes, they are experienced, but they are not real, because they change. When we see a magician saw a lady in half she does not die. When the mind is dismissed, awareness remains. Now, investigate awareness and try to dismiss it. It cannot be dismissed because the one making the investigation is awareness. You can never get rid of your self, because you are eternal.

Materialists believe that consciousness evolved out of matter and it therefore needs objects in order to exist. Does awareness cease to experience itself when the objects appearing in it have been removed? If you look at the instrument of knowledge, the intellect, it is clear that it can illumine objects in its field because it is illumined by awareness, but it cannot illumine awareness, because awareness is subtler than it. But if you, awareness, investigate yourself carefully, you will discover that you perceive yourself whether or not the intellect is present. You are self knowing, self existent. You do not depend on anything for your existence.

## Nothing Ever Happened

Of the billions of souls inhabiting the earth, only a few understand the meaning of the statement "nothing ever happened." If it is true, experience, which is the basis of our everyday identity, never happened. When you think about who you are, you invariably think about the long string of events that happened to you over the course of your life. You cobble them all together and the total seems to add up to your identity. But does it? If a stranger wants to know who you are, you identify yourself with reference to things that happened in your life, because nothing is happening at the moment to identify you. Although you are there and you exist—how could anyone ask the question if you did not exist?—it is assumed that you are someone other than what you appear to be. This is how ignorance works.

When asked "Who are you?" you never say, "I am pure consciousness," which is a real show stopper. Or, "Have a look, you moron!" which would invite the awareness in them to recognize the awareness in you. You start with your name, which is just a bunch of sounds. To make these sounds meaningful, you need to augment them with other information that is always related to what your body and mind apparently experienced in the past. If you are your experiences, why is it not clear to the person who is asking? It is not clear, because your experiences no longer exist, just like your words, which appear in awareness for a few seconds and dissolve back into awareness. If your words were real, they would cluster around you in space and never go away. But they do not hover around your head speaking themselves, eternally informing the world who you are.

What we call life is very similar to a dream viewed from the perspective of the waking state. When we are in the dream, things seem to be happening. We take them to be real and experience them accordingly. But when we wake up, we realize that we were in fact asleep in bed during the whole dream existence.

So did something actually happen? It did, but it did not. The person I take myself to be, the one on my driver's license, lives in a tiny provisional sliver of reality, a miniscule island of time that dissolves into thin air as soon as I inquire into it.

If I have invested everything in the idea that I am so and so from such and such a place who did this and that, I will not be interested in self inquiry. I will dismiss this "nothing ever happened" talk as the prattling of fools. But it is impossible to avoid this idea, because death is hovering nearby. Nothing is definitely going to happen when I die, if I think of myself as the body. It is just many bits and pieces, an assemblage, a sand castle, arranged for the sport of a fickle awareness that quickly grows bored of its forms. Nobody welcomes death, except perhaps some of the aged and infirm because they believe it spells the end of their existence. In reality, it is impossible to not exist, because awareness is eternal and all there is. If you subtract all your experiences and the memory of all your experiences, there is still something left over. And if you investigate what or who is left over, you will discover that you always existed and will continue to exist long past the time when the universe ceases to exist.

This is why enlightenment is equivalent to immortality. We want to be immortal because we love ourselves. Because I love myself and I do not understand my true nature, I would like to have my body and mind live forever so that I can experience myself endlessly in the form of objects. The joke is that the experiencer, who merely enjoys a relative existence, is just another object caught in the web of time. And the joke on top of this joke is: I am self aware, self experiencing. I do not need objects—a body and a mind and a world—to experience myself.

If you do not want to accept your limitless identity and insist that you are who you think you are, it is helpful to understand that your life is like a delicate bubble floating on the surface of an infinite ocean of awareness, and to live in such a way that when the bubble bursts, you welcome it.

## The Opposite Thought

The conviction that I am awareness and not the body-mind entity is only liberation if it frees you from dependence on objects. Objects are anything appearing in awareness, the whole gamut of subjective experience: beliefs, opinions, judgments, fantasies, memories, fears, desires, etc. Self inquiry lumps them all into one category and calls them ignorance. Ignorance is not stupidity. Some very intelligent individuals are ignorant that they are awareness and some not so intelligent individuals are aware that they are awareness. When an individual is ignorant of his or her identity, he or she takes ignorance to be knowledge and identifies with it. That I am awareness is knowledge because it cannot be negated. Only information can be negated when subsequent information shows that it is untrue.

Unfortunately, when I realize that I am awareness, I realize that my whole thought system does not agree. It developed when I did not understand who I was, so it has a completely different opinion. This situation is a little like being two people. One person says, "I am limited, inadequate and incomplete" and the other says "I am limitless awareness. I am capable of dealing with anything life has to offer. Far from being incomplete, I am fullness itself."

Because I am now convinced, for whatever reason, that I am limitless awareness, the first voice is not acceptable. After all, in a non-dual reality, the mind is also the self, so I would like my mind to be on the same page with me. If I know that I am awareness and my mind continues to spout ignorance—unless it knows it is ignorance—how enlightened am I? Ignorance and knowledge cannot exist simultaneously. At every moment the self ignorant ego identifies with beliefs, judgments, opinions, feelings and ideas that express its limited view of itself and the world, thereby continuing to reinforce its ignorance.

This discrimination involves diligently monitoring the thought flow and applying knowledge in the form of the opposite thought to the seemingly endless ignorance the mind cooks up. It can be knowledge in the form of any of the teachings presented so far.

For example, the popular view that "I can have it all" is ignorance, because the ego is limited and not in control of the fruits of its actions, life is a zero sum game, and it already does have it all, because it is actually the self.

The view that "I am special" is ignorance, because you are just the five elements, mind, intellect, ego, tendencies and awareness like everyone else.

The view that someone other than myself can make me happy is ignorance, because there is not anyone else.

The view that something is right or wrong with the world is ignorance, because the world is only in your mind and your mind is not real. If it is real, where is your mind and the world in deep sleep? Why does the world not bother you when you sleep?

The thought that I may get sick and die is ignorance, because what is born dies and what is never born never dies. Since I am awareness, I am never born. Therefore, death has nothing to do with me.

To catalogue all the ideas that ignorance inspires would take centuries. To make it easy, self inquiry has reduced them to a short list—I am the body-mind-intellect-ego—because this is where they all come from.

The "I" sits behind the subtle body. There is only one "I." When it thinks it is incomplete and limited, it is under the spell of core ignorance. When it thinks "I am limitless," it is under the spell of core knowledge. If you want enlightenment, it is much better to have the "I" temporarily under the spell of knowledge.

Core knowledge and core ignorance are like David and Goliath: it is not a fair fight. It would be nice to think that poor little David might get lucky and knock Goliath out with a small stone, but let us be realistic. This scenario is equivalent to chanting a mantra once and expecting to get enlightened. David has a much better chance if he does pushups, takes steroids, bulks up and gets a big club like Golilath's. How would he do it?

He applies the opposite thought. He consciously substitutes the "I am complete" thought for the "I am incomplete" thought when it arises—which it does with every illegitimate fear and desire. Fears and desires are just proxies for the idea that I am incomplete and inadequate. If you feel depressed because you are not getting what you think you want at work or in your relationship, ask yourself who is depressed and who wants the depression to go. Then, with the help of the knowledge "I am the one in whom this depressing feeling is occurring," notice the natural separation between you and the feeling. Identify with the one who sees, not the feeling. The feeling dissolves. Knowledge is very powerful. Nothing more than the conscious thought of awareness is required to reach awareness because you are awareness, even when you think you are someone or something else.

Substituting truth for untruth builds a truth vasana, which neutralizes the likes and dislikes that keep us tied to the wheel of action. It will eventually neutralize the ego-doer completely. Nothing can be done to make you complete and whole except to cancel the thinker-feeler-ego-doer. You were complete and whole before your body was born. You are not a doer.

The doer will object. It will say that it cannot assert the truth because it does not *feel* it. Aside from the fact that the truth does not feel like anything, except perhaps the absence of suffering, the doer should be encouraged to take its steroids. In other words, it is precisely when you do not feel good that you need to remind—bring the knowledge back to your mind—yourself who you are. Who you are is not a feel-good experience. Yes, practicing the opposite thought is not easy; it may even seem dishonest because we are so attached to our feelings. But it is necessary to fake it until you make it. If you practice diligently, the bad feelings will dissolve as the truth vasana burns up the ignorance vasana.

Substituting the true for the false is not mindless brainwashing. It involves a constant dialogue with your ego. This solution only works for mature people who desire freedom strongly, have created lifestyles that allow them to monitor the mind on a moment to moment basis, and who know the difference between knowledge and ignorance. It does not work for extroverted people with a weak or middling desire for liberation. Neutralizing the doer does not mean that actions are meant to be given up, only that the true source of action is known. The true source of action is not the doer; it is a complex web of impersonal forces, illumined by awareness, that animate the body-mind like a battery animates a toy.

If attention is not properly introverted and the lifestyle is too active, the practice of applying the opposite thought will not work. In this case, the mind can be purified with the karma yoga attitude, until it becomes prepared for the direct application of self knowledge.

Those who take enlightenment to be a thought-free state dismiss this practice. They say that the presence of any thought, including the thought "I am awareness," shows that the goal has not been reached. Aside from the fact that enlightenment is not a state of consciousness that can be reached, no thought, including the thought "I am a limited ignorant suffering person," stands in the way of the self, because the self is present before, during and after every thought. It is a different order of reality. If you shoot a person's shadow, the person is not injured. Many discover the self precisely when they are completely identified with the suffering ego. Identification with the idea that the self suffers or enjoys is all that stands in the way of enlightenment. The knowledge just attacks the ignorance that brings on the identification.

It does not turn the individual into an enlightenment zombie who blurts out "I am the self" every time his or her identity is requested because this idea is stuck in the mind. Imagine how helpful it would be to offer this assessment of your identity to a prospective employer. The application of self knowledge might be called Alka-Seltzer yoga. The ignorance "I am limited" causes an upset mind, and the knowledge "I am the self" relieves the upset. For it to bear fruit, this practice should become continuous, so that it builds a strong truth vasana, one that is automatically triggered when fears and desires arise, just as the thought of your beloved arises when you hear her favorite song. Eventually, when the last doubt about who you are is destroyed, the practice is no longer necessary, even though the knowledge is always present. It is always present because you are always present. But it no more stands in the way of using the mind for everyday tasks or creative thinking than the knowledge of your name. It stands in the background, like a good butler, while you go about the business of life. It is instantly available should you need it.

## Name and Form

Every experience involves awareness plus name and form. When stimuli enter the mind through the senses, the mind takes the form of the object, is illumined by awareness, and therefore it is known. The object is never experienced out there in the world. It is experienced in awareness. To make the experience of the form useful, a word is assigned to it. You perceive a cat and say "That is a cat." If awareness is fascinated with experience as name and form, it forgets who it is. So, to return attention back to itself, it needs to subtract the name and the form. It is easy to dismiss the name as not-self, but what about the form? If you study the form as it appears in your awareness, you will see that you cannot find a boundary between the form and the awareness in which it appears. If there is no way to experientially distinguish the form from its substance, the form can be dismissed, because it is actually the substance. Consistent application of this analysis causes happiness. However, happiness is not due to the technique. It is due to the revelation of the self when pure experience is divested of its name and form.

## The Mirror of Awareness

If one wall in a room is a single mirror, all the objects that appear in the mirror will be identical with the objects in the room, and the space in which the objects appear will also be identical with the room space. If you try to grasp an object appearing in the mirror, a door knob, for example, you cannot do so. The door knob does not protrude into the mirror space as it does in the room space. It is in exactly the same dimension as the mirror. It is non-separate from the mirror. In fact it is just the mirror. Similarly, consciousness is like a multi-dimensional mirror in which all existence appears. When you touch any object, you are actually touching consciousness. When you perceive a tree, you are actually perceiving yourself. If you have this understanding, then objects need not be removed from awareness, for awareness to realize itself. They do not obscure the self. They reveal it.

Because awareness is formless, it cannot be directly perceived as an object is perceived, just as the glass of which a mirror is constructed is invisible until objects appear in it. When the vasanas cause a subtle object, like a thought or a feeling, to appear, it enables awareness to experience itself in form.

The argument that awareness can be known only through objects is untrue. It does not need an object, like a person, to know itself. It knows itself in the presence and the absence of objects. The objects in awareness, like the notions that you have about yourself, do not actually affect you at all, just as the images appearing in a mirror leave no trace on the mirror.

## Something to Work Out

Do I see the world because it is there, or is the world there because I see it?

CHAPTER THIRTEEN

# Meditation

Meditation is my nature. It is consciousness's direct appreciation of itself as immediate, unchanging, self luminous being.

The practice of meditation only works when I do not know that I am consciousness. It is a means that can lead to the realization that the meditator and the object of mediation are non-separate. It is an act of mind, wherein consciousness as attention is fixed on silence, its most subtle manifestation, and begins to experience itself, even though it is always experiencing itself. It is the inquiry that arises when the self is experienced.

Meditation practice does not work unless it is supported by the other yogas, because the extroverting pressure of unconscious tendencies carries attention away from the self into the world of objects. Meditation is keeping the mind turned inward. Invariably, individuals who find meditation difficult do not practice the other yogas. Trying to meditate without the aid of the methods discussed so far is like treading water; the vasanas that are burned in meditation are replaced as soon as the individual leaves the seat of meditation and contacts the world.

The subtle body, the mind-intellect-ego, is relaxed, open and flexible in its natural state. When ignorance is operating, it becomes tight and contracted.

It takes pleasure in protecting itself and vigorously defends its notion of itself as incomplete, inadequate and separate from everything. Although ignorance seems to be passive, it is actually aggressive. See how passionately it clings to objects! Perversely, its contractions become hard and fast subconscious tendencies and eventually seem to be quite natural. Meditation, not to mention the other yogas, unwinds these tendencies, relaxes the ego, and provides a platform for direct inquiry.

The science of meditation is the result of the knowledge that arose from patient analysis of unsolicited meditative states, consciousness breaking through and revealing itself to the mind. Meditation practice is the result of reverse engineering. The ancients looked at the factors involved in spiritual experience and experimented with them until they could recreate the subjective conditions that produced transcendence, thereby accelerating the soul's evolution.

Because meditation provides a stable platform for self inquiry, it is useful to develop a meditation vasana. When the mind is in contact with the self, healing energy floods the mind. Although most epiphanies wear off in a matter of hours, they produce vasanas that inspire practice and keep the mind focused on the goal. Practiced diligently, meditation purifies the mind, because it brings awareness to dysfunctional patterns of thought and feeling.

When the meditator transcends the mind and sees from the level of the self—which is not a level—the need to "maintain" consciousness—not that consciousness can be maintained—dissolves because the self is effortless awareness. Knowledge of the subtle body's patterns and complexes is more accurate from the self's point of view than knowledge derived from a witness created out of one part of the mind. Furthermore, transcendence breaks attachment to the mind, making it easier to purify.

Finally, transcendence can produce self knowledge, the ultimate purifier, if it is accompanied by self inquiry. In fact, the self-realized meditator realizes the absurdity in trying to purify something that will again become impure. The purpose of purification is not to become perfectly pure. You are already purity itself. It is to produce a reasonably problem-free mind, one that can calmly inquire into awareness.

Before we introduce a powerful meditation, designed to put the mind in contact with the self and initiate self inquiry, it may be helpful to look into a number of popular meditations in light of the idea of self knowledge.

## The Arrested Mind[35]

Meditation as a thought-free state that is tantamount to happiness is one of the most common theories. It is true that when the mind is arrested in the waking state, bliss is experienced. It is also true that deep sleep is blissful because the divisions that create conflicting thoughts are absent. It does not follow, however, that thoughts are the enemy of happiness.

When you feel good, it is logical to think that bliss should last forever. It is less logical to think that bliss caused by an activity could last forever, because the results of finite actions are finite, and the unconscious tendencies that cause thought can never be completely eliminated. Additionally, the mind is just a bundle of thoughts and feelings and the desire to stop the mind is merely another thought in it. How will it eat up the existing thoughts? In fact it will fatten, not starve, the mind. Finally, how will we work out what needs to be worked out in the world, if the mind is not available? True freedom and lasting happiness are attained only through the knowledge "I am happiness itself," which is not possible with a dead mind.

## Happy Thoughts

Most of us have common sense and are not willing to go to the trouble of stopping or controlling the mind to attain happiness. Another theory suggests replacing unhappy thoughts with happy thoughts. The popular modern meditation practice of using affirmations involves making positive statements about oneself or the world. This approach seems easier than going for a blank

---

35. This idea of meditation was discussed in chapter 2 and will be exhaustively examined in chapter 14.

mind, but creating and maintaining happy thoughts is hard work, so happiness is also held hostage to incessant effort.

And if you think about it, creating happy thoughts is actually just another way of saying "I am unhappy," which reinforces the view that I am an incomplete being. Supposedly, the happy thoughts crowd out their unhappy companions, but negative thoughts and feelings can be very useful, because they illumine areas that require attention. In fact, because mental and emotional pain is a symptom of a much deeper complaint, separation from the source of happiness, trying to correct the symptom without addressing the cause is ultimately futile.

However, visualization, a happy thought variant, which utilizes the mind's tendency to think in images, can purify the mind. Visualizations invented by neophytes and created solely from imagination, beyond an immediate feel good factor, are not very useful because they are not based on a clear understanding of the relationship of the psyche to the consciousness. For a symbol to be effective, it needs to be a powerful self archetype, the contemplation of which clears the mind and brings single-pointed attention to the self.

## Mantra Meditation

A mantra is a spiritually charged sound syllable or syllables which purifies the nervous system, consumes thoughts and feelings, and awakens the mind to the self when it is repeated with feeling and understanding. Mantras are composed of seed syllables, fine vibrations that generate bliss. Unless there is an inclination to chant endlessly, chanting is a limited solution to the question of happiness. Yet, bliss calms the mind and aids concentration. When concentration is highly developed and directed to the self, inquiry is possible.

Mantras have specific spiritual meanings, the consistent and deep contemplation of which can lead to self realization. *Om namah shivaya* is a popular mantra chanted daily by millions worldwide. What does it mean? The first word, *om*, is the Vedic sound symbol of the self, pure consciousness. It is customarily chanted at the beginning and end of every meditation, because consciousness exists before the beginning and after the end of everything. *Namah* refers to the individual. It is a statement of the relationship between the individual and the consciousness. Namah is composed of two syllables, *na* and *ma*. *Na* means *not*. *Ma* means *me*. Namah negates the limited self. The negation of the limited self is called surrender. I am prostrating to my limitless self, acknowledging it as my sole support, the real me.

If *om* and *namah* bubble with meaning, *shivaya* overflows. Both shivaya and om symbolize the self. *Shivaya* means "that which is always auspicious." What is it about us that is always good? It is the fact that we exist and that our existence is eternal. You can throw away everything you have, even the body. But nobody, not even God, can throw you away.

"Because I am other than the body, I don't suffer its changes. I am not born, nor do I die. I have no sense organs, so I am uninvolved in the world. Because I am other than the mind, I am free from sorrow, attachment, malice and fear. I am pure, without thought and desire—and so I am. I have no attributes. I live without breathing. I am eternal, formless and ever free. I am the same in all, filling all things with being. I am infinite, non-dual, pure consciousness."

Mantras describing the self, like the one above, are exceptionally effective meditations if they are consistently repeated with full understanding of the meaning.[36]

## Insight Meditation

Vipassana meditation requires neither a blank mind, special imagery, nor the repetition of a mantra. It trains the mind to dispassionately observe the phenomena constantly appearing on its luminous screen. This ancient and respectable meditation asks the meditator not to identify with, react to, or act out samskara-motivated impulses. When both objective and subjective sources of sensation are identified and objectified, the meditator is asked to inquire if there is a separate self apart from consciousness to which they belong. The realization of the impermanence of all phenomena and the discovery of the non-existence of ego that comes from dispassionate observation causes knotty

---

36. Mantras from Shankaracharya's Atma Bodh, Self Knowledge

samskaras to unravel, freeing the mind of limitations. When this condition is achieved, evidently enlightenment happens by default.

However, if a meditation technique asks one part of the mind to observe the other part, the split will eventually need to be healed, so witnessing meditations eventually have to deal with the removal of the witness. Furthermore, if witnessing is maintained by effort, the benefits will cease when the witnessing stops. Still, vipassana, which mimics the witnessing power of awareness, is based on the fact that if you watch an object exclusively for an extended period, awareness turns around and becomes aware of itself, not that it is ever unaware of itself.

Practiced with an inquiry into the nature of the witness, it can awaken the meditator to the knowledge "I am effortless awareness." Short of that, vipassana is an excellent, arduous technique that purifies unhelpful samskaras and grants a relatively peaceful state of mind.

## The Gap

Another theory defines meditation as attention on the space between thoughts or the gap between the waking and sleep states. That, contrary to appearances, nothing in the universe is substantial is the basis of this technique. On analysis, a material object, though seemingly solid to the senses, strings out into waves and completely loses its form. Similarly, the mind, which is capable of thinking only one thought at a time, is an apparently opaque flow of thought. Yet gaps exist between each thought. A moment after a thought ends, its successor begins. Since the omnipresent, all-pervasive self is the substrate on which the mind dances, it pervades the space between thoughts. Therefore, if the karmic pressure that jams up the thoughts is reduced, the thoughts slow down and induce a heightened state of awareness that allows the meditator to see into the gap and realize the self.

The idea combines nicely with mantra, a conscious thought. Most mental activity is unconscious patterns of quasi-logical associations, specific to the samskara sprouting in the mind. Associative thinking, where one thought connects to another like a link in a chain, is spiritually useless because the mind can end up anywhere. But mantra is a specific conscious thought of the self, introduced into the mind in place of everyday thoughts, and practiced with a gap. If the mantra is not simply interjected between random thoughts, or chanted on top of the samskara-produced associations, but allowed to absorb the mind's energy and become the only thought, stopping the mantra stops the mind momentarily, and at that moment, if attention is directed to the gap, the self in the form of silence, peace, light or energy can be experienced.

Meditation on the interval between waking and sleep, when the waking ego is dissolving into its constituent elements, is another gap meditation. If concentration can be maintained when the mind-ego entity dies, as it does immediately prior to sleep, one can "enter" the self through this gateway.

## Meditation Practice

Meditation practice is a means to an end, not the end in itself. However, the meditator should enjoy sitting for its own sake and not allow the anxiety to experience transcendence prevent transcendence. Only when the mind is quiet and observant is it possible to notice the self. Transcendence is not necessarily a dramatic experience. In fact, it works because we are already always beyond our bodies and minds. Meditation practice should strip off our identification with the body and mind, allowing us to appreciate the natural separation of the self from its vehicles.

Aside from enlightenment, meditation can be practiced for purely psychological and physical benefits: increased energy, heightened senses and reactions, strengthened immunity, improved intelligence, creativity, efficiency, power, pleasure, discrimination, dispassion, sense of purpose, peace of mind, expanded awareness, selflessness, compassion and more.

If you were blessed with a contemplative temperament, or gained one through righteous living, meditation is easy. If not, it is difficult, because your ego will quickly become bored and send you off to do other activities. It will also be inclined to resist your efforts, because meditation moves it from the center to the periphery of consciousness. Individuals who find themselves struggling or bored should abandon meditation and stick with karma yoga, until more vasanas are exhausted and the mind attains a state of relative tranquility.

## An Excellent Technique

Meditation is awareness as attention, flowing to the self like the flow of oil through a wick to the flame. In the following ancient meditation, attention is moved from the sense world to the breath and finally to the self.

If holding the body upright is difficult, lying down is acceptable as long as the tendency to sleep can be overcome when the mind empties. In India, where yoga evolved, people have no furniture, and sitting cross-legged on the ground is natural. Traditional yoga poses like the lotus and the accomplished pose are excellent, but if you find yourself thinking about pain because your feet are resting on top of the thighs, it is better to opt for an easy chair. Except for the attempt to awaken dormant energies in the body, a practice not recommended for neophytes, the position of the body is not critical. The body should be comfortable and the meditator should be prepared to take a short vacation from it.

On the mental level assume a gracious, upright, noble pose. Get into a sensitive, inquiring state of mind, like a botanist patiently examining a delicate flower. The meditator should think of meditation as an afternoon on the beach, not a shift in the mines.

Make a resolution to leave your worries and involvements behind. Feel satisfied you are making an effort to meditate. Next, clear the mind of memories of previous meditations, good or bad. Trying to improve a bad meditation or reproduce a good one is futile, and will only agitate the mind.

With the eyes closed, settle in and ask for help. Obviously if you knew who you were, you would not be meditating, so you are really saying that you do not know anything, an essential ingredient for a successful meditation. Most meditators believe in a higher power, God, a spirit guide, a guru figure, the universe, guidance or some kind of deity. The self, which knows every thought and feeling, understands the need and will respond. It put the meditation idea into the mind in the first place, so the meditator need not worry; everything that needs to happen will happen.

After the invocation, scan and relax the body from the feet up. If you have a hard time relaxing, consider this helpful visualization. Imagine you are a warm, peaceful, light-filled ball of consciousness inside your feet and expand until the feet feel light and empty. Next, bore your way up the legs, hollowing out the ankles, knees, and hips. Take your time. It may seem to be a silly trick but it works because the body is actually a vast field of consciousness, not a dense slab of meat. If the ball of light does not work, use any method you wish to relax. Because they are associated with waste removal, the stomach and abdominal organs often carry negative energy, so spend sufficient time working in this area. Move up and explore the chest. Its association with the emotional center causes angry and unforgiving feelings to lodge there, so the muscles are often tight. Scan leisurely, leaving it light-filled and relaxed, then move up to the neck and shoulders. Much tension accumulates here, so take your time. When this area is relaxed, move out to the tips of the fingers and hollow out the arms like you did the legs. Then redo the neck and shoulders.

The face we carry around in the world is not usually our real face, so we need to do something to get it back to normal. Work around the chin, mouth, and cheeks first and then work up to the eyes and forehead. Many tiny vibrations hover around these areas, so release the muscles supporting them and let them dissipate. A smile or frown means too much energy has been left behind. Aim for the indifferent look of a Buddha or the peaceful face of the dead.

The idea behind all this scanning and relaxing is to prepare the body for your exit. Think of the body as an automobile and yourself as the driver. The driver just returned from a long day on the road, parks the car in the garage and enters his or her home for the evening. Before you park it for good, re-scan the whole thing to make sure it is comfortable and turn your attention to the breath.

## The Breath

The breath goes in and out nicely on its own. Simply observe it, do not breathe consciously, although observing the breath tends to interfere with it. It will settle down and return to its normal pattern. The purpose of meditation is to relax physically and mentally. Watching the breath occupies the mind with a simple rhythmic object. At this point, give the mind a challenge: try to synchronize attention with the breath. This is called "the mind riding on the breath." When the breath flows out, attention should flow out, and when the breath comes flowing in, attention should come with it. The mind will wander. Pull it back and synchronize it with the breath. It need not ride perfectly on every breath. Do not get upset if it does not work immediately. Take your time.

Meditation is not about the breath. The breath is only a tool. How long should one work with it? There is no hard and fast rule, sometimes five minutes, no longer than ten. If it takes more than ten minutes, give up and do something else until the mind is calmer. You are looking for a sign that the mind is getting quiet, because it stills quickly once you can synchronize it with the breath.

As the mind and breath harmonize, use surplus attention to release pent-up energy on the out breath. Just as the out breath cleanses the body, releasing energy detoxifies the mind. Energy in the form of tension and frustration distorts the mind and makes it unable to reflect the light of awareness as it is. Do not try to analyze any thoughts or feelings that arise during this phase of the procedure. Later, when you are seeing the self or seeing from the self, you can analyze them if you wish, although ultimately all thoughts are basically useless. We are not trying to psychoanalyze the ego, only to take pressure off the mind.

## The Silence

The mind is becoming quiet when you become conscious of all sorts of sounds of which you were previously unaware. It is like going to sleep; you never hear the clock ticking until you want to sleep, because the mind, formerly occupied with its thoughts, is emptying. You may hear the heartbeat, the scratching of the breath as it goes in and out, snippets of conversation taking place blocks away, the hum of the kitchen refrigerator or a fly buzzing lazily in an adjoining room. The thoughts may be amplified or slow, as if they were slogging through molasses. You might start picking up on them as they begin, rather than midway through their cycle. You will notice these things because you are now surrounded by a bubble of silence that, depending on the quietude of the mind, is hardly noticeable or that might seem to roar, as it does on the Great Plains in the dead of a summer night.

When the silence appears as a tangible presence, take your attention from the breath and fix it on the silence. Because it has served its purpose, the breath should drop out of consciousness. Occasionally, the silence completely swallows the mind and you find yourself deep within and unaware of the breath, the noises in the room, your thoughts and absolutely everything, a state similar to conscious sleep. Time dissolves and you might be overcome with ecstasy.

Many unusual experiences can happen when the mind is quiet. One would not think to visualize or chant, because the experience of the silence is so fulfilling. However, sometimes a mantra arises spontaneously, chanting itself. Occasionally, meditation activates particularly subtle parts of the causal body and wonderful visions appear. Or not. Let them happen, do not cling. All experiences are transitory and not under the control of the ego. Moreover, the purpose of meditation is self inquiry.

If the mind remains active and the senses report information, thoughts and sounds enter into and disappear out of the silence like phantoms. The awareness in which they appear is a rocklike, real, luminous and eternal presence. The experience of the silence is the essence of meditation. By bringing the background of experience to the forefront, meditation allows the meditator to observe the transitory, insubstantial nature of the body-mind instrument.

See the silence as the altar of the inner temple and take great pleasure witnessing the thoughts and feelings worshipping it. It is always a struggle to keep attention fixed on the self in the form of the silence. If the silence is particularly deep and radiant, attention will naturally gravitate toward it and meditation will be effortless. If not, vasanas will pull it away. Keeping attention fixed on the silence is meditation. Once you have a reasonable lock on it, gently begin to relax concentration, allowing attention to dissolve into the silence, until experiencing the silence is effortless. If you fall asleep, it is a sign that the mind is completely empty. You want to get to the point where the mind is virtually dead, but you are still awake.

The purpose of meditation, working with the breath and mind, is to create an inner environment conducive to the study of the self. The meditation is not creating the silence, although it may seem so. The silence is the substrate of experience, self-luminous consciousness. This technique simply withdraws enough consciousness from the body and mind to allow the ever present and apparently hidden silence to manifest.

Simply being there in the presence of the silence causes inquiry. What illumines the silence? Is someone or something other than it illumining it, or is it illumining itself? How does it relate to the "me" I think I am? Of course you know the answer, but it is necessary to *see* the answer for yourself.

# CHAPTER FOURTEEN

# After and Beyond Enlightenment

Enlightenment as an event—the hard and fast knowledge I am limitless awareness—changes everything and changes nothing. Yes, your vision has undergone a complete makeover, from duality to non-duality. But the famous statement "before enlightenment I chopped wood and carried water, after enlightenment I chopped wood and carried water" accurately sums up your post-enlightenment life. You will not suddenly leap tall buildings with a single bound like Superman when you realize who you are, although it may feel as if you could. Your bank account will not miraculously fill up with money, although you will be rich beyond measure. The world will not suddenly worship you, even though you have love in spades. Karma does not care if you are enlightened and you will not care that karma does not care. The karma standing in your account will continue to fructify and the Internal Revenue Service will expect you to pay your taxes. If you want an exciting life, it is better to take up skydiving or to win the lottery.

## Pseudo-Enlightenment or Enlightenment Sickness

Usually a strong sense of goodwill toward everyone arises at this time, and you almost invariably feel that you should share what you know with others. But before you set out to do so, it is wise to double check to see if you are suffering the disease of enlightenment. It is similar to enlightenment and difficult for the sufferer to diagnose, although it is a well known malady. It should be treated quickly before it becomes a chronic condition.

One benign symptom of enlightenment sickness is transcendental boredom. It is an understandable and slightly negative feeling born of the realization that you have accomplished everything that had to be accomplished in this life, the realization that what you do from now on will not fundamentally make a difference—ignorance is here to stay, after all—and the crystal clarity about the basic emptiness of life. It is caused by a residual sense of doership and unpurified traces of rajas. You may long for a little bit of the excitement and confusion that marked your life in ignorance, but you know you cannot go back.

If you interpret the "no-thingness" of reality as a void and become vaguely disillusioned, know that you have a mild case of enlightenment sickness, due to unpurified traces of tamas. Enlightenment is not the experience of the void. There is no void, only the fullness of awareness appearing as a void. Knowing that experience is only apparent does not involve the destruction of experience, so it is possible to see the world as a vacuous dream and still take pleasure in it. The enjoyment that comes from watching a magic show provides amusement, even though the audience knows that what it is experiencing is unreal.

If self knowledge came after a long period of diligent spiritual practice under the tutelage of a pure teacher, you will probably not catch enlightenment sickness. You would have lived in such a simple way that you were already happy before you discovered who you are, and there will be virtually no change in your inner life. You would have associated with enough truly enlightened people to understand that enlightenment is nothing special. But if you were not blessed with a sattvic disposition and excellent karma and you struggled

long and hard, you will probably be so eager to make the most of your enlightenment that you will not take time to tidy up the last bits of ignorance.

If you formulate your enlightenment as a grand happening and turn it into
a big story, you have the enlightenment disease. In reality, you should be happy
to keep your mouth shut because you did not get something you did not have
all along. Awareness is your nature. By making a fuss about it, you are only
calling attention to a long stay in ignorance, not to a special accomplishment.

If you hear yourself telling others that you are awakened or enlightened or
"cooked," you have enlightenment sickness. Awakening is not enlightenment,
because the self never slept. You are the fire that cooks, not the cooked food.
Awakening means that some kind of insight or mystical experience happened,
which you define as enlightenment. Enlightenment cancels the ego, so there is
no one left to claim he or she is presently awakened. Or if the ego survived, it
knows that the self—not it—is enlightened. At best you can say, "I am not enlightened, nor am I unenlightened," because both enlightenment and endarkenment are simply ideas to you, awareness.

Here are two examples of the specious logic of someone who has allowed
the ego to co-opt his or her enlightenment. "Consciousness is non-dual. This
means that everything is the same as everything else. Therefore, the moral distinctions operating in the creation have no meaning. That is why I do what I
want without regard for anyone or anything." Or, "reality is non-dual, therefore
nothing ever happened. Therefore I do not exist. If I do not exist—I'm so not
here!—my dualistic orientation does not exist. So if you see me acting like a
self-centered jerk, it is a projection of your ignorance."

If you believe that your words are gospel and that your deeds, whether
or not they correspond to common sense and reason or whether they are in
harmony with dharma and tradition, are a teaching stratagem, you need help.
Although the Western spiritual world is maturing and seems to be on to this
con, there are still crazy wisdom gurus who count stealing your money, having
their way with you in bed, and turning you into a slave to further their gurugic
ambitions as a pedagogical device.

It is natural to feel compassion when you know who you are, but if you
think it qualifies you to save the world, it is just a pedestrian desire for fame

masquerading as compassion, another symptom of the enlightenment disease. If you find yourself collecting worker bees to spread the word, setting up tax exempt institutions to keep the cash from the government, conducting expensive retreats, seminars and intensives, and starting up newsletters featuring glowing testimonials highlighting your tremendous compassion, accompanied by photos of you surrounded by wholesome smiling "devotees," you need to check into the emergency room.

Enlightenment entails no duties or responsibilities. It is not an ideal that demands a particular kind of behavior. If you think it has turned you into a pure saint and requires you to live an austere and holy life and behave with perfect love, you have enlightenment sickness. Enlightenment cannot be equated with sainthood, because behavior depends on the nature of the instrument through which awareness functions, not on the self. For example, electricity flowing through a light bulb produces light. Functioning through a stereo, it produces sound. Operating through a heater, it causes heat. If only sattvic samskaras remain, saintly behavior will manifest, but rajas and tamas can never be completely eliminated. Traces of rajas and tamas, associated with the belief "I am enlightened/awakened," quickly become carcinogenic cells in the mind that metastasize into the cancer of enlightenment sickness and taint your thoughts, words and deeds with self interest, unless they are recognized for what they are. Ambition and enlightenment are like oil and water.

Symptoms of this disease involve taking a fancy new name or names, pasting a smarmy blissful smile on your newly enlightened face, flaunting monk's robes, shaved heads, holy beads, wooden staffs and what not. If you meet an enlightened master giving teachings in a low voice in such a way that it takes him five minutes to complete a simple sentence, you are witnessing enlightenment sickness, not a profound transmission from deep within. Our newly minted Buddha may be prone to ostentatious devotional behavior, particularly repeated bowing like a bobble-head doll. One of the most pretentious symptoms is the habit of referring to oneself in the third person to demonstrate detachment from the ego. Some years ago, an American woman came to India and *experienced* enlightenment as soon as she stepped off the plane in Delhi, or so she said. She made her way to Rishikesh, a holy town on the banks of the Ganges. It so happens that beggars congregate in holy places, because it is the dharma of pilgrims to give once they have worshipped at the local temples. Indian beggars are not shy. They come right up with folded palms and say, "Ram Ram," the name of one of India's most revered deities. "Ram Ram" in this context means "In the name of god, give me money," but she thought everyone was seeing her as the god Ram, now that she was *fully* enlightened. If you have enlightenment sickness, you may also believe that you are entitled to your little sensualities, extravagances, vanities and larcenies—because your very presence here on earth is a great blessing for all and sundry.

The notion that you need to "live the wisdom of love each moment" is enlightenment sickness. Of course you are free to demonstrate it, but demonstrate to whom? If you know who you are, no demonstration is required. Love is not something you do. It is what you are. If you are love and you are alive, every action will be automatically saturated with love. If you cannot see it and feel that you need to do something about it, there is still doership and you are not enlightened. Enlightenment means there will be no one to "consciously choose from moment to moment" to be loving or not. What cup of sugar worth its salt will say, "Oh, I think I will be sweet every moment of my days now that I know who I am!" It has no choice because it is always sweet. Sweetness is not an action. The fact that you are the self is all that is required to bring love and wisdom to the world.

If the mind on which you, awareness, shines is sattvic, love and wisdom will manifest. If, not, not. The presence or absence of sattva in the mind is not a statement of enlightenment. Although the scriptures of self inquiry exhort the seeker to cultivate a sattvic mind—love and wisdom are the hallmarks of a sattvic mind—they do not do so for the sake of creating a loving and wise ego. They encourage it because a sattvic mind is necessary for self inquiry. Self inquiry is not about proving something to yourself or manifesting something for the benefit of the world; it is about understanding and appreciating yourself as you are, warts and all. Once self inquiry has borne fruit, the whole issue of manifesting and demonstrating does not arise. You need not prove that you are enlightened, to yourself or others. It only arises when there is a doubt about who you are.

If you claim to be enlightened and say that God gave you a mandate to do something with your enlightenment, you fail to understand that you are beyond God and need not take orders. Without you, awareness, God cannot lift a finger. You also fail to understand that God is not in the business of issuing mandates, because God sees no difference. To God you are God. To say that God is telling you to be compassionate and enlighten the world means that God does not know who God is—or who you are. And presumably, if God is someone other than you, God is omnipotent and can enlighten the world at will, without your assistance. If this is so, why would he or she exhort you to demonstrate compassion and enlighten the world? To remove this symptom, you need to understand that virtue is not the result of what you do. It is what you are. Those who want to be virtuous find it convenient to imagine that God is telling them to be wise and compassionate, as if wisdom and compassion were anything but common sense values.

Cultivating wisdom and compassion may be helpful to prepare the mind for enlightenment, but it is not necessarily a sign of enlightenment, although many enlightened beings are wise and compassionate. This idea appeals to that part of the mind that can never accept reality as it is. When you assimilate the knowledge "I am awareness" everything is included: wisdom, compassion and everything else in the apparent creation. You understand that nothing can be done about it. And if something is done about it, it is an apparent doing with apparent results. But if you have only assimilated this knowledge intellectually, you may add a stipulation; you may choose to believe that you are not *fully* enlightened unless you demonstrate compassion and wisdom, whatever that means to you. Is it churlish to point out that the world is full of wise and compassionate individuals who are not enlightened?

If you want to define enlightenment as wisdom or compassion, fine, but wisdom and compassion are not equal to self knowledge, although they are related to it. Wisdom is the application of self knowledge to life and compassion is awareness shining on a pure heart. It is the non-assimilation of the vision of non-duality that gives rise to the notion that enlightenment is wisdom and compassion. Wisdom and compassion are the self, but the self is not wisdom and compassion. If you are the self, you are free of wisdom and compassion.

Enlightenment is not an identity, nor is it a career opportunity. Although several famous modern teachers have succumbed to enlightenment sickness, to the point where they lost their reputations and institutions, ran afoul of the law or died unhappy, and others seem to delight in making fools of themselves, it is a reasonably benign disease caused by insufficient respect for the power of residual samskaras, positive and negative.

The good news? It can be cured with a strong dose of honest self inquiry, a dollop of humility and a simple life away from the spotlight. If you are so afflicted, do not bite your cyanide capsule. It is understandable that an inspired and happy person will throw caution to the winds and set out to make up for lost time, by achieving in happiness what he or she had formerly failed to achieve in unhappiness. But the belief that you can have your cake and eat it too is evidence of an unpurified understanding. Little by little, in the most innocent and imperceptible way, you will re-identify with the body-mind entity and have to start over again. This too is not the kiss of death. The self is always present, just waiting to be realized once more. I once met an honest man who said he had realized the self five hundred times, so there is hope.

## The Liberated Person

If you analyze nature carefully, you will see that there are no sharp edges, no revolutionary changes. Because it is supported by unchanging consciousness, the laws that govern change see to it that transitions between events are gradual and orderly. In five years, the media will speak of the financial collapse of 2008 as if it were a dramatic and isolated event. But hundreds of millions of barely noticeable changes, over a forty-year period, transpired before the bubble burst. And even before it broke, the changes needed to correct it had already begun. Yes, it is natural to want suffering to end once and for all in a dramatic fashion, but that is not how it is. The human mind is a particularly conservative instrument and it is attached to its suffering. It has barely evolved since the day the first organism crawled out of the Precambrian ooze and set up residence on dry land. So the notion that you will suddenly be a newer, better model when you realize who you are is not supported by the evidence.

Indeed, your resistance to change will be less, but the law of karma takes its own sweet time. Fortunately, the real you has plenty of tolerance for the foibles of the apparent you and can patiently suffer your transition to a glorious human being in good humor. Spiritual growth is measured in millimeters, not miles, in millennia, not minutes.

If an individual cultivated a pure mind during his or her seeking phase, he or she will manifest divine qualities once the knowledge is firm. But very often, strange as it seems, someone who has not lived a particularly pure life assimilates the knowledge. In this case, there will appear to be a conflict between his or her behavior and the knowledge of non-duality. If the knowledge is firm, it is not a problem, although it may confuse others. Eventually, the understanding will purify the remaining traces of duality and the higher qualities will manifest in full measure.

In any case, the scriptures that make up the science of self inquiry contain numerous verses that describe the effect of hard and fast self knowledge on the individual. It is difficult to know if someone is enlightened because there are no outward signs, so these descriptions discuss the enlightened person's relationship to the mind and the world.

An enlightened person is someone who can, without effort, renounce desires as they arise in the mind. If the renunciation of desire is an effort, it means that self knowledge is not firm, because the vasana in question still has a hold on the individual. Some scriptures insist that only when desire is completely eradicated can the individual be said to be enlightened. But this notion calls into account the very rationale for pursuing enlightenment. To say that I am enlightened only when all my desires are gone is to say that I am enlightened only when I am asleep or dead. In the meantime, I am privileged to suffer and enjoy along with the unenlightened. It also assumes that desire and awareness enjoy the same degree of reality. Desire is insentient consciousness, but the self is sentient consciousness. The insentient depends on the sentient, but the sentient does not depend on the insentient. So there is no contradiction between them. Finally, not all desires produce suffering. Many desires make the desirer happy and make a positive contribution to the world when they fructify.

Desires are present in the enlightened, but they arise spontaneously without the individual's will. Consequently they produce no suffering, just as a grain of roasted wheat cannot germinate. Because they have been neutralized by the knowledge of completeness, they do not produce positive and negative vasanas. Although a roasted seed cannot sprout, it can be used as food. Similarly, the desires of the enlightened yield experience. Experience involves pleasure and pain for both the enlightened and the unenlightened, but it does not produce suffering in the enlightened.

The statement that an enlightened individual is free of ignorance, not free of desire, bears scrutiny because ignorance is the cause of desire. Is it true that where there is no ignorance of wholeness, there is no desire? Yes and no. There is no desire for completeness, but there may be desire for practical things in the apparent world that are necessary for the maintenance of the body. These desires do not belong to the enlightened person, however. To identify an enlightened person with desire or the absence of desire is not correct, because the enlightened know that desire is just the gunas playing out. In fact, they see desire as a positive creative force. The Bhagavad Gita, one of self inquiry's premier texts, says that the self is the desire that is not opposed to dharma. In terms of action, therefore, the desires of an enlightened person have a beneficial effect on the world because they are just the desire of consciousness creating, sustaining and destroying the world.

Desire is just an outward flowing, creative energy playing in the subtle body that moves the mind to think and the body to act. It is not a problem if I do not identify with it, because I know that it is happening only in the apparent reality. A rainbow is an apparent bridge in the sky, but I will not try to walk on it even though it is a thing of beauty. Shorn of the belief that objects in the apparent reality can fulfill me, I see the world is a beautiful place, reflecting as it does the marvelous light of awareness that I am.

When I dream, I take the dream world to be real, and I suffer and enjoy according to what happens in it. But the enlightened are not in the dream of life. The dream of life appears in them. Therefore, whatever desires appear are also dream desires, not real desires. This, however, does not mean that the enlightened act out desires that are opposed to dharma, because they are only dream desires. An enlightened person will not engage in actions that injure himself or herself or others, because he or she sees no difference.

Negative impulses do appear in the minds of the enlightened, but they are known for what they are. The enlightened can easily entertain unenlightened thoughts like "I am not the self" or "I am the doer." They are not bothered by selfish impulses and negative feelings, because they know that these are the result of slowly exhausting prarabdha karma. If the knowledge is not firm, the ego will identify with these thoughts and feelings.

Enlightenment destroys the personal connection with desire. Desire causes the fear in the unenlightened that they will not get what they want. But the enlightened know that they always have what they want, because fullness is the nature of the self. Therefore, there is no anxiety concerning the results of their actions. An enlightened person is free of the fear that he or she can become unenlightened, because self knowledge is not memory based. It is possible to forget something that was formerly known if the object is not present or the memory is deficient, but the self is always present. So when the self is directly known, it cannot be forgotten. It is the one to whom remembering and forgetting happens. This is why the scriptures say you can never go back to what you once were. Once you know what a tree is, can you forget that it is a tree?

If scripture says enlightenment is self knowledge and the self is not a doer, then it would seem to mean that anyone doing anything would not be enlightened. Yet, we see so-called enlightened beings engaged dynamically in all walks of life. How can this paradox be resolved? The enlightened person understands that when something is happening, nothing is actually happening, and that when nothing is happening, something—awareness—is happening, not that awareness happens. In other words, he or she does not confuse reality with appearances, the self with the not-self. He or she knows that it is the apparent body, activated by apparent vasanas, that produces apparent action and that from the self's point of view, no action is taking place. Having permanently identified with the self as the self, he or she acts without the feeling that he or she is acting. Because enlightenment cancels the doer's karmic account, the results of the actions of an enlightened person benefit others, since the enlightened person has nothing to gain.

The enlightened person does not think he or she is an enlightened person. He or she is quite happy with the person that was there before, during and after enlightenment, not that choice is actually involved. To see no difference not only means to see no difference between the subject and the objects, it also means to see no difference between the light and dark sides of the mind. Practically, this means that the enlightened love their apparent selves, warts and all. They see the perfection in imperfection. They know that what *is* could not be otherwise.

An enlightened person is never unsatisfied with the self. Dissatisfaction is the hallmark of the unenlightened. Enlightenment is freedom from suffering, not experience, although the self is free of experience. Fructifying karma provides ample experience. If your enlightenment motivates ambitious undertakings, know that you have enlightenment sickness, not enlightenment. Ambition and enlightenment are like oil and water. Existing karma plays out and as time passes the experience of peace and bliss grows. It is like being awake while sleeping. In sleep we experience complete peace and bliss without consciously appreciating it. The enlightened experience limitless peace and bliss in the waking state and know the reason: because they are fullness itself. This sense of supreme satisfaction comes because they know that all that was meant to be achieved in life has been achieved and all that was to be enjoyed has been enjoyed. They would not go back to samsara, even if they could.

An enlightened person understands that there is nothing personal about life, that the idea that I am an "I" who does certain actions and to whom certain things belong, is purely fiction. Yet his or her story is worth telling. It is a play worth acting, so the enlightened sport joyfully in the apparent reality, playing their roles to the hilt.

## More or Less Enlightened?

Obviously, if reality is non-dual and enlightenment is the hard and fast knowledge "I am limitless, non-dual, actionless ordinary awareness," there is only one enlightened being. Awareness realizes what it is and that is the end of it. It does not, nor did it ever involve anyone else, although it seemed to. There are no stages or levels, no full or partial enlightenments.

If we are going to play the "who is *more* enlightened?" or "am I *fully* enlightened" game, we should have a rational basis for making a determination, otherwise anyone can be enlightened. At least nine hundred very dead people thought Jim Jones of Guyanese Kool-Aid fame was fully enlightened. Known child molesters claim to be enlightened and are believed to be enlightened by many.

If we take the apparent world into account, we can say that there are different types of enlightened beings, owing to the nature of the qualities at play in their subtle bodies. But what standard do we apply to rate these qualities? Is peace superior to compassion? Is wisdom superior to radiance? Is dispassion inferior to love? Is the yogi sitting in silence superior to the sage who teaches scripture?

Because self knowledge removes ignorance, it purifies unhelpful rajas and tamas from the mind. But whether the knowledge does the work or an ego, blessed with the knowledge, actively roots out the impurities of the mind, enlightenment predisposes the intellect to sattva. So in the fullness of time, all things being equal, enlightenment will tend to produce a peaceful, clear, radiant, compassionate and wise mind.

At the same time, rajas need not be a problem if the knowledge is firm. Many enlightened beings, with predominately rajasic subtle bodies, are intensely inspired and do marvelous good works. It is also quite possible for an enlightened individual to lead a tamasic life. Although non-doing is an understanding that has little to do with action per se, it often boils down to physical laziness—which is bad only if you think it is. It is also a matter of fact that the three gunas cycle endlessly through all minds, enlightened or not. So, is an individual more enlightened when sattva is present, less enlightened when rajas is present, and unenlightened when tamas is present? The only conclusion that we can reasonably draw is that there are no rules and that anything is possible for the enlightened.

Having said all that, your enlightenment is only as good as you are. If you want to evaluate yourself or others, enlightenment is a very poor standard, in so far as there are many saintly unenlightened individuals and many enlightened scoundrels. It is better to leave enlightenment alone in the shining world of knowledge. If you want to evaluate yourself or others, common sense dharma is a reasonable standard. Am I kind and loving to myself? Am I polite and friendly to others? Am I fair minded? Do I respond naturally and sympathetically to life?

## Beyond Enlightenment

Enlightenment, as an event, spells the end of suffering, and I call myself an enlightened being as defined above. I did not catch enlightenment sickness. So far so good. But the idea that there is an enlightened being implies that the same one who once suffered is now free of suffering. But what if enlightenment is the realization that I never suffered in the first place? What if I am not a person who has realized the self—an enlightened being—what if I am the self? How would I see things, if that was true? What would I have to say about myself?

I cannot be objectified. I neither exist nor do I not exist, because existence and non-existence are dualistic concepts that are useful for the self ignorant, but of no use to me. I am neither a person nor a non-person. I was not born, nor am I unborn. I am not male, female, or neuter. I am neither finite nor infinite. I am not dual or non-dual, one or separate, subject or object, empty or full. I am not perfect or imperfect. I never lived or died. I am not pure, nor am I impure. I am neither righteous nor unrighteous. I do not do anything, nor do I do nothing. I am a sun that that never sets, neither bound nor free. I am not describable, nor am I indescribable. I am not discriminating nor non-discriminating. I am neither passionate nor dispassionate. I pervade nothing and nothing pervades me. Spirit and matter are the same to me. I am not the higher or the lower self. I am not the knower or the known. I am known only to myself. I cannot understand, nor am I understood. I am not afraid to say I am pure knowingness, the reality of everything, not that there is anything for me to be the reality of.

When I talk to my mind, I tell it to stop complaining and realize who it is. I tell it that there is no cause for worry, that the things it thinks are real are not real at all. I inform it that it should not cry, because it is everything. I encourage it to stop being bad and stop trying to be good. I tell it to quit longing for a big experience and realize the self, step by step. I say that the knowledge of the self is difficult to obtain and that what it experiences is not the self. I warn it about passion and always tell it that it cannot realize who it is with its feelings. I say, "You are not the one who feels good when things are going your way, nor are you the one who feels bad when life is against you." I offer it the eyeglass of non-duality to correct its defective vision. I tell it to renounce the world, then to renounce renunciation and then to renounce the absence of renunciation.

I am not the essence of anything, because there is nothing to be the essence of. I am neither gross nor subtle. I come from nowhere and I am going nowhere. I have no karmas. I have no body and no home. I destroy all bodies and homes. I am within and without everything, like space, yet there is no *in* or *out* for me. You cannot take anything away from me, nor can you give me anything. I am not made up of parts, nor am I a partless whole. You cannot worship me because I am not an object. I am not attached, nor am I non-attached. I am not foolish, nor am I wise. I am free from thought and the taint of no thought. I am not silence or words. I do not say that the world is real, or unreal, or apparently real, or non-existent or an illusion. I am pure knowing, even though there is nothing to know.

Nothing can touch me. No yoga can purify me. I purify everything without doing anything. I look on righteousness, prosperity, heaven, compassion and liberation as meaningless values.

# CHAPTER FIFTEEN

# The Teachings of Ramana Maharshi

A few years ago, I was interviewed by a friend at my flat in Tiruvannamalai behind Ramanashram, about the teachings of Ramana Maharshi, one of India's greatest sages and presently the most famous symbol of self inquiry in the West. While examining some of Ramana's teachings, I have tried to introduce the reader to the spiritual context of Ramana's enlightenment, because most Westerners, in spite of their appreciation of and devotion to Ramana, have almost no appreciation of it. The centerpiece of this interview is an in-depth analysis of Ramana's enlightenment experience.

Interviewer: I have some quotations from Ramana's teachings that I have been thinking about and I would like your take on them. After saying that the self is existence, consciousness and bliss, Ramana is asked "When will the realization of the self be gained?" and he replies, "When the world which is what is seen has been removed, there will be realization of the self, which is the seer."

James: Let me give you a little background on Ramana's statements. There are two great traditions under the umbrella of Vedic culture: Yoga and Vedanta—the science of self inquiry. Yoga deals with the experiential side of spiritual life and is for the purpose of purifying the mind. It is not a valid means for self knowledge, because its stated aim is a particular type of experience called samadhi. Yogis sometimes attain enlightenment because they develop curiosity about consciousness, the self, as a result of the subtle experiences their practices generate. They may intuitively draw the correct conclusion about the self and their identity as consciousness during one of their samadhis, like Ramana did during his death experience. Or they may gain enlightenment by reflecting on their experiences over a period of time.

Many have epiphanies similar to Ramana's. But almost no one becomes enlightened during a particular experience, because the meaning of the experience or the significance of the one to whom the experience is occurring is not assimilated. The hard and fast understanding "I am the self" needs to come out of self experience to set you free.

The question "when will the realization of the self be gained" is a typically yogic question. Yoga is for doers, achievers. The questioner believes the self is something that is not available all the time, something to be gained. It is natural to want what you do not have, if you think it will benefit you in some way. One of the meanings of the word *yoga* is "to obtain." Obviously, you can only obtain something you do not already possess.

Vedanta, the science of self inquiry, contends that the self cannot be gained at some time in the future, as a result of action. It is a path of understanding and employs a language of identity. For example, it says, "You are consciousness." Notice that this sentence is not an injunction. It is a statement of fact. It says that the self cannot be gained, because you are the self already. If there is anything to gain, it will be self knowledge. Self knowledge is only a loss of ignorance, not a gain of the self.

In any case, Ramana's response is in harmony with traditional Vedanta. Ramana had the greatest respect for the knowledge enshrined in the science of self inquiry. Contrary to the notion in vogue today concerning the irrelevance of the ancient tradition of Vedanta, he was very scripturally astute. He even wrote a scripture, Upadesha Saram, which has been granted the status of an Upanishad by the traditional Vedanta community, a great honor.

This teaching is called the discrimination between the subject—the seer—and the seen—the objects. It establishes the understanding that what you see—meaning experience, including all mystic experiences—is "not-self." The one who sees them is you, the self. He says that you will realize who you are, meaning understand that you are the self, when you have separated the seer, you, from what you experience.

One thing I admire about Ramana was that he refused, unlike many modern teachers, to cook up a fancy personal teaching on the subject of self realization. His statements were in harmony with the scriptures on Yoga or Vedanta. Even though Ramana died a half century ago, he was a very "modern" sage, if you consider the fact that the Vedic spiritual tradition is thousands of years old.

Why did he refuse to do so? Because no modern teaching is required. The whole enlightenment business was worked out a long time ago. Enlightenment is a simple understanding of the self and its relationship to experience, the ego-experiencer, and the forms the ego experiences. In a nutshell, it is the understanding that while the forms depend on the self, the self does not depend on the forms. This freedom from attachment to experience is called *moksha*, liberation. It is not something you obtain. It is something you are. The operative words in his response ("When the world which is what is seen has been removed, there will be realization of the self, which is the seer") are "has been removed." What kind of removal is it? Does the complete destruction of the unconscious tendencies, vasanas, allow you to gain the self? Or is enlightenment the removal of the notion that the world is separate from the self?

In Ramana's teachings you will find both ideas. The word *world* is actually a psychological term. It does not mean the physical world. The physical world, in so far as it is actually physical, is the self. It is impersonal. No individual created it and no individual is going to remove it. But the world that Ramana says must be removed is that of the psychological projections that make up an individual's personal world. These projections are based on a belief that the self is separate, inadequate or incomplete.

Ramana's teaching is not Ramana's teaching. It is called *vichara*, inquiry, and goes back several thousand years. The purpose of inquiry is knowledge, not the physical removal of the mind. If he had been teaching Yoga as a means of liberation, he would not have encouraged inquiry, because Yoga is committed to the experience of samadhi, not understanding that one is the self.

Interviewer: This is interesting. I never heard it stated this way before. But I thought the goal was sahaja samadhi.

James: Contrary to conventional wisdom, the samadhis are not the final goal. *Sama* means equal and *dhi* is a contracted form of *buddhi*, intellect. So it means a mind that values everything equally. *Sahaja* means continuous and natural, so it is a mind that has continuous non-dual vision. Perhaps you can gain this kind of mind by the long and difficult practice of Ashtanga Yoga. I don't know. But why go to all this trouble, when you actually have this samadhi naturally all the time, without doing a lick of work.

Interviewer: Oh, how is that?

James: As the self. Self realization is not continuous, because the self is out of time, but it is natural to the self. It is your nature.

Anyway, no samadhi is equivalent to enlightenment, because samadhis are only states of mind or no mind, no mind being a state of mind. Samadhi helps purify the mind by burning subconscious tendencies and is a great aid to inquiry, but if you remove the mind, how will you make an inquiry? Who will make an inquiry? You make an inquiry with the mind for the mind, so it can shed its ignorance and no longer trouble you. The mind is a very useful God-given instrument. Would God have given us a mind if He had intended for it be destroyed? And in fact, Yoga isn't about killing the mind either, because how will you experience a samadhi if you don't have a mind? The mind is the instrument of experience.

If you argue that you are aiming at nirvikalpa samadhi where there is no mind, fine. Unfortunately, a fly landing on your nose can bring you out of nirvikalpa samadhi, not that there is anyone there to come out of it. And when the "you" who wasn't there does come back, as I just mentioned, you are just as self ignorant as you were before. Why? Because you were not there in the samadhi to understand that the samadhi is you. If you are the samadhi, you will have it all the time, because you have you all the time. Therefore, there will be no anxiety about making it continuous or permanent.

Interviewer: OK. You're saying that samadhi is not the goal, that it is just the means?

James: Yes. Not *the* means. A means. There are many other ways to purify the mind. Misunderstanding this teaching is perhaps responsible for more despair, confusion and downright frustration for seekers than any other. It is commonly believed that all the vasanas need to be physically eradicated for enlightenment to happen. And many people believe that Ramana had achieved that *extraordinary* state. It may be extraordinary, but it is not enlightenment.

If you study Ramana's life, you will see that by and large he was a very regular guy, head in the clouds, feet firmly planted on the earth. He walked, talked, cooked, read and listened to the radio. I love the story of him returning to the ashram at one in the afternoon, to see a sign saying the ashram was closed from noon until two pm. What did he do? He sat down outside and waited for it to open. If he did not have a mind, who or what was doing all these things? No vasanas means no mind, because the vasanas are the cause of the mind. How did he go about the business of life? So I think we need to look at the word *removal* in a different way.

Ramana was called a *jnani*, a knower of the self, because he had removed the idea of himself as a doer—it is called *sarva karma sannyasa*—which happens when you realize you are the self. Or you realize you are the self when you realize you are not the doer. "Not the doer" means the self. It doesn't mean that the ego becomes a non-doer. The ego is always a doer. As the self, he understood that while the few non-binding vasanas he had left were dependent on him, he was not dependent on them. How can a thought or a feeling affect the self? For a person who thinks he or she is the doer, allowing the vasanas to express or not is not an option. Actions happen uncontrollably because the ego is pressurized to act in a certain way by the vasanas. They happen without the will of an enlightened person too, but acting on them is entirely elective.

So the removal that Ramana talks about is only in terms of understanding. He often uses another metaphor that he borrowed from Vedanta, the snake and the rope. In the twilight, a weary, thirsty traveler mistook the well rope attached to a bucket for a snake and recoiled in fear. When he got his bearings and his fear subsided, he realized that the snake was actually only the rope. There was no reason to take a stick and beat the snake to death, which is equivalent to trying to destroy the mind, because the snake was only a misperception. When he calmed down and regained his wits, he inquired into the snake and realized that it was just a rope. And in that realization the snake was removed.

Interviewer: My understanding is that he meant the removal of all the attachments to our conditioned mind.

James: That was because he understood he was the self. The way you lose attachment all at once is to understand you are the self.

Interviewer: It is often called "a constant experience."

James: Sure, but the self is "constant experience" anyway. Or put it this way, if this is a non-dual reality and this reality is the self, then each and every experience is the self. So nobody is short of self experience, the ignorant and the enlightened alike. The problem is that very few people understand that everything is the self. So they seek all these incredible self experiences.

Interviewer: The self is a constant experience?

Ram: No, the self is "constant experience" if there is such a thing. In fact "constant experience" is a contradiction with reference to the self, although experience is constant in the apparent reality. The self becomes experience, but it does not sacrifice its nature as a non-doing, non-experiencing witness to do it. This means you are free of your experiences. Let's put it a better way: experience is the self, but the self is not experience.

Interviewer: When one says "constant experience," would that mean remembering the self constantly?

James: Remembrance is helpful up to a point. But you can never make remembrance constant. Knowledge is constant. When self knowledge takes place, you no longer chase experience, thinking it will complete you. Remembering is a mental activity that implies forgetting. Once you know you are the self, there is nothing to remember any more. How can you remember what you are? You are the one who is doing the remembering. You are prior to the act of remembrance. You cannot forget, because you are always present. If you were somewhere else or someone else, you could forget.

Interviewer: The next question Ramana is asked is "Will there not be realization of the self, even while the world is there (taken as real)?" He replies, "There will not be."

James: If I do not take the world to be real, I will not seek happiness in it. When I seek happiness in the world, I expect it to fulfill me, but there is no lasting fulfillment in the world because the things in the world do not last. I want the objects that give me happiness to last when things are going well and I expect them not to last when things are going poorly. But life does not care how things are going for me.

Ramana was a wise man because he removed his self ignorance. I don't think he sat there all day, trying to break his attachments. I would think that because he was so young when he woke up, his vasanas were not entrenched. Indian culture was pretty pure in those days and he came from a decent family, so he did not have deep negative attachments, like sex and money and so on.

Interviewer: Yes, when you think of a teenage boy sitting for long hours in samadhi in the temple, he must have been taken care of, so the people there recognized him, to some extent. But how about him? Would he really know what is happening to him? He never read any spiritual books, never had a teacher, and is sitting there for hours.

James: That's a good question. He probably did know because there were mahatmas running about, role models if you will. So he knew how they lived, and probably got help from the sadhus whom he came in contact with. The Indian spiritual scene is a vast network. Word of someone's enlightenment gets around very fast. Many great men must have shared certain things that would be helpful. After all, he was sitting at the hub of one of India's most holy sites, Arunachala, which has been attracting mahatmas for thousands of years.

I stayed with a great mahatma in Kerala, Swami Abhedananda, who was a guru's guru. Many enlightened people came to see him and he would invite them up to his room and I'm sure everyone benefitted. Many of the Westerners who come to India, even those who have been here a long time and who have been associated only with the "export" gurus, often have peculiar notions about saints like Ramana. They believe that he was a kind of lonely figure, the only one of his kind, head and shoulders above the crowd, lived in a cave like a hermit who sat in silence most of the time, and didn't have a social life. He probably was quite distant and emotionally reserved like most Tamil men, but he had love in spades and if you have love, people come and give you what you need.

And then, too, you have to understand that his sense of himself being the self never left him, so he wouldn't be that concerned about his emotional needs. And finally, self knowledge is not something that you have any doubt about, if it is the real thing. You just know.

Interviewer: Did he know the self?

James: Yes. He may have thought of it as an object at first, which is natural. It's hard to tell and it really doesn't matter, although the Ramana devotees bristle at the notion that the reason he sat in the caves alone was to erase whatever sense of duality there was left in his understanding. To me that only adds to his glory, if it is true. But then enlightenment will come only to a very mature person, regardless of his age. Usually, the self appears first as an object and then, when one keeps the mind on the self and repeatedly inquires into it, the bedrock understanding eventually comes that one is the self that one is enquiring into. This is certainly what he taught. And he taught it with authority that is based on personal experience. But it really doesn't matter because he realized who he was and was a fine example of a realized soul, unlike so many of these modern people claiming enlightenment.

The problem of language comes in at this level. He uses the language of experience more than he does the language of identity. If you read the statement describing his enlightenment experience in the temple, you get the sense that he knew he was it, perhaps a little vaguely in the beginning, but more clearly as time passed. Again, it is very difficult to tell from the words.

It is probably not correct to say that he knew the self. It is more accurate to say he knew he was the self. That is the meaning of the word *Ramana*.

Interviewer: That seems like a very subtle distinction.

James: It is, but there is a world of difference. To say that you know the self means that you see the self as an object, as something separate. To say that you are the self means that there is no duality in your experience or understanding of yourself. Let's talk about his famous enlightenment experience now. I think it can shed light on this subject of what knowing the self actually is.

Interviewer: Yes. It's right here. I copied it from the board in the Mother's Shrine.

> I felt I was going to die and that I had to solve the problem myself, there and then. The shock of the fear of death drove my mind inwards and I said to myself mentally without forming the words "Now death has come, what does it mean? What is it that is dying? This body dies." And I at once dramatized the occurrence of death. I lay with my

limbs stretched out still as though rigor mortis had set in and imitated a corpse so as to give greater reality to the inquiry. I held my breath and kept my lips tightly closed so that no sound could escape so that neither the word *I* nor any other word could be uttered. "Well then," I said to myself, "the body is dead. It will be carried stiff to the burning ground and there reduced to ashes. But with the death of the body am I dead? Is the body "I"? It is silent and inert, but I could feel the full force of my personality and even the voice of the "I" within me, apart from it. So I am spirit transcending the body. The body dies but the spirit that transcends it cannot be touched by death. That means that I am the deathless spirit." All this was not a dull thought. It flashed through me vividly as living truth which I perceived directly, almost without thought process.

"I" was something very real, the only real thing about my present state, and all the conscious activity connected with my body was centered on that "I." From that moment onwards the "I" or "self" focused attention on itself by a powerful fascination. Fear of death had vanished once and for all. Absorption in the self continued unbroken from that time on. Other thoughts might come and go like the various notes of music but the "I" continued like the fundamental *sruti* note that underlies and blends with all other states. Whether the body was engaged in talking, reading, or anything else I was still centered on the "I." Previous to that crisis I had felt no perceptible or direct interest in it, much less any inclination to dwell permanently in it.

James: First, this is a typical self experience. It, or something like it, happens somewhere to someone every day. Remember that lovely piece of writing by Wren Lewis that you gave me—the guy who got poisoned in Thailand and had what is now called a "near death experience"?

Interviewer: Yes, that would be another interesting one to talk about.

James: It certainly would. My point is that there is a vast literature of these kinds of experiences. First, let's take the statement, "the shock of the fear of death drove my mind inwards."

The mind was previously facing the world. Now it is looking inwards.

Next we have Ramana's reaction to the experience. This is important because it reveals the nature of Ramana's mind very clearly. Ordinarily, when we have intense experiences involving great pleasure or great pain, our emotions take over and cloud our appreciation of the experience. We either get so frightened we cannot report what happened accurately, or we get so ecstatic we cannot report what happened accurately. But Ramana stayed cool as a cucumber. He says, "Now death has come, what does it mean? What is it that is dying? This body dies."

I mentioned earlier that Vedanta is concerned with meaning. Here you have an inquiring mind, one not fascinated by the experience, seeking to understand the experience. Although the majority of the people coming to Tiruvannamalai are experience-happy, quite a few have this kind of mind to some degree. They want to know. But very few have it to the degree that Ramana did. This shows that he was a lover of knowledge.

And using logic he draws the right conclusion, "This body dies." Already we can see by implication that he knows he is other than the body. He has completely objectified it. Then he dramatizes it "to give greater reality to the inquiry." The rest of his musings up to "it is silent and inert" are further confirmation of his understanding that he is not the body.

Next we come to the realization of the self. This is the positive side—what happens when the world is negated. He says, "but I could feel the full force of my personality and even the voice of the 'I' within me, apart from it." The word *personality* is quite interesting. I don't know if this was an accurate translation of Ramana's words. But what he probably meant was the *jivatman*, the self embodied as an individual. I'm sorry to use these fancy Sanskrit terms, but there is simply no English equivalent. The self is unembodied, but it is capable of embodiment. It is called the jivatman. OK, we can call it the soul or the person, but it is not quite right because it throws up too many imprecise associations.

So now he is aware of the dead body and the subtle body, what is called the personality, and "even the voice of the 'I' within me, apart from it." You see the whole structure of the self in this experience. Then, he concludes correctly, "So I am spirit transcending the body." He has answered the "Who am I?" question, which up to this point he had never even considered.

And then the icing on the cake, he describes self knowledge. "All this was not a dull thought. It flashed through me vividly as living truth which I perceived directly, almost without thought process."

When you have any experience, the knowledge of that experience arises in the mind. This knowledge needs to be grasped, owned, if you will. In this case, he witnessed the knowledge "flashing vividly through me as living truth." This should quiet the people who say that the mind has to be dead for enlightenment. The operative words are *almost without thought process.* This means there was thought.

Interviewer: So how does this relate to liberation?

James: Many people have these kinds of experiences, but do not realize that they are "spirit transcending body." It is this knowledge that is called liberation. Why is it liberation? Because thinking you are the body is a huge problem. It makes the world and everything in it seem to be real. But to the self, the world appears as a kind of dream, so all the experiences you have in it cannot bind you. In the next statement he addresses this issue of what is real. He says, "'I' was something very real, the only real thing about my present state, and all the conscious activity connected with my body was centered on that 'I.'" This is knowledge. The "I" is real. The body-mind entity is not "taken to be real."

Interviewer: Surely, if it is the self, it has to be real, doesn't it?

James: That's a good point. There is a statement in Vedanta that says "*Brahma satyam, jagan mithya.*" It means the limitless self is real and the world—the body-mind—is apparently real. Real is defined in spiritual science as what never changes, what lasts forever. So experience and the body don't fit that definition. But experience is not actually unreal either. It has a peculiar status, neither completely real, nor completely unreal. There is a famous Vedantic text, the Vacarambana Sruti, that explains how it is. I won't digress into it because we are just getting to the meat of Ramana's experience.

There is one more thing to understand in this passage. Ramana is not quite through with the process he's experiencing. He is at the intermediate stage. Before this experience came, and he realized he was the self, he thought that the body was real. But this experience has shown him that with reference to the self, the body is not real. It is important that he completely negate his belief in the reality of the body. So he has to say that it isn't real. Then later, when the knowledge that he is the self is completely firm, he can take the body back as real or apparently real, because it is non-separate from him. The only actual problem with the body is the belief that it is an independent entity and that the "I" depends on it. But Ramana realized that the "I" was free of the body. He says—and this is very important—"all the conscious activity connected with my body was centered on that 'I.'"

People who are ignorant that they are the immortal self, what you would call materialists, believe that the "I" is centered on the body, that it is the body that gives life to the "I." But scripture and direct experience reveal that the body is centered on the "I." In other words, the "I" is the living principle, and the body is just matter. Ramana realized that fact.

The next statement is very difficult to understand. In a way, we would have been much happier if Ramana had packed up his meditation carpet and stole silently away into the night. He is the self and he knows it. Shouldn't that be the end? But as usual, life always has another surprise in store. He says, "From that moment onwards the 'I' or 'self' focused attention on itself by a powerful fascination."

Which "I" did what? If I'm the "I," the one without a second, how do we get two "I's" here? Has Ramana lost his realization? How can the self be fascinated with anything? It would be fascinated only if it felt there was something to experience or know. But we know that it is whole and complete, lacking nothing, so why is it acting as if it weren't? Furthermore, if it is self aware, it is already *focused* on itself.

This experience was not the end. In fact, it was just the beginning of Ramana's spiritual journey. He has just become self realized, but he has not become enlightened, if we take these words at face value.

Interviewer: What do you mean by that?

James: The last paragraph shows clearly that he thinks of the self as an object and that he sees himself as separate from it. He is experiencing it, no doubt—it would remain as a permanent experience—but he has yet to see himself solely as the non-dual self. He does. He gets there. We do not know when, probably sometime during his meditation phase when he was living in the caves, but he gains the last little bit of knowledge.

Interviewer: How do you know?

James: The language. Let's take the language at face value, although it is very risky to trust a translator. Ramana was a very straightforward person. He says, "Absorption in the self continued unbroken from that time on." So the natural question is "Who is absorbed in what?" Was the self absorbed in the self or was Ramana absorbed in the self? We understand what he means a couple of sentences later when he says, "I was centered on the 'I.'" And one gets the impression that the first "I" was different from the second. This is a statement of the self realization phase of the spiritual journey. If there was no duality left, why doesn't he just say, "I, the self, was centered on myself." This is how it is in non-duality, not that the self is centered on anything. The "I" is self knowing by nature and requires no centering.

And it fits in with the self inquiry that Ramana taught, which was based on his own experience and backed by scripture. One of the definitions of self inquiry that Ramana gives is "Holding the mind on the self is inquiry." So here he is, a young boy of seventeen who did not have a clue about the self, with his mind fixed permanently on the self.

Interviewer: So what is the next phase? How does it happen?

James: You keep watching the self. You stay alert, which is not hard because the self is very beautiful. And the more you watch it the more it sets you to thinking. You become fascinated. The words Ramana uses are "a powerful fascination." When you are in this phase, you need a cave or something like it. You do not want to be in the world. If you stay in the world your connection might be broken.

You fall in love. When you are in love you do not stop thinking. One thing that we need to point out here is very important. You know how I have been saying that this belief that the mind has to stop completely is not true, that it does happen but it need not happen, that having a dead mind can be a big problem?

Interviewer: Yes.

James: Well, it is clear by Ramana's own admission that his mind had not stopped completely. He says, "Other thoughts might come and go like the various notes of music..." This state he is in is *savikalpa samadhi*, to use the Yogic term. It is a state of clear seeing in which *vikalpas*—thoughts—arise and fall. But the thoughts do not obscure the vision of the self. This is very important. Ramana says so.

Anyway, where was I? Yes...love. You fall in love. When you are in love you do not stop thinking. On the contrary, you think more; you want to know where your beloved is, what he or she is doing. This thinking is inquiry. Ramana already had the knowledge from his experience to guide him in his inquiry. He knew about himself and the "I beyond the body."

You are getting it all straight about who you are and what your relationship is to this beautiful being. And then one day something happens. We cannot say when. It just happens, if you stay focused on the beloved. There is an Aha! and at that moment, the you that was looking at the self becomes the self. There is actually no becoming. You were it all along. The becoming is a recognition, a knowing. But the becoming changes your perspective. You are no

longer the individual looking in at the self, awareness, you are awareness looking out at the individual. And what do you know? That awareness and the individual are one. Or in the words of scripture, "*Tat Tvam Asi.*" That (self) you
are. Formulated from the self's perspective, the words are "*Aham Brahmasmi,*"
I am limitless. Ramana the form is limited. Ramana the self is unlimited.

This is what Vedanta calls enlightenment. From that point on, you do not
abide *in* the self, you abide *as* the self. You have only one, non-dual identity.

Interviewer: That's a very important analysis that will help many people who
are nearing the end of their spiritual journeys. Now let's consider this. At the
end of his book *Self Inquiry* he says, "He who is thus endowed with a mind
that has become subtle, and who has the experience of the self is called a
Jivanmukta."

James: Here's a vindication from Ramana's mouth of what I have been saying
about the mind. The mind does not have to be killed. When enough gross
vasanas are exhausted, the mind becomes subtle. It still has thoughts, but the
thoughts do not unbalance it. This kind of mind comes about through simple
restrained living and clear thinking. It is capable of self realization.

But I have to take issue with this statement. Experience of the self is not
enlightenment. When is the self not experienced? It may be self realization
but it is not enlightenment, for the simple reason that it implies that there is
an experiencer other than the self. It is enlightenment when the experiencer
realizes that he or she is what is being experienced, i.e., the self. Enlightenment
is knowledge, not experience of anything. People erroneously believe that enlightenment is gaining some permanent incredible experience of the self. But
a jivanmukta is free of everything, especially experience. A jivanmukta is the
self. *Jivanmukta* simply means someone who has realized he or she is the self
and has no sense of duality.

Interviewer: Ramana goes on to say, "It is the state of jivanmukta that is referred to as the attributeless Brahman and as Turiya. When even the subtle
mind gets resolved."

James: Well, this is not a correct understanding of jivanmukta. In the first place, it is not a "state." States are experience-based and come and go. Attributeless Brahman would not have any states in it, nor would it be a state. A state is an attribute. *Attributeless* and *Brahman* are two words that describe awareness, the self. It has no attributes and is limitless, which is the meaning of the word *Brahman*. The resolution of the mind is simply a resolution in understanding. The mind understands that it is the self and that makes it peaceful, and finishes it as an independent entity. It does not mean that the mind dies, never to think a thought again.

Interviewer: "…and when one is immersed in the ocean of bliss and has become one with it without any differentiated existence, one is called a *Videhamukta*. It is the state of Videhamukti that is referred to as the transcendent Turiya. This is the final goal." So is he saying this is enlightenment?

James: That's the way it seems. He is describing enlightenment in the language of experience or Yoga. If you analyze that language you can find the problem. He is experiencing limitless bliss, yet he is talking about it being a goal, something to be gained. But in the language of identity, it is something that you are.

We have to resort to linguistic analysis because Ramana is dead and we have no idea if the translator knew what Ramana meant and used the correct words. Even if Ramana was speaking to us directly it would be possible to misunderstand the meaning, unless we knew the self. The only way to get the proper idea of the meaning of these words is to hold them up to scripture and see how well they fit. This will be a useful interview for seekers, but it will not make me a lot of friends among the Ramana devotees, because Ramana has attained the status of deity of late and you cannot have your gods with feet of clay. Ramana was a realized soul and a human being of the highest caliber. But we have only his words to go on, and I don't want this to be my opinion on the teachings of Ramana, although it will certainly be taken as such. My idea is to discuss Ramana in light of the science of self inquiry. Mind you, I am not saying that Ramana was not enlightened. But he was not a scriptural master and spoke to many individuals at different stages of their spiritual journey, and did not issue a "big picture" statement about his teachings, one that would resolve the apparent contradictions.

Let's pick apart this statement a little more. In the first place, what do the words *immersed in* mean? These are experiential words. They indicate a person having a particular kind of experience, in this case bliss. The next words of interest are "has become one with it." What do they mean? What kind of becoming is it? If the becoming is experiential, the experience of bliss stops because the one who was experiencing it is no more. In oneness, non-duality, the subject and object necessary for experience are not present. So if somebody is going to lose the experience of "the ocean of bliss," why will they merge into the self? It doesn't make sense.

This is why the Bhakti tradition scoffs at the liberation tradition. The bhaktas say, "Why would I want to be God, when I can experience God all the time?" It's a valid point. However, it doesn't take into account the fact that you can be God and experience God. There is only a contradiction when you have a flawed understanding of the nature of God and the world.

But what if this becoming is the coming of understanding? By understanding I mean the recognition that the subject, the mind-ego—the one experiencing the bliss—and the object, the bliss, are one. *Bliss* is a common but inaccurate word because of its experiential implications. One way to describe this understanding experientially is that it is a shift during which the foreground—the ego—which has been experiencing the self in the form of bliss, becomes the background, and the self—which has been the object of experience—becomes the foreground, as I mentioned. So now the "I" is the self looking out at the ego, looking in at it. And when this shift takes place there is an instant recognition that "I" is the self. One's identification of "I" with the ego-mind ends once and for all. From that point on there is no foreground or background, no in or out. The mind is purified of these concepts.

*Videhamukti* exoterically is usually taken to mean liberation when the body dies. Why would you have to wait until the body dies to realize the self, since the self is always present when you are alive? This liberation at death is just a belief. Death is just a belief. The actual meaning is "freedom from the body." *Vi* means *without* and *dehi* means *the body* and *mukti* means *liberation*.

So it is not an experiential term; it is a statement of knowledge. It means that when you realize that you are not the body, you are free. The realization that one is not the body, if it is a hard and fast knowledge, is enlightenment. We can include the mind-ego in the word *body* too because it is a body, albeit a subtle one. Body means embodied. This experience and the understanding that arises with it means that from this point on, you are no longer embodied. The bodies are in the self but the self is not in the bodies. This is why it is called liberation.

Interviewer: You have always been the self; it's like a recognition.

James: That's right.

Interviewer: It's an embracing.

James: Yes, one owns it.

Interviewer: It's the moment the wave sinks into the ocean. It's when the wave stops being this wave.

James: Yes, but—here's that famous "but"—the wave can be there. If there is a wave in the ocean, you know that it is not just an independent wave; it is the ocean as well. It won't be a wave unless it is the ocean. The wave depends on the ocean, but the ocean does not depend on the wave. So even if there is a wave, it has no effect on the ocean. Enlightenment does not destroy dualistic experience. One just realizes that experience depends on me, the self, but that I am always free of experience. Acting in the world with this knowledge is quite different from acting in this world without it.

Interviewer: Right. What you are saying now is very important. It's completely contrary to what I have been led to believe. It's a vital point. I can remember talking about this elsewhere. Recently, a woman came to me quite disturbed because she could not do anything about her mind. She had the idea she must kill her mind completely.

James: All that so-called teaching does is deflate people; it doesn't give them encouragement and is patently untrue. Mind you, you need to get some mind out of the way—your neuroses, your binding likes and dislikes—and for that you need to do some work. The mind is not the problem, the mess you have made of it is. That's why Ramana encourages spiritual practice. This is what Vedanta says too. The mind needs to be quiet, but that does not mean that the mind has to disappear completely. It may disappear momentarily, but it always reconstitutes itself.

If self realization only happens when the mind is non-existent, then the self and the mind enjoy exactly the same order of reality, like sickness and health. When you are healthy you are not sick. The scriptures say that this is not so. Experience shows that it is not so.

The self is knowable directly when the mind is functioning. The self doesn't need any knowledge. The mind needs it and to get it, it has to be functioning clearly. But when the mind is overcome with heavy activity and dullness, it is impossible to know the self.

Interviewer: So the mind does experience the self, then? This seems contrary to what you were saying before.

James: That's good, picking up on an apparent contradiction. The answer is yes and no. What is experienced is the reflection of the self in a pure mind. The pure mind is like a highly polished mirror and the self illumines it, so it is experienceable there. There can be no direct experience because the mind and the self enjoy different orders of reality. The self is subtler than the mind. Ramana defines inquiry as holding the mind on the self, which means keeping your attention on the reflection of the self in a pure mind.

You hold your attention on it to get knowledge. When you get knowledge, you can relax. You are trying to figure out what it is and what it has to do with you. And if you do not involve yourself with the modifications arising in the mind, there will eventually come a point when there is the 'Aha!' And that 'Aha!' is simply the recognition that what I am experiencing is me, not some consciousness other than my own.

When you grasp the knowledge "I am the self," you are no longer excluding yourself from the experience of the self. As long as you are experiencing the self, you are excluding yourself from the self. You are saying "I am here, the self is there and I am experiencing it."

Interviewer: Ramana makes a strong statement when asked, "Will there not be realization when the world is there (taken to be real)?" He says, "There will not be."

James: I think we spoke about this before. The statement means it will seem to be real if you see the world as an independent reality. They put the phrase "taken to be real" in because "is there" makes it seem that the world has to be physically not seen for realization to happen. One might believe that perceptually, experientially the world is going to disappear. It's a common belief among spiritual types.

Interviewer: That's right. And that makes it even worse. It makes it scary.

James: They think that if it hasn't disappeared they aren't enlightened.

Interviewer: And they also think that the enlightened are walking around in some sort of deep grey void.

James: Maybe that's what all these zombie types that congregate at the spiritual centers are doing. Maybe they are the only really enlightened ones. Language is very important, because these people are getting their ideas from somewhere. Failure to understand explains why so many seekers do not become finders. There are many people in the spiritual world who would be classified as self realized, according to the stages of enlightenment mentioned above.

This is what Ramana calls *antar mukha*, turning the mind inward, watching or realizing or experiencing the self.

But, rightly, these people are not satisfied and continue to entertain doubts about their state. Usually, the doubt has to do with making the state permanent, which is impossible, since the person and his pure mind are still in the realm of time. In other words, there is always the realistic fear that the experience will not last. And even though they are so close to enlightenment experientially, it still eludes them.

And the reason? Because they are prisoners of the language of experience. The language we use indicates the way we think. And at this stage, when the experience is more or less continually available, the only barrier to converting the experience to a "permanent" state, not that enlightenment is a state, is the way one thinks. What needs to happen at this point is that the individual needs to convert the language of experience to the language of identity. The language of identity states that the experiencer and what is being experienced are not two separate things, that they are in fact the same. When any object is experienced the knowledge of that object arises simultaneously in the intellect. And if the mind in which the reflection of the self appears is pure, the knowledge of the self will arise with it in the intellect. This knowledge is in the form of an insight, an *akandakara vritti*, that I am the whole and complete, actionless awareness that I am experiencing. Let's recall Ramana's statement of this situation. "All this was not a dull thought. It flashed through me vividly as living truth which I perceived directly, almost without thought process."

If the person is accustomed to thinking of the self as an object, he or she will be reluctant to surrender the experiencer, and the self will continue to remain as an experienced object. The surrender is in terms of letting go of the idea of oneself as an experiencer and embracing one's limitless identity. This is the "destruction of the mind" that yogis talk about. This phrase "destruction of the mind" is very unfortunate. It should be "destruction of ignorance." The destruction of ignorance does not destroy the mind.

Were the person to be trained in the language of identity, this problem would not arise. In fact the person would immediately recognize the content of the experience as "I" and that would finish the work. Clinging to experience is hanging on to the container and sacrificing the content. It is like a person pouring the Coke out of the bottle and drinking the bottle. We can throw away the container. It is non-essential. We need the contents, the self.

The whole of Vedanta can be reduced to one simple equation found in the Upanishads: "You are that." *That* is the self and *you* is the self in the form of the experiencer and the verb *are* indicates the identity between the two.

Interviewer: Probably that is where I am struggling right now, existentially speaking. Because I think that's probably true of me. I see everything as an experience.

James: That's what I've observed. You describe everything to do with you in terms of what's happening. I believe that "Nothing ever happened" teaching of Papaji's is meant to neutralize the belief that what happens has something to do with you.

Experience isn't bossing me. I'm bossing it. Without me it doesn't amount to a hill of beans. That's freedom. I don't have to erase it. I just take it as I please. This is why bad days are good days for the enlightened. They can see themselves in everything. Looking to experience for validation is the tail wagging the dog. We're trying to set things straight and get the dog to wag the tail. That's how it is. Dogs wag their tails, not the other way around. Yoga says that if you get this experience, nirvikalpa samadhi, then you are enlightened. Vedanta says that you are the self, no matter what experience you are having.

Interviewer: Here's another of Ramana's statements on self inquiry that I think is very interesting. "How could this search be done in books? All the texts say that in order to gain liberation, you must make the mind quiet. Once this has been understood, there is no need for endless reading. In order to quiet the mind, one has only to enquire within oneself what oneself is."

James: This statement may lead a person to conclude that no scriptural information would be useful in self inquiry. But you can't make an inquiry without knowledge. In fact he supports scripture with the statement "all the texts say..." You can't perform inquiry without the knowledge that I am not the body, mind, etc. You can't just sit there without any information like a dodo and say, "Uh...Who am I? Duh...Hey God...who am I?" This is not going to work, even if the heavens are rent asunder with the booming voice of God... "YOU ARE PURE CONSCIOUSNESS!!!"

Interviewer: Ha ha ha!

James: Even if He tells you to your face, you will have no way to evaluate this information. "Uh? I am? What does that mean?" I need knowledge. I need to know how who I am relates to my body and mind and the world around. It has to be contextualized, or it is useless. Scripture does an excellent job of contextualizing the "I," telling you what it means to be the self. And anyway, Ramana is only dissing "endless reading." In fact, you should not *read* scripture. It should be taught to you. Then you should reflect on it until its truths are assimilated. Nothing, except perhaps inspiration, will come of just reading.

Interviewer: I've mentioned several times that we should talk about self inquiry as a practice, and I came across an interesting question and answer that addresses this issue. Someone asks Ramana "What is the method of practice?" and he replies, "As the self of a person who tries to attain self-realization is not different from him and as there is nothing other than or superior to him to be attained by him, self-realization being only the realization of one's own nature, the seeker of liberation realizes, without doubts or misconceptions, his real nature by distinguishing the eternal from the transient and never swerves from this natural state. This is known as the practice of knowledge. This is the inquiry leading to self-realization."

He seems to be saying that self inquiry is more than just asking "Who am I?"

James: That's right. From speaking with people who come here looking for self-realization, I've learned that many think all one has to do is say "Who am I?" and somehow the answer will be revealed. But this isn't how it is. The fact is that the nature of the "I" is well known. If you have a doubt, just read the Upanishads or Shankara or any Vedantic text. It is very clear. Even these Neo-Advaita teachers have it right on this issue. There are many words that indicate the self and there is a brilliant proven methodology that can destroy your self ignorance.

There is a peculiar belief that the self is some mysterious unknown presence, only apprehended through mystic means, about which one can say nothing. Unspeakable. Indefinable. Beyond words, etc. But actually, the self is the only thing one can speak about with precision and certainty because it is the only reality. All the rest of it, what people think of as real, cannot really be described because it is neither completely real nor is it completely unreal.

In this statement Ramana uses perhaps the most common word to indicate the nature of the self. He says it is eternal. This distinguishes it from the body-mind-ego complex and the world around, which is constantly changing. We think of the body as real, but when you look into the body you cannot come up with anything substantial. It keeps resolving into subtler and subtler elements until it disappears altogether. But no matter how much you analyze it, you cannot reduce the self to anything else. It cannot be dissolved.

Interviewer: So inquiry is not a matter of getting knowledge then, it is a matter of applying it?

James: Yes, Ramana says that inquiry is separating the real from the unreal, the eternal from the transient. So it is a practice. Before you can practice you need to know what is real and what isn't. Twelve centuries before Ramana, Shankar uses the exact same words, "practice of knowledge (jnanabyasa)" in Atma Bodh and elsewhere to describe this process. And it was already part of the tradition when Shankar came along. The practice is called *viveka* and it is the proven method of liberation.

Interviewer: It seems quite intellectual. How does it work?

James: It isn't "intellectual" in the pejorative sense that one hears the word used today. But it definitely relies on an astute use of the intellect. There is this notion that Ramana taught in silence and that only by sitting in silence, not by using the mind in any way, can one realize the self. This is patently untrue. Here Ramana is not recommending silence. Mind you, meditation, sitting in silence, is a very useful practice, but Ramana himself makes it very clear that in self inquiry, the intellect is the instrument of realization.

In his description of his own awakening, one can see that he was obviously conscious and thinking and discriminating. And there is no reason one cannot think when the mind is silent. In fact in that state, conscious thinking is beautiful, a real joy. There is even a yogic term for it, *savikalpa samadhi*. It means samadhi with thought. *Vikalpas* are thoughts.

Interviewer: This is quite surprising. The common notion is that the intellect needs to be shut down for the self to be realized.

James: That is the view of Yoga. Controlling the mind is useful to prepare the mind for self realization, but it is not tantamount to self realization. We need to remember that the mind is transient and therefore unreal. So how are you going to control something that is non-eternal? The one who is trying to change, the ego, is non-eternal and what is meant not to change is non-eternal. Therefore, how can there be any permanent change? Even if there is change as a result of your efforts, you will have to keep up the effort to keep the changes operational. So you find yourself having to do all these things to be what you want to be. This is always the problem when you try to change the mind or stop the mind. Inquiry is not a question of controlling the mind. It is a question of observing the mind.

Interviewer: So how does this discrimination work?

James: Well, first we need to know that not any Tom, Dick or Harry can just practice inquiry. In the first line of the very next paragraph Ramana says, "This is suitable only for the ripe soul." You need to be prepared. Prepared means mature, indifferent to the blandishments the world has to offer. And secondly, one needs a burning desire to be free of his or her own mind. This is different from saying that one needs a dead or different mind. The mind is going to be with you in one form or another, whether you like it or not, so the only sensible question is how to live happily with it. When you realize what the self is and that you are it, you see that you have always been free of the mind.

Discrimination or inquiry is the moment to moment practice of the understanding that the experiencer and its experience are not real and that awareness is real.

It works like this: whenever an impulse to do something, possess something, feel something or change something comes up in the mind, as it does all the time, one does not just mindlessly set out to manifest the desired result. Instead, you think "What lasting benefit will I get by doing, getting, experiencing this? Will I be more, better, different? Will I gain lasting happiness or will I still be what I am?" Assuming that the one doing the practice is the ego, which it would necessarily be, will that person be any wiser with reference to his or her own self by doing/thinking/feeling/experiencing something? And the answer is always no. True, you may be wiser with reference to a specific idea, but will you actually become whole and complete and free of your mind by doing what you are contemplating doing? For example, you may invest in the stock market and lose a bundle because the corporate fat cats are cooking the books. So you learn to not trust people's word concerning money, but are you fundamentally different because you don't have the money you once had? Or are you fundamentally different because you are more wary? You are still what you are.

Interviewer: So self transformation is not self realization.

James: It may be useful to clean up your ego a bit before you set out to set it free, but the very fact that you are trying to change means that you are not free.

Interviewer: A friend and I rented a house we found on the internet recently from a woman who was going on vacation and when we moved, I noticed a collage on the wall celebrating her recent spiritual awakening. And pasted on the collage were different sized words from different periodicals that said, "One day I got tired of being the same, so I made the BIG JUMP."

James: What you have here is a spiritual awakening, but not self realization. This is a person who has been stuck with some bad values, and consequently caught up in some unhealthy habits, who finally gets the courage to confront herself and make changes in the way she lives. And this is very good, an important first step. But this is not self realization. Awakening is not self realization, although during an awakening you may come to experience and understand that there is a self.

Interviewer: This is an important distinction, I think.

James: Yes it is. This experience is not self realization because the one who landed is the same one who made the jump. Once the proper values and good habits are in place, a new problem will surface: is this all? Because you haven't addressed the fundamental problem, you have just corrected some karmic mistakes the ego made. I'm not saying that spiritual awakenings aren't good, but once you are awake to how foolish you are and the possibility of getting out of it, then you can perhaps start to seek wisdom, which at some point will entail asking who made the jump.

Now, if Ramana is saying that the self never changes and you are the self and the self is endless bliss, then you will never want to jump out of yourself. So what we have in the case of this woman is an ego changing itself. And no matter how much the ego changes for the better, it is never going to change into the self. When you realize that you are the self, it doesn't matter to you what the ego is. You accept it as it is. You understand that it wouldn't be the way it is if it could help it and you let it be. Or you work on it dispassionately, if that is your karma. When you no longer see yourself as the ego, it will gradually become more pure and radiant but it will never become the self. So thinking that you are going to become different is not the way to go.

Interviewer: I have another teaching that I would like to discuss. Ramana says "As the self of a person who tries to attain self-realization is not different from him and as there is nothing other than or superior to him to be attained by him, self-realization being only the realization of one's own nature"…etc.

James: I think this statement should be required reading for anyone who wants to understand what enlightenment is. Ramana makes it very clear that it is not about being different from what you are or getting something that is better than what you already have—like a high state of consciousness. He uses a very interesting word here—*only*—to make the point that incredible spiritual experiences or altered states of consciousness or transforming oneself is not enlightenment. He says it is "only" realizing what you are.

Interviewer: But isn't this realization something unique?

James: No. What is being realized might be considered unique if you had been ignorant for a long time, but this realization is no different from realizing or understanding or knowing anything. When it happens, there is always a sense of irony because it is something that has always been known. What could be more familiar to you than you? It may seem like a big deal because something that is so obvious can easily be taken for granted and forgotten. So self realization is always a re-discovery, not a discovery.

Interviewer: So this is the whole cosmic joke idea.

James: Yes. To solve the riddle you need a trick, a technique, which Ramana calls inquiry or *viveka*. You need to be reminded that you are eternal, that nothing can be added to or subtracted from you, that experience is impermanent and that you need to start paying attention to your own mind and its ideas to the contrary. Then you get to work dismissing them. As long as you hold erroneous views about yourself, you will not hold the right view about yourself.

Interviewer: Which is that you are whole and complete.

James: Yes, that experience depends on you, but that you do not depend on experience.

Interviewer: That nothing can affect you.

James: That you don't need anything at all to make yourself happy.

# CHAPTER SIXTEEN

# Neo-Advaita

Mystics have proclaimed the oneness of all things for thousands of years. The science of self inquiry that culminated in the teachings of Adi Shankara in the eighth century has had a profound effect on Eastern religion and spirituality. Although we see the idea of non-duality popping up in Western thought from the time of Christ until the present day, it did not develop into a systematic means of self realization and has virtually no impact on Christianity, Islam and Judaism, unlike self inquiry, which deeply conditioned Indian culture. Until the colonial era, contact between the East and West was limited, but slowly the West became aware of the social, political and religious philosophies of the once powerful Oriental nations. During the last half of the nineteenth century, the New Thought movement sprang up in America. The founders of Christian Science, Unity, and Science of Mind and the transcendental poets were certainly familiar with non-dual thought. Around the turn of the last century, a few Indian mahatmas visited the West and more or less formally introduced us to the idea of non-duality. The powerful speech given by Swami Vivekananda at the Congress of World Religions in Chicago in 1893 was a milestone in the East-West spiritual relationship, proclaiming as it did the oneness of all religions.

For some reason, Vivekananda put his own spin on the traditional teachings, emphasizing Yoga at the expense of Vedanta. It is possible that he felt that the West was not properly prepared. Whatever the reason, the Vedanta he introduced to the West was not strictly traditional and became known as New Vedanta or Modern Vedanta, a contradiction in terms, if ever there was one.

## Multi-Path Confusion

New Vedanta introduced the idea of four paths or yogas—action, devotion, knowledge and meditation—which were supposedly suitable for different personality types, whereas the Vedas only sanction two: action and knowledge. The path of karma is intended for extroverts with a heavy vasana load, and the path of knowledge is for contemplative types whose vasanas are predominately sattvic. How the multi-path idea was meant to be an improvement is difficult to discern. Traditionally Yoga is considered to be a subset of the science of self knowledge, not a separate path to enlightenment. The practices of Yoga are not inferior to self inquiry but, as laboriously pointed out so far, are not suitable as a means of liberation. They are, however, extremely valuable to prepare the mind for liberation because without a pure mind, liberation is not possible.

So with the ascendancy of the Yoga teachings, enlightenment came to be considered a permanent experience of samadhi, in contrast with the mundane experiences of everyday life, which it obviously cannot be if reality is non-dual. In any case, the experiential notion of enlightenment has been the dominant view for the last one hundred years in the West, although it dates back to a few centuries BC, where it is given voice in the Yoga scriptures of Patanjali. It has obviously been around for a very long time because we can trace the Yoga Sutra's origins to the Upanishads, which are records of mankind's earliest spiritual thinking.

Air travel increased the East-West dialogue. By and large, the tsunami of export gurus that inundated the West in the 1960s peddled Modern Vedanta. The emphasis on Yoga was necessary because materialism had corrupted the Western mind. Although there was a strong spiritual hunger in the West, it was not really prepared to assimilate the essence of self inquiry. Materialists are doers and enjoyers and the idea of experiencing enlightenment is good enough for them. As the world became increasingly interconnected and spirituality gained respectability, the bond between East and West deepened.

## Ramana Maharshi, Osho, Papaji and the Rise of Neo-Advaita

In the eighties, the Western spiritual world became reacquainted with Ramana Maharshi, a great Indian sage, who had achieved a certain degree of international recognition around the middle of the last century, but who had been all but forgotten since his death. Ramana realized the non-dual nature of the self and taught self inquiry and Yoga. Neo-Advaita, sometimes called Pseudo-Advaita, the West's latest idea of the wisdom of the East, came about mainly through a disciple of Ramana, HWL Poonjaji, commonly known as Papaji, although J. Krishnamurti, Jean Klein, Ramesh Balsekar and others contributed to it.

Papaji, who was virtually unknown in India during his life, came to the attention of the Western spiritual world shortly after Bhagawan Shree Rajneesh, the notorious ninety-three-Rolls-Royce guru died. Rajneesh, the horse's mouth concerning the topic of enlightenment for Westerners for many years, was a particularly clever man who created a very large following by wedding two largely incompatible concepts, sense enjoyment and enlightenment. His "Zorba the Buddha" idea gave a whole generation of rebellious, disaffected, community-seeking Westerners good reason to party hearty on their way to God. When Rajneesh, who rechristened himself Osho to avoid the bad karma his notoriety produced, died, his devotees, ever on the lookout for the next master, "discovered" Papaji, by this time an old man languishing in Lucknow, a hot, dirty, noisy city on the banks of the Gomati river, a tributary of the Ganges.

Papaji, like Osho, was a clever man with an outsized personality. He was a *shaktipat* guru with a super-abundance of "spiritual" energy, which some people claim he transmitted to his disciples. A shaktipat guru transmits shakti, spiritual energy, which causes an epiphany. After the transmission, Papaji informed them that they were enlightened. He should have known better—and perhaps he did—because there is only one self and it has always been enlightened. But this distinction was definitely lost on his followers. As it so happened, many got high on "the energy" and imagined themselves to be enlightened, a condition known in yogic culture as *manolaya*, a temporary cessation of thought, or if you prefer an English term, an epiphany.

It so happens that Osho's followers, in spite of the fact that most of them spent long periods in India, had virtually no knowledge of self inquiry, even though they called themselves "neo-sannyasins" which translates as "new renunciates." Renunciation is a tried and true Vedic spiritual idea, but in their case it is not clear what they actually renounced. Buddha was certainly a renunciate, but it would be a stretch to expect Zorba to renounce anything that interfered with his enthusiastic celebration of life.

On the upside, his followers busied themselves developing sometimes effective therapies to deal with their manifold neuroses. Osho was a Jain, not a Hindu, and seems to have more or less ignored the great spiritual tradition that surrounded him, at least after he became famous. His role models, whom he was not above criticizing, were Christ and the Buddha. Papaji, on the other hand, was a died-in-the-wool Hindu from a Brahmin family of Krishna devotees. His contribution to the spiritual education of this group was two-fold. He introduced them to Ramana Maharshi, whom he claimed was his guru, thus giving himself a golden, nay platinum, credential. And he familiarized them with the word *advaita*, which means non-duality. Hence, the advaita movement, which has attracted many thousands of Westerners. Although Ramana was Papaji's guru, their ideas of spiritual practice, self inquiry, were quite different. Ramana's involved persistent and intense effort on a moment-to-moment basis to dispel the mind/ego's idea of duality, while Papaji's involved only asking the question "Who am I?" and "keeping quiet" until the answer appeared, the absurdity of which was lost on them.

## Neo-Advaita Versus Traditional Vedanta

On the surface Neo-Advaita, which has no worthwhile methodology, seems fairly reasonable. By and large it teaches that you are not the body-mind-ego entity and that you are non-dual awareness, both of which are in harmony with tradition. If reality is non-dual, then there is no one that is ignorant of his or her self because knowledge and ignorance are duality. If there is no ignorance of who we are, there is no need for a teaching, a teacher or a student. In non-dual reality there is no body and mind to be something other than the self—awareness—so there is no bondage and no liberation, no suffering and enjoying, no joy and no sorrow. If you are non-dual awareness you cannot do anything, so there are no right and wrong actions. You were never born and you never die and experience does not exist.

This teaching causes a problem because it does not take experience into account. So you either have to deny the existence of experience, which can only take place in duality, or modify the teaching. You cannot deny the existence of experience—although Neo-Advaita does its level best—because it exists. So to tell someone caught in the experiential world that he or she does not exist, or that nothing can be done to attain enlightenment, is not helpful. The sages who gave us self inquiry were considerably more sophisticated and worked out an intelligent solution. They assigned a provisional reality to duality that is in harmony with the experience of everyone and then proceeded to destroy it, using teachings that correspond with the common sense logic of the seeker's own experience.

Without the notion of a provisional or apparent reality, which experience confirms, you are forced to superimpose the idea that all is consciousness on empirical reality. Needless to say, it does not apply to this level of reality. A verse in the scriptures on Yoga says, "a yogi in samadhi sees no difference between a lump of gold and the excreta of a crow." Presumably, an enlightened Neo-Advaitan, in dire financial straits, might attempt to pawn a handful of crow poop and sweep his lump of gold into the garbage can. Non-duality, non-difference, does not mean sameness. It means that from the self's perspective there is no difference, but from the level of the body and mind there are only differences. This discrimination between what is real and what is apparent is the signature of an enlightened person. In fact, one of the definitions of enlightenment found in the scriptures of self inquiry is "the discrimination between what is real and what is apparent." When you superimpose the notion of non-duality on multiplicity, you add a belief that will eventually have to be discarded at some point. This kind of spiritual belief, which is just ignorance, is exceedingly hard to investigate if it is taken to be the truth.

## No Teacher, Seeker, Path, Knowledge or Ignorance

If reality is non-dual and a special experience of consciousness or a dead mind is not enlightenment, only self knowledge could be enlightenment. But Neo-Advaita does not accept the view that ignorance, which shows up as a lack of discrimination, is the problem, because it says that ignorance does not exist. This is a convenient teaching that plays to the strong anti-intellectual bias of modern seekers. It is true that it does not exist from the self's point of view, but a seeker does not know that he or she is the self or he or she would not be seeking, so this teaching is not a teaching at all. It leaves the seeker with no avenue to actualize the desire for freedom that attracts him or her to the idea of enlightenment, and is tailor made to produce frustration. That enlightenment is a blank mind or the absence of ego is an equally ill-considered notion that inevitably produces suffering when it is pursued. Both of these ideas are the result of level confusion, assigning the same degree of reality to pure consciousness and reflected consciousness—the experiential world.

Of course, if there is no knowledge and no ignorance, there is no seeker either. And if there is no seeker, there necessarily cannot be a path. How Neo-Advaita squares this idea with its very existence is difficult to determine. If there is no knowledge and no ignorance, there is no teacher to pass on the knowledge that there is no path, seeker, knowledge, ignorance, or doer, etc.

This is not to say that negation is not useful. Traditional self inquiry employs negation liberally. But it is half the loaf. The other half is the teachings that reveal the self, using the positive methods described throughout this book. The self is not a big empty void. Because Neo-Advaita is a nihilistic denial of the obvious, it has no methodology apart from its mindless negations.

## Being Present, Dropping Suffering

Another popular teaching, "being present," is unskillful because it does not take the vasanas into account. It is the vasanas that keep the mind worrying about the future and obsessing about the past. Desire needs to be addressed, not repressed with the technique of "being present." The absurdity of such a teaching is evident when we look at it from the self's point of view too. When are you not present? For you to know that you are not present, you would have to be present. If you were absent, how would you know? The karma yoga view is a simple and obvious solution to this problem, but Neo-Advaita has not discovered it, even though it is as old as the hills.

A further teaching, an injunction actually, informs the non-existent seeker to "drop" his or her suffering. How a non-existent ego would drop non-existent suffering is beyond comprehension, but let us assume that there is an ego, and that suffering is undesirable. Suffering is a powerful tendency brought on by ignorance of the nature of the self. It is subtler than the ego and not under its control. It can be removed by inquiry, but it cannot be dropped at will like a hot potato.

Another glaring contradiction found in Neo-Advaita is the claim by the teachers that their statements stem from their own experience. It seems almost gratuitous to point out that from the self's point of view, which seems to be the only point of view Neo-Advaita espouses, there is no experiencer either. It is not the intention of the author to question the enlightenment or lack thereof of any Neo-Advaita teacher, although it is always wise for seekers to do so. It is my intention, however, to point out that enlightenment does not in any way qualify one to teach enlightenment. Furthermore, satsang, as it is conceived by Neo-Advaita, is completely insufficient as a means of self realization.

To avoid the sticky question of a teaching and a teaching methodology, with its abysmal ignorance of the tradition of self inquiry Neo-Advaita uses the argument that their titular inspiration, Ramana Maharshi, gained enlightenment without a teaching and a teacher. Aside from the fact that it is, in very rare cases, possible to realize the self without help, the odds are about the same as winning the lottery, perhaps less. Additionally, this idea does not take into account Ramana's extreme dispassion and the fact that after his enlightenment, he became a dedicated student of the science of self inquiry and actually wrote a scripture, The Essence of the Teaching,[37] that has been accepted by the traditional Vedanta community as having the status of an Upanishad.

---

37. *Upadesha Saram*

## Qualifications for Enlightenment

Perhaps the best way to approach Neo-Advaita is not by what it teaches as by what it does not. Probably the most obvious omission is the notion of qualifications necessary for enlightenment. Neo-Advaita is burdened with an understandably democratic ethos, the idea being that anyone who walks into one of its meetings off the street can gain instant enlightenment, which is possible if you define enlightenment as an epiphany. But then again, you can also fall down a non-dual flight of stairs and have an epiphany.

Because self inquiry defines enlightenment differently however, it insists that a person be discriminating, dispassionate, calm of mind and endowed with a burning desire for liberation along with secondary qualifications like devotion, faith and perseverance. In other words, it requires a mature adult with a one-pointed desire to know the self. The reason for these qualifications, which were discussed in chapter four, is the fact that enlightenment is a hard and fast recognition by the mind of its non-separation from everything; only a very rare individual will let go of his or her sense of individuality to gain another, albeit greater, identity. The mind must be capable of inquiring into, grasping and retaining the knowledge "I am limitless Awareness and not this body-mind." To accomplish this, its extroverted tendency must be checked and attention directed to the self. To put forth the required effort, the individual needs to have the settled conviction that nothing in the world can bring lasting satisfaction. This conviction is what self inquiry calls maturity. To my knowledge, no Neo-Advaita teacher espouses this view. The reason is obvious: he or she would have no one to teach.

## I Am Not the Doer

Perhaps the centerpiece of Neo-Advaita teachings is the idea that there is no doer, a traditional teaching that was carefully unfolded at the beginning of chapter seven. It has achieved considerable popularity in the Neo-Advaita world because it appeals to the something-for-nothing mentality. "You mean I can get enlightened without doing anything? Where do I sign up?" It also dovetails nicely with the idea of enlightenment as the absence of ego. If I do any spiritual work, I am strengthening my ego, or so the logic goes. It is true that the ego can co-opt the practice, but only if practice is done without the right understanding. This teaching, as is the case with all dogmatic statements from the self's point of view, contradicts experience. Everyone sees himself or herself as a doer and identifies to some degree with the actions done by the body and mind at the behest of the vasanas. If a teaching denies my existence, it condemns me to remain as the doer I think I am. Traditional Vedanta agrees that you cannot do anything to be what you are, but it suggests that you allow the science of self inquiry to help you remove your ignorance of who you are because enlightenment is a matter of understanding, not action.

## Importance of Karma Yoga for Self Inquiry

It would be impossible to underestimate the importance of karma yoga for self inquiry. Karma yoga is not taught in the Neo-Advaita world because it is for the doer. Furthermore, it requires discipline and considerable patience, qualities not in evidence in people seeking instant enlightenment. It also requires continuous monitoring of one's motivations and reactions to events. Additionally, it requires a willingness to change one's attitudes. Finally, it demands a pure lifestyle because the vasanas continually divert attention away from the self. None of this is possible if I do not exist. And if I do exist, it is hard work.

Not doing will not create karma—good or bad. But, because it is impossible not to do, the idea that there is nothing to do means that the entry-level seekers will just continue to do what they have always done. No blame, but the idea that there is nothing to do will not result in enlightenment or growth. To fill the non-doing void, Neo-Advaita, thanks to Rajneesh's Zorba the Buddha idea, keeps the seeker hooked with an apparently positive injunction, "celebrate life." How celebrating is not a doing is difficult to understand, but intellectual contradictions rarely stand in the way of an immature seeker's desire to have fun. In contrast, self inquiry encourages sacrifice, the idea being that the ego cannot have its cake and eat it too. The desires that extrovert the mind need to be sacrificed for the sake of a quiet mind, one capable of meditating on the self, reflecting on the non-dual teachings, and assimilating the knowledge.

When actions conform to dharma, binding vasanas are neutralized. Dharma means that I do what has to be done, irrespective of how I personally feel about it. I do not want to pay my taxes, but I pay my taxes. I may not get a vasana for paying taxes, but I will certainly eliminate any agitation associated with noncompliance. But when my desires are all that matter, is it any wonder that whatever non-dual experience happens in the satsang, when the mind is temporarily arrested by the group energy, quickly vanishes with the appearance of the next binding desire? This is why the Neo-Advaita world is little more than thousands of people, including the teachers, who have had scores of non-dual experiences, but who at the end of the day are still prisoners of their desires. Enlightenment is freedom from dependence on desired and feared objects.

Ramana Maharshi, who had an experience of the self at the tender age of seventeen, understood the wisdom of practice. He sat in meditation on the self in caves for about twenty years and studied the texts of both Yoga and self inquiry after he was awakened, although this is not the party line of Ramana devotees. Had he been a Neo-Advaitan, he would have immediately advertised satsang and begun instantly enlightening the world. But he had the wisdom to understand that while the epiphany was the end of his seeking, it was not the end of his work. Had it been, he could have returned home, eaten this mother's *iddlies* and played cricket like any normal seventeen year old Tamil boy. Is it unreasonable to assume that he applied the knowledge he gained during his experience, until the mind's dualistic orientation was reduced to ash in the fire of self knowledge? The notion that his epiphany destroyed his sense of duality once and for all does not jibe with common sense.

## Devotion to God

Another essential component of any valid spiritual path is devotion to God, as explained in chapter nine. Ramana gave devotion to God, meaning glad acceptance of the fruits of action, equal status with self inquiry as a spiritual path because devotion to God exhausts vasanas and breaks down the concept of doership. "Not my will, but Thine." It also teaches that God, not the ego, is the dispenser of the fruits of one's actions. But Neo-Advaita sees devotion as "duality" and has nothing to do with it. In fact, devotion works just as well as the idea of non-duality to prepare the mind for self realization because the self functions through the chosen symbol or practice to bring the necessary qualities for self inquiry into full flower.

One view that needs to be examined in this context is the notion that enlightenment can be transmitted in some subtle experiential way via the physical proximity of a "master." Traditional Advaita disagrees with this view for the reason that ignorance is deeply entrenched in the aspirant's thinking and that it is only by deep reflection on the teachings that the ultimate assimilation of the knowledge is achieved. This assimilation is often called full or complete enlightenment. On the other hand, the transmission fantasy fits nicely into the Neo-Adviatic conception of easy enlightenment, as it does away with the need for serious practice. One need do nothing more than sit in the presence of a master and presto-chango!—I wake up for good. If this were true, however, the thousands who sit at the feet of enlightened masters everywhere would be enlightened.

Another half-baked idea that has gained currency in the Neo-Advaita world is the notion of "awakening." While sleep and waking are reasonable metaphors to describe the states of self ignorance and self knowledge, Neo-Advaita assigns to them an experiential meaning that is not justified. Just as anything that lives dies, anything that wakes sleeps. The self never slept nor does it awaken. The mind does. This waking up and going back to sleep—all of which takes place in the waking state incidentally—is a consequence of the play of the gunas in the mind. When the mind is sattvic, the reflection of the awareness shining on it causes the individual to "wake up," i.e., to experience the self, but when rajas or tamas reappear, as they inevitably do, the mind is clouded over, the experience is lost, and the mind "sleeps." Until the extroverting and dulling vasanas are purified, the seeker is condemned to a frustrating cycle of waking and sleeping.

## Where's the Methodology?

Finally, self inquiry has survived as a viable means of knowledge because it reveals the truth with a refined methodology. Many realize non-duality within and outside the tradition but are incapable of teaching non-duality because they are either unsuited to teach or lack a viable method—or both. Neo-Advaita's statements to "be the space for the thoughts" or "be as you are" are not skillful teachings, because they deliver a non-dual teaching of identity in experiential language. Such teachings give the impression that something can be done to achieve awareness and that self realization can come about through an act of will. In traditional Advaita, not only should the teacher have realized his or her identity as the self in such a way that he or she never re-identifies with the belief that the "I" is limited, but he or she should be able to wield the means of knowledge skillfully.

Many Neo-Advaita satsang teachers use a picture of Ramana to lend legitimacy and gravitas to their satsangs, while they promote one of the most famous Ramana myths, that silence is somehow the ultimate teaching. While understanding the nature of the self in silence apparently finishes seeking for a very few highly qualified individuals, silence is certainly not superior to the skillful use of words in bringing about enlightenment. This is so because silence is in harmony, not in conflict, with self ignorance, as it is with everything. One can sit in silence without instruction for lifetimes and never realize that one *is* the silence, meaning limitless awareness. Knowledge, however, which is a legitimate means of knowledge, destroys self ignorance like light destroys darkness. Additionally no experience, including the experience of silence, can change thinking patterns. An experience of non-duality may temporarily suspend thought or increase one's resolve to see oneself as limitless awareness, but the notion that the "I" is limited, inadequate, incomplete and separate is hard wired. It is only by diligent practice of the knowledge "I am limitless, ordinary awareness and not this body-mind" that the mind's understanding of reality gets in line with the nature of the self.

Why are binding desires such a major problem for anyone seeking enlightenment? Because they disturb the mind to such a degree that contact with the self as it reflects in the mind is broken, making self inquiry impossible. It is contemplation on the reflection of the self in the mind that allows the intellect to investigate the self in line with the teachings of self inquiry and gain the knowledge "I am the self." Neo-Advaita characteristically wiggles out of the sticky trap of desire by claiming that the self is free of desire, which it is, but if I take myself to be a human being, it is definitely an impediment. If you swallow Neo-Advaita's idea—and what experience-hungry ego would not?—it can lead to an unhealthy moral indifference. You can pursue your desires without reference to dharma and justify your behavior with the knowledge that you are not the desirer. You are "just playing in consciousness."

## Seeking Emotional Fulfillment

There is no way to know for certain, but Neo-Advaita seems to be more about emotionally unfulfilled individuals looking for an alternative to a hectic modern lifestyle, one that offers a sense of community, than a proper spiritual path. Far from the idea of relying on the self to supply emotional needs from within, most believe that enlightenment will help them gain the worldly things that have so far eluded them, particularly love. The attenuated hugs that the followers of Osho made famous and are favored by devotees of the famous Hugging Saint are much in evidence in the meetings of popular Neo-Advaita teachers. And it is clear from the behavior of many of the teachers of Neo-Advaita who have supposedly "got it," that their enlightenment has not significantly diminished their lust for fame, wealth, power and pleasure.

Keeping in mind the fact that everything in empirical reality is actually consciousness seeking its way back to itself, it would be unfair to suggest that there is anything sinister about Neo-Advaita. However its teachings, as I have tried to show by contrasting them with self inquiry, suffer from a lack of understanding of the nature of reality. To pass off ignorance as knowledge is not a crime; it does, however, have unfortunate effects on the unsuspecting. Although the truth is eternal and has been known forever, the comprehensive, systematic and refined teachings that crystallized into the science of self inquiry over twelve hundred years ago are obviously the last word in the enlightenment business. There is no need to reinvent the wheel, nor is an adaptation for the benefit of modern world necessary. Yes, self inquiry can always benefit from a linguistic update, but that is all. The teachings stand on their own.

I was informed recently by a friend who has considerable knowledge of the Neo-Advaita satsang world that we have now entered the "Post-Neo Advaita" period. Not surprisingly, Neo-Advaita has not lived up to its promise as a quick and easy means of liberation and people are now looking for the next most incredible path to enlightenment. It seems their prayers have been answered with the appearance of the yang-yin duo, Kalki Avatar and his Mother God wife, founders of the illustrious Oneness University. This compassionate team will—for the modest fee of $11,500 for a two-week enlightenment course—direct special energy from a golden ball into your poor confused human cranium and rewire your brain for enlightenment. As an added benefit, you will miraculously survive the global calamity about to befall the earth in 2012, which is slated to wipe out a significant fraction of humanity. Evidently this promise of personal and global enlightenment is thinning the ranks of the Neo-Advaitans who, in typically Western fashion, are always looking for the most efficient shortcut to limitless bliss.

Does Neo-Advaita have any redeeming virtues? Just as high school is a prerequisite for university, seekers need to start somewhere and Neo-Advaita, imperfect as it is as a vehicle for spiritual practice or self realization, provides entry-level access to the idea of non-duality. Finally, because Neo-Advaita is probably more of a support group for like-minded spiritually inclined individuals than a rigorous investigation into the truth, it will continue in some form or other for the foreseeable future. But it will probably remain a lifestyle fad unless it investigates its roots and discovers the teachings of self inquiry.

# About the Author

JAMES SWARTZ grew up in Montana and attended Lawrence University in Appleton, Wisconsin and the University of California at Berkeley before finding his niche in the world of business. He saw great success as a businessman, but in 1967 he experienced a major epiphany that turned him away from that path. He traveled to India on a spiritual journey, searching for the path to enlightenment. It was here that he learned of the famous Indian sage Swami Chinmayananda, whose knowledge and teachings proved to be the means to set James free.

Now a disciple of the sage, James travels extensively to cities in America, Europe, and India to hold seminars on Vedanta, the science of self-inquiry. He provides resources for understanding non-duality through his website, www.shiningworld.com.

James has previously self-published two non-fiction books: *Meditation: An Inquiry into the Self* (1998) and *The Mystery Beyond the Trinity* (1998).

Sentient Publications, LLC publishes books on cultural creativity, experimental education, transformative spirituality, holistic health, new science, ecology, and other topics, approached from an integral viewpoint. Our authors are intensely interested in exploring the nature of life from fresh perspectives, addressing life's great questions, and fostering the full expression of the human potential. Sentient Publications' books arise from the spirit of inquiry and the richness of the inherent dialogue between writer and reader.

Our Culture Tools series is designed to give social catalyzers and cultural entrepreneurs the essential information, technology, and inspiration to forge a sustainable, creative, and compassionate world.

We are very interested in hearing from our readers. To direct suggestions or comments to us, or to be added to our mailing list, please contact:

### SENTIENT PUBLICATIONS, LLC

1113 Spruce Street
Boulder, CO 80302
303-443-2188
contact@sentientpublications.com
www.sentientpublications.com